THE LIGHT OF PARIS ASSOULINE

New York School of Interior Design

HOME

THE
FOUNDATIONS
of
ENDURING
SPACES

ELLEN S. FISHER *with* JEN RENZI

PHOTOGRAPHS BY MARK LA ROSA

FOREWORD BY ALEXA HAMPTON

CLARKSON POTTER/PUBLISHERS

NEW YORK

All rights reserved.

Published in the United States by Clarkson Potter/Publishers, an imprint of the
Crown Publishing Group, a division of Penguin Random House LLC, New York.
crownpublishing.com
clarksonpotter.com

CLARKSON POTTER is a trademark and POTTER with colophon is a registered trademark
of Penguin Random House LLC.

Library of Congress Cataloging-in-Publication Data
Names: Fisher, Ellen S., author. | Renzi, Jen, author. | Hampton, Alexa, writer of foreword.
Title: New York School of Interior Design Home / Ellen S. Fisher with Jen Renzi;
    Foreword by Alexa Hampton; Photographs by Mark LaRosa.
Description: First Edition. | New York: Clarkson Potter/Publishers, 2018.
Identifiers: LCCN 2015049380
Subjects: LCSH: Interior decoration. | New York School of Interior Design.
Classification: LCC NK2110 .F57 2018 | DDC 747—dc23
LC record available at http://lccn.loc.gov/2015049380.

ISBN 978-0-8041-3719-5
Ebook ISBN 978-0-8041-3720-1

Printed in China

Book design by Rita Sowins / Sowins Design
Illustrations by Taruan R. Mabry
Cover design by Ian Dingman
Cover illustration copyright © Parish Family, courtesy of the NYSID Archives
    and Special Collections
Additional credits appear on page 452.

10 9 8 7 6

First Edition

TO S.R.K.

CONTENTS

FOREWORD

For decades, the business of interior design has thrived. The discipline's success—and that of its practitioners—has largely been based on talent in *design* over talent in *business.* That equation has borne rooms of unspeakable beauty at the very time that it has doomed some careers to brevity. Never has it been more essential to be successful in both halves of the profession than it is now. The present day thankfully demands seriousness in all aspects of the business of design. Talent and instinctual gifts will always be intrinsically important to the production of great art. However, those ingredients are not enough by themselves. As such, education is of course the cornerstone of any proper design endeavor.

No one is more qualified to "write the book" (figuratively and literally) on the practice than the New York School of Interior Design. In this book, design strategies walk hand in hand with the more mundane, though no less important, practices and intricacies of the profession. The distillation of vital though sometimes nebulous or abstract topics—ranging from how to address color to the implementation of various types of lighting—lives on these pages. So does that which contends with more concrete, quantifiable issues like space planning and how to address a design brief, all while working with clients to achieve their goals.

This book is an essential text for all students of design. Furthermore, it is inspiration and intel for those simply interested in the art and practice of the discipline. I am glad to welcome this book to the important canon of interior design, where it will help make this very worthy career all the more credible through its acknowledgment of the seriousness of its pursuit.

—ALEXA HAMPTON
Principal, Mark Hampton LLC,
and member of the board of trustees for the New York School of Interior Design

PREFACE

At the New York School of Interior Design, we cover the full spectrum of the profession, from commercial office and retail to hospitality and health care. But even as the practice of design becomes increasingly multidisciplinary, its foundation rests firmly on residential roots. An understanding of the domestic environment is integral to our thinking about spaces of all scales and project types. Whether teaching students how to design a luxury spa, a hotel lobby, or the headquarters of a Silicon Valley start-up, we plumb the complex relationship between individuals and their physical surroundings—*home* being a microcosm of every facet of that dynamic.

Professionalism underwrites every course we teach, even those that cater to novices or continuing education students who may not be pursuing an undergraduate or graduate degree in interior design. As educators, we never underestimate anyone who wants to embark on a comprehensive study of the field.

—DAVID SPROULS
President, New York School of Interior Design

INTRODUCTION

Over the past decade, residential design has become a cultural passion. Home-renovation television shows, DIY blogs, and shelter magazines treat the domestic sanctum as protagonist, not just scenery. Such exposure has stoked widespread enthusiasm about all things house and home and brought renewed attention to the profession. No longer perceived as strictly the purview of those with a large house and deep pockets, interior design is universally attainable, relevant and applicable to any abode—no matter how modest—and available to every buyer.

For design enthusiasts, such accessibility is a source of not only empowerment but also consternation, because democratization is not the same as demystification. One might read an article about how to estimate the yardage needed to reupholster a sofa, but in order to figure out what and how much fabric to buy, it's still necessary to understand yarn and weave types and how patterns are applied so they line up at the seams. And, yes, thanks to the Internet, consumers can now enjoy flash sales of designer products and access to formerly exclusive resources such as "to the trade only" showrooms. But pricing structures for custom products, decorative wall finishes, and built-in cabinetry can be hard to understand, leading to unrealistic expectations about budgets. The glut of confusing (and often conflicting) information is a disservice to anyone embarking on a design project, whether a new homeowner seeking to furnish her entire abode, a renter in the market for custom curtains to spruce up his apartment, or any dweller who plans to hire a professional for interior work.

So we created this book, an exhaustive residential design bible, to explain every aspect of the process. Our mission is to nurture better-informed design practitioners *and* consumers, leading to more resolved and refined interiors. It covers the full gamut—from finding inspiration to final installation—and the complete chain of decision making along the way, including the critical details on elements such as millwork and properly scaled furniture. Although it is structured in a modular format, with self-contained sections on specific rooms and features that can be digested à la carte, reading from start to finish first is the best way to gain a big-picture understanding of the complexities and to prevent costly mistakes such as ordering an inappropriate countertop material for the kitchen.

This book was written with specific audiences in mind, including the intrepid DIYer who wants to tackle as much as possible on his own. Many people just love designing their own space and would rather go it alone, armed with encyclopedic and authoritative information. Other readers may simply not be in the financial position to retain professional services.

This book will show motivated amateurs how to make informed choices about everything from the selection of wallcoverings to determining the correct height of a built-in work surface in a home office. They will glean real information about how the process unfolds, how furnishings and finishes are fabricated and installed, what missteps to avoid, and when it might be wise to enlist the aid of a pro.

Those new to the process will gain perspective on all that goes into an interior scheme so that they can make smart decisions on their own or determine whether they need to hire a professional—a decorative painter, a fabricator of custom window treatments, an artisan to create a bespoke rug to fit the odd proportions of their living room, a cabinetmaker to build shelving in the library, a general contractor to rehab the guest bathroom, or an interior designer to realize their dream home from top to bottom.

People who are hiring an interior designer for the first time will discover how to find a professional whose philosophy aligns with their own. Guidance is offered on a variety of topics, including contracts (what they cover and how to decode them); how design fees are structured; in what order the process progresses; how the designer will interface with not only clients but also architects, general contractors, and other related professionals; and why vacating one's home for a few days during the installation process is recommended.

Because this book offers a comprehensive and in-depth explanation of the design process and the myriad decisions a practitioner makes in creating an interior, professionals at all levels can use it as a resource manual. It serves as a primer for those just entering the field, helping readers to connect the dots between diverse topics and better understand how they interrelate and fit into the overall timeline, from purchasing to final punch list. And while a majority of the content will be familiar to seasoned professionals, midcareer practitioners can use this book to brush up on dormant skills or learn insider tips—secrets to creating a budget and "never thought of that" questions to ask during client interviews, for instance—from fellow designers who share their expertise and advice in these pages. Readers with a commercial design or architecture background will appreciate the master classes on decorative elements more specific to residential interiors, such as lampshade details and living room floor plans.

Interior design is equal parts art and science. It is problem solving with an added value: the designer's unique creative twist and ability to refine solutions with an eye for beauty and empathy. A good interior designer is a problem solver and a storyteller. Her role is to create a narrative for the space—one that will thread it all together. As such, interior design demands both blue-sky dreaming and logical reasoning. Practitioners and amateur design enthusiasts alike need foresight and panoptic vision to keep the big picture in mind, along with laser focus to see how every minute detail clicks into place. But at its heart, interior design is so much more than the sum of its parts. It transcends the selection of beautiful finishes and the creation of custom furnishings. Ultimately, it is about place making: imbuing spaces with meaning and relevance, heart and soul. That's the very definition of home.

the DESIGN PROCESS

Interior design is a rigorous process built on many decisions. Whether the project in question is new construction or pre-existing, a studio apartment or a grand domicile, it requires a methodical, orderly, and organized approach. A specific sequencing of events is necessary to get from concept to completion. Planning ahead, thinking through myriad problems in advance, and sizing up one's needs and spatial constraints to determine the most appropriate and inspired solution are indispensable skills. From day one, every element—from the tiniest detail to the most comprehensive architectural modification—needs to be considered as a whole and managed with informed decision making, scrupulous oversight, and a lot of quick thinking, as things can and will inevitably go awry.

Anyone who takes on a serious design project discovers the unexpected complexity of interior design. Intertwined decisions lead to creative and operational challenges. Even seasoned pros confess that much of their work involves troubleshooting and problem solving—and that's part of the fun. For design enthusiasts of all stripes, the excitement of seeing a vision fulfilled trumps the hiccups that occur along the way.

THE PROFESSIONAL MIND-SET

Most people design their homes in an ad hoc manner, one step at a time: over the course of a few years, they save up enough money or muster the energy to tackle the next room. For instance, a young couple upgrading to a larger abode might use their old furniture plus a few family heirlooms donated by a sympathetic parent to fill the yawning spaces. Months later, as their budget frees up, they buy a few items to plug in the gaping holes. When they become fed up with sitting on a too-small sofa, they buy a new one. Off-the-shelf curtains are upgraded to a custom design; a plain rug is exchanged for a more lush version.

Such a piecemeal approach to interior design can certainly result in a lovely home. But a strategic plan is necessary to achieve the level of finish, resolve, and customization that distinguishes a well-executed space. From information gathering to installation, either the homeowner or a practitioner will need to follow the professional design process as closely as possible—and embrace the professional mind-set:

PLAN AHEAD

Set the vision in advance. Every detail is interrelated, so having the big picture in mind can help you organize and edit as you proceed through the design process. That way, you'll know whether to say yes to the quirky lamp you spy on a leisurely Sunday stroll through the flea market. "You cannot look at a job through tunnel vision," says designer Vicente Wolf. "Everything hinges on something else; it's like fitting together pieces of a puzzle."

BE ORGANIZED

Designing a space is a job for a person who relishes bringing order to chaos. Use lists, charts, and spreadsheets, and store it all in three-ring or digital binders. Cross-reference every detail.

EMBRACE TROUBLESHOOTING AS A CREATIVE EXERCISE

Even if you have designed a residential interior before, something will always throw you for a loop, because the system has a million moving parts, and you can't quite know what you are getting yourself into until you're in the middle of it. But for professional designers, troubleshooting is an exciting challenge: instead of doing things the same way over and over again to avoid problems, most prefer to push themselves to find new solutions to enhance a space. "We'd go stale if we just did things the same way each time," explains designer Katie Ridder. "Part of the challenge—part of the art—is to figure out how to create something you've never created before."

RESEARCH AND ASK QUESTIONS

Interior design is the ultimate continuing education pursuit. Designers learn something new on each project, because their work entails an ongoing dialogue—with vendors and specialists—that helps them to refine their knowledge.

OPPOSITE: Designer Paul Siskin cleverly set apart a slim settee from a living room seating area, allowing a circulation corridor through the space. **PREVIOUS SPREAD:** Pamela Durante showcased a sitting room's loftlike proportions by mounting curtain panels and artwork close to the ceiling plane.

KNOW YOUR LIMITATIONS

Be realistic about your strengths and weaknesses, your capacity for organization, and the amount of time you have to devote to a project. Some tasks are very challenging for DIYers who lack the proper knowledge and experience. You may want to engage the services of an interior designer for your project if a certain level of sophistication requiring custom elements is called for, the timeline is tight (for instance, you want a remodel done all at once instead of over the course of a few years), or the scope of the project is too much to handle solo.

HIRING AN INTERIOR DESIGNER

For many homeowners and renters taking on a design project, the best solution is to hire a practitioner to determine the goals and requirements, outline an appropriate budget and schedule, develop space plans, select and purchase furniture, fixtures, and equipment, and commission custom millwork. An interior designer can team with and help the client engage allied professionals—from architects to AV consultants to structural engineers. He can spearhead every aspect of the project or help his clients to structure or phase the work so that they can oversee certain tasks on their own. Regardless of how the collaboration unfolds, designers welcome—and indeed rely on—input from their clients. Interior design is not only an applied art but also a service business, and the practitioner's goal is to fulfill his clients' needs and to help them define their vision.

Consider hiring an interior designer as early in the process as possible to reduce the chances of potentially costly mistakes, even if an architect has already been retained to oversee a renovation or a new construction. An interior designer can work with the architect to select finishes, from flooring and ceiling treatments to hardware and architectural lighting, and her keen understanding of how people use rooms is instrumental in finessing a floor plan to suit a client's lifestyle.

A fireplace with mirror above forms the focal point of a traditionally appointed living room by Cullman & Kravis.

Each interior design firm develops its own process and procedures, but here are the steps you can expect to encounter:

1 INITIAL INTERVIEW

The client meets with prospective designers—the ideal candidates will have both an academic grounding and hands-on experience in the field. During the interview the client outlines the project's parameters and reviews the designer's qualifications and portfolio. Designers are often hired after this initial get-to-know-you appointment, but some clients need a few more meetings before making their decision.

2 CONTRACT

The designer will prepare either a proposal or a more formal letter of agreement based on the initial conversations. A proposal for services will contain a brief statement about the project and the work it will entail. A letter of agreement is an official contract requiring signature by the client, and sets forth details about the project, the scope of the designer's work, compensation and fees, and other terms and provisions. Once the contract is signed, the project begins.

3 INFORMATION GATHERING

Every project starts with a discovery process, a fact-gathering phase to give the designer a deep understanding of the clients, their needs, their possessions, and the character of the space. This "programming" stage—also referred to as "pre-design"—defines the key problems, challenges, and goals that will shape the resulting design. Ideally, the designer meets the clients at home and/or project site to better grasp their lifestyle and assess and document the physical condition of the space and any belongings.

4 ADDITIONAL FOLLOW-UP

The initial Q&A session often generates more questions than answers. Follow-up meetings or conversations are sometimes needed to get a crystal-clear picture of the project's parameters. The designer may even give the client "homework" in the form of a questionnaire to fill out at leisure. The get-to-know-you phase can last for a few weeks or even months.

5 PROGRAM DEVELOPMENT

The programming stage culminates in a written summary (or program) that details the project's parameters. The designer presents this to the client, who carefully reviews it, makes any necessary corrections ("actually, our library will need to house five hundred books, not two hundred"), and ultimately approves it.

6 ANALYSIS AND IDEATION

The designer takes time to analyze the project's challenges and parameters and to cull ideas and inspiration. This "schematic design" phase sparks a concept that will unify every decision, from spatial layout to color palette. This thinking-through stage is when the practitioner uses her imagination, creativity, knowledge, and wit to create potential solutions.

7 SCHEMATIC PRESENTATION

The designer proposes the concept and a preliminary scheme to the client. This might take the form of a mood board and impressionistic sketches of the space, or it might be more involved: furniture plans, swatches of materials, tear sheets of furnishings. The client approves the scheme—in writing—or requests modifications to be implemented in the next step.

8 REFINING

After the client approves the proposed direction, the designer begins to flesh out the scheme. She has just *defined* her vision; now she *refines* it. Ideas begin to evolve from the general (a round dining table) to the specific (a 60-inch-wide Eero Saarinen black marble–topped table). The designer will determine the exact height and profile of the baseboards, figure out the best placement of electrical outlets, choose final paint colors, furnishings, and much more.

9 DESIGN DEVELOPMENT PRESENTATION

The designer invites the client to her studio in order to share the complete scheme. She will present renderings of each space being designed, floor and furniture plans, samples of wood and other materials, and fabric swatches. By taking in every space and detail in relation to one another, the client is able to better understand the overarching design concept and unifying sensibility. At the end of the meeting, the client is asked to approve the scheme and is sent home with a project binder organized by room, which includes the cost of the proposed elements, and takes some time to mull the proposal and express concerns about various features.

10 CONTRACT DOCUMENTATION

Once the client approves the scheme, the designer generates final floor and furniture plans. Purchase orders for furnishings and custom features are issued. At this stage the designer coordinates with the architect or other licensed professionals and, if the scope of the project warrants it, helps the client solicit bids to hire a GC.

11 CONTRACT ADMINISTRATION

The designer purchases the specified fabrics and furnishings, enlists vendors to initiate custom commissions, and hires any necessary collaborators, such as AV or lighting consultants. If construction is involved, the designer will review the documentation generated by the architect and/or GC. The designer's role in the build-out includes visiting the construction site, managing some of the craftsmen, and generating the final punch list of unresolved items.

12 INSTALLATION

Once construction wraps, the designer works with various tradespeople to complete elements such as wallcovering and decorative finishes. She then oversees delivery and installation of all furnishings, lighting, and accessories. For large projects and those involving construction, items are stored in a warehouse until the space is ready; then the installation happens within a tight time frame. Otherwise, the designer will be present as needed over the course of a few weeks or months to receive deliveries.

13 AFTERMATH

After the installation is complete, a few items inevitably linger on the punch list: a console with a long lead time arrives a few weeks late, or the painter has to return to fix some nicks. The designer ensures that all details are resolved. Sometimes the client waits until the space is 90 percent complete before making decisions about the final layer—accessories and artworks. Fees for additional work will need to be renegotiated if the designer's contract has an end date.

DEFINING THE PROJECT

The first step of any design project is to determine its scope: What will the work entail? Defining the contours as concretely as possible provides clarity, context, and direction. Is the scope narrow (new window treatments for a bedroom) or broad (renovating and furnishing a large home)? The objective may be to improve function, as in the case of revamping an underutilized dining room to double as a home office. Or the goal may be more abstract, such as conjuring a nurturing mood in a nursery. No matter how modest the objective is, every step should be executed with the big-picture vision for an entire room (or home) in mind.

Identifying the users of the space is also an integral part of defining the project. Each room tends to be dominated by a particular family member; a designer will ask questions to connect a certain space to a specific individual and to determine whether any areas are shared. He will also assess the needs, desires, lifestyle, and interests of the inhabitants. How do they envision using the space? How do they want their home to feel? How should it function (for dining, lounging, sleeping)? Technology or other special considerations that affect the planning or infrastructure should also be carefully taken into account.

Designers call this analysis the programming or pre-design phase. It is the foundation of every well-managed interior design project, no matter the size. A thorough consideration of these variables up front—by both the client and the professional—will mean a smoother process and a more satisfactory result.

QUESTIONS TO ASK

Whether you are a homeowner or a designer, you can determine the parameters of your project by asking the following questions:

WHO LIVES HERE?

Consider all inhabitants who will primarily use the space: don't forget kids and pets, the au pair, and live-in grandparents, for example. The needs of empty nesters will be very different from those of young couples with three kids and a dog, or recent graduates living on their own for the first time. Even if the project is to remodel just one room occupied by a single family member, it's still a good idea to keep in mind everybody else who lives in the home. A teenage boy may see his bedroom as a private sanctum, but his parents will pop in on occasion to chat or assist with homework.

WHO ARE THE OTHER USERS?

Assess the needs of any person who enters the home on a regular basis for work or another reason, such as a housekeeper, a caretaker, or a nanny. Does the homeowner entertain often or host overnight guests? If the answer is yes, then their use and comfort should also factor into the design scheme.

When David Scott was hired to design the interior of an oceanfront home, he envisioned a decorative scheme that drew from the site. Part of the challenge was to instill a balance of openness and enclosure in the airy, double-height main living area, which he achieved by using textured finishes evocative of the beach.

SHOULD THE LOCATION—THE GEOGRAPHIC AREA AND THE BUILDING ITSELF—INFLUENCE THE DESIGN?

The structure's architectural character and the surrounding environment will inevitably inform the interior scheme. Generally, the best strategy is either to be consistent with the existing style or to deliberately play against type. Take cues from the locale by redoing a waterfront living room in a spectrum of aqueous hues and finishes. Or give a colonial home an ultramodern interior, using the design principle of contrast to conjure aesthetic frisson.

HOW WILL THE INHABITANTS USE THE SPACE?

Get a handle on how the inhabitants will use the space. Is the kitchen just for cooking, or will the family eat here too? A library may need to accommodate both quiet reading and laptop use.

WHAT ARE THE ADDITIONAL FUNCTIONS OF THE SPACE?

Some spaces will have a singular focus, and others will be called upon to multitask—for example, a den is occasionally used to sleep overnight guests, or a bedroom also functions as a sitting room or a home office. A generously sized kitchen is an ideal spot to incorporate a laundry nook, a command center, or a play area.

WHEN WILL THE SPACE BE USED?

Account for the season and time of day when a space is inhabited. Is it a year-round residence, a pied-à-terre, or a weekend or summer home? Will a room be occupied throughout the day or just in the morning or evening? When the space is used and what it will be used for must inform everything from the type of lighting needed to the optimal texture of the finishes.

WHAT STYLE WILL REFLECT THE HOMEOWNER'S AESTHETIC SENSIBILITY?

An interior design scheme should address a desired atmosphere and account for color preferences and historical influences—for example, French art deco or Scandinavian modern.

DO THE INHABITANTS HAVE SPECIAL NEEDS OR SENSITIVITIES THAT THE SPACE MUST ACCOMMODATE?

Ramps, open shelving, or other accessible solutions may be required if residents' sensitivities, disabilities, or physical limitations are a consideration. If the homeowner intends to "age in place"—that is, remain in the space for a lifetime if possible—then features such as wide doorways for easy wheelchair passage are helpful. Blackout shades can be used in window treatments to make light-sensitive residents more comfortable, and additional insulation or wallcoverings and flooring that cushion sound are good design choices to muffle noise. When dust allergies are a concern, minimize the use of textiles.

HOW SHOULD THE SPACE ADDRESS THE INHABITANTS' PSYCHOLOGICAL NEEDS?

Physical space influences how people feel on a very subconscious level. Yearnings for privacy, personal space, and access to light and nature are important factors to consider. Good design anticipates and supports these needs.

WHAT TECHNOLOGY WILL BE INCORPORATED INTO THE SPACE?

Security systems and smart-home or whole-house automation require touch pads, routers, wireless communication devices, and other gadgets that may affect infrastructure; if planned for in advance, such technology can be integrated into the design or hidden from view.

IS ENVIRONMENTAL CONSCIOUSNESS A CONCERN?

Because they will affect infrastructure, ecological requirements should be addressed from the project's inception. Everyone has different standards (not to mention budgets). That being said, homeowners' philosophies often change over time. "Many clients don't think about eco-friendliness until they have their first baby or the pet gets sick, and then healthy materials and finishes suddenly become a priority," says designer Kati Curtis. Changing an element such as cabinetry—which can off-gas formaldehyde—after it's been installed is tricky and expensive, so think ahead.

HAVE ANY SCHEDULING ISSUES BEEN IDENTIFIED?

Is this space currently being used for another purpose? Will anybody be living in the space while it's being redesigned? What's the ideal move-in date? Does the baby's room need to be completed before the due date? Construction that needs to be wrapped up prior to a big party or a major life event is particularly stressful.

A carefully illuminated side table becomes a spotlit pedestal for art in a living room by David Scott, which features a custom sofa upholstered in masculine pinstripes.

4

1: For his New York home, Geoffrey Bradfield designed a library that doubles as a den and an entertaining salon. A U-shaped banquette anchors the room, creating a sort of conversation pit in reverse. 2: A living room by Matthew Patrick Smyth showcases pale tones and an eclectic mix of delicately scaled furnishings—a formal space designed for formal occasions. 3: The dining room of Joan Dineen's townhouse is used primarily in the evenings and for formal occasions. Dark wood finishes, a moody lighting scheme, and a formal ambience suit the room's nighttime-only character. 4: To create a bedroom that would grow up with its youthful inhabitant, Suzanne Lovell combined a tasteful gray-on-gray palette and furnishings with whimsical artworks.

Eco-consciousness was a consideration in a living room by Kati Curtis, which features sustainably sourced textiles and VOC-free paints and finishes. The scheme contrasts rough, natural textures and elegant gray tones.

CREATING
A BUDGET

Developing the budget for a project can prove vexing, especially for those new to the interior design process. Novices tend to have an inaccurate sense of the pricing of various elements and services. (And indeed there exists quite a range; consider a 32-inch-long metal console table, which can cost $400 or $100,000 or anywhere in between.) While some people can readily identify a maximum amount they feel comfortable allocating to a project, for many homeowners the budget is a question mark. Some lucky ones are concerned with value—at whatever price point—rather than an actual dollar amount.

Still, it is essential to earmark an acceptable figure at the project's inception, prior to making any decisions—or even beginning to design, for that matter. "It makes no sense to go down a route that might be completely unrealistic," says designer Jamie Drake. (In fact, many professionals won't start working with a client until a budget has been solidified; it's often written into the contract.) Creating a budget, especially for a large or complex job, is a task for which a layperson can benefit from professional advice. Experienced designers can approximate what the project might cost given comparable jobs they've completed, or suggest an appropriate range.

One way to approach budgeting is to ask *how much do I want to invest in the space?* versus *how much is it going to cost?* "Think about the interior design budget as a percentage of what the property itself costs," designer Vicente Wolf advises. "Ten percent is a good baseline."

Projects can be phased so expenditures are spread out over time; with a master plan in mind, the job can proceed in a sound and logical fashion but as the budget allows. Designers can also advise about where to splurge and where to save. A good start is to invest in a few key pieces you love and then build the room around them over time.

Interior designer Allison Caccoma prepares a rigorously detailed budget for clients before a project gets under way. She creates a spreadsheet itemizing each projected purchase—from the carpet installation to bedside sconces—with columns listing a high and low estimate, figures based on similar previous jobs. "As elements are specified, I fill in the actual amount in a third column. The spreadsheet is constantly updated, so clients know how much they've spent already, and where they are in terms of what they hoped to spend," she explains. Although replicating that method could be complicated, it's nonetheless a savvy organizing tool. Many design-management software programs have budgeting capabilities that can prove helpful for professionals and amateurs alike.

Keep in mind that design and renovation projects invariably cost more than anticipated. Along the way, it's easy to be tempted by the nicer fabric or higher-end furniture, or to tack on a redesign of another room. "We often observe the phenomenon of budget creep: 'Actually, while we're moving out to finish the master bath, we might as well renovate the kitchen too,'" says Chip Brian of Best & Company, a general contracting and construction management firm.

After an order for custom furniture has been placed, shipping and delivery charges are calcu-

lated (estimate 15 percent of the cost of an item); also account for applicable sales taxes on design services and purchases. Those fees alone may add up to an additional 10 percent of the base cost of furnishings and materials. Whatever the anticipated budget, a smart homeowner or designer will set aside a cushion of at least 25 percent of the overall budget. The unexpected *will* arise— and the unexpected *always* costs money.

Custom details like decorative wall finishes and bespoke upholstery—as in this living room by Phillip Thomas—can eat up a sizeable portion of a design budget. Fine art and antiques are always worthwhile investments.

ASSESSING THE "GIVENS"

After identifying the project parameters and the end users, the next key step is scrutinizing the site and itemizing any existing furnishings. During this survey phase—or predesign—information is gathered about the configuration and condition of the room or rooms, from big-picture characteristics (what is the quality of light?) to granular details (are there any odd bumps and pipes?). The survey entails a painstaking evaluation of the positive and negative attributes of a space. Close examination helps determine what features and qualities can be emphasized or celebrated, and what should be toned down, accommodated, or altered. A room's bones will also reveal what can be changed and what cannot. This is when assets and liabilities are pinpointed that will be dealt with later, during design development.

The site survey can also be a time of reckoning. Problems are singled out that may require expert help to resolve. A homeowner who thought she could get by without any major rehabbing may realize she'll need to hire a specialist to tear up a hearthstone and refinish the floors. Turns out the dining room will have to be skim-coated by a painter before the scenic wallpaper can be hung. Or an interior designer uncovers structural challenges that will require the aid of an architect.

However, this is also the step when a space's potential for beauty is uncovered. Such an intimate appraisal sparks the imagination, planting a seed about how the design might ultimately take shape, and the many possible scenarios to be explored.

"INTERIOR DESIGN IS NOT JUST ABOUT PRETTY; IT'S ABOUT CREATING A LIFE AND A LIFESTYLE THAT'S ENJOYABLE AND FITS THE HOMEOWNER'S BUDGETARY AND FUNCTIONAL PARAMETERS."
—Jim Druckman, president and CEO of the New York Design Center

Neal Beckstedt was challenged to maximize a bedroom's assets (amazing views, high ceilings) while working around its limitations: small size, not enough wall space, bland architecture. He layered textures and hung artworks in intriguing locations to counteract the lack of architectural interest, and created a built-in to house the HVAC and serve as the headboard. Sheers soften the glare without screening the views.

SIZING UP
THE SPACE

It is important to evaluate the spatial characteristics of the room from an *objective* point of view, independent of the future design or even the intended use. Take stock of existing elements and their condition—from floorboards and ceilings to the location of doors and power outlets. Scrutinize the location of windows, overhead lighting, and any existing built-ins. Are areas of the room significantly different when examined at one foot above the floor, at five feet above, or closer to the ceiling? Imperfections make their appearance at every level and need to be accounted for as the design is developed. If the project is not yet built, the space can be judged by examining the architectural plans and construction documents.

The following checklist will help in discerning a space's potential and limitations—whether the space has already been secured or during a hunt for real estate.

Scale

Note the overall scale of the room (i.e., its size in comparison to the human body). A room is judged as cozy or impressive by how big or small a person feels in it. How high is the ceiling? How wide or large or snug is the room? Does one feel dwarfed, crowded, or comfortable there? Perception of scale is often affected by the path or transition from one room into another.

Frank Lloyd Wright famously exploited this quality, often designing a very low, restrictive entry that opened into a high-ceilinged room.

This created a jolt of expansion that enhanced the loftlike impression.

The scale of a room has the most impact on what must be done to create the desired ambience. If a room has a high ceiling and grand moldings, it will be difficult to create a sense of coziness. Similarly, if a room is on the small side and the goal is formality, then special attention will have to be paid to the windows and entries, the size of the furnishings, and the lighting in order to fulfill the vision.

Proportion

While scale concerns the relationship of one thing to another (i.e., a person to a room), proportion is the relationship of parts to the whole. Look at the overall shape of the floor plan. A rectangular space whose height approximates the width of its shortest side is considered to have balance and stability.

Balance

Just as people seek balance in life, so too do they seek it in their surroundings. A sense of visual equilibrium is often established through symmetry, as in the case of a matching pair of windows that are equally spaced on a wall. But balance can also derive from asymmetry; consider a seating group with a sofa anchoring one side and, opposite, two chairs. Note any opportunities to create symmetrical or asymmetrical balance by using the architectural elements or the decor. Look for the existence of a strong centerline or focal point. Is there a centrally located fireplace, for instance? Also be attentive to what's called a "local" symmetry: just one part of an overall plan allows for a symmetrical arrangement, such as a seating alcove in a larger room.

Axis and Alignment

Note how key architectural features align along cross axes, which are lines drawn through the middle of opposing walls. Is the main entryway or other focal point centered on the wall? Are windows symmetrically placed or offset? Do they line up along an axis? Are any of them directly opposed or otherwise aligned? Often, a strong axis will align with the center of a major architectural element.

Vistas/Sight Lines

A sight line is a kind of visual axis, leading the eye toward an interior focal point or an exterior view. During this initial evaluation of a room, it is important to note exactly what is seen upon entering: A wall? A view of the garden? A specific feature? What is viewed from other key vantage points within the room? What's visible through each window and doorway?

Circulation

This term refers to the flow of foot traffic through a space. A strong entry point and a linear path—visual or physical—aimed directly at an important focal point or destination within the room is an asset. Paths of movement are largely based on the placement of doorways. Is there an overabundance of them, and might sealing one off improve the sense of circulation? Does the room provide access to another? The placement of furniture can control the circulation through a room; at the same time, the circulation must be appropriately directed so furniture can be grouped together as islands of conversation and repose.

Natural Light and Views

Windows, doors, and skylights are assessed both as portals to a view and as conduits of daylight. They can frame a view or create moments of pause—transitions between one space and the next. Note what type of view each door or window frames, and if those vistas should be obscured or celebrated. How much direct or indirect illumination does each window admit? Will windows or open doorways need to be treated for visual privacy or light control?

ARCHITECTURAL ELEMENTS

Construction

Is the room or structure wood-framed or built of concrete? (Retrieving the original architectural construction plans or those from the most recent renovation can provide insight if this is not obvious.) Also critical is identifying what rooms or areas are directly above and below the work being done. Is the laundry room one flight above a dining room, for instance, and will vibrations from the washing machine preclude hanging a delicate chandelier below?

Openings as Architectural Features

Windows and doors are physical elements in a room, not just apertures to admit daylight. Are the windows large or small? Are they well placed on the wall and in relation to each other? Are they flush to the inside wall surface or recessed with a deep or shallow sill? Do they feature moldings, mullions, or other trim? Proportionally speaking, how do the windows and doors relate to the height of the room?

WINDOWS

How do the windows operate: double-hung, hopper, etc.? Will the opening and closing of the window have any bearing on the installation of treatments? How will the windows be cleaned?

DOORS AND DOORWAYS

Can any of the existing interior doors be removed? What are they made of and how do they operate: by swinging, folding, or sliding? If sliding, which door panel is stationary? How much wall space is above doors leading to the outside, and do they swing in or out?

ARCHWAYS

What is the sense of entrance? Do any archways mark the transition from one space to another? What views do they frame?

Built-ins and Architectural Woodwork

Note the existence of any built-in elements and millwork, including cabinets, bookcases, mantels, hearths, and steps or level changes. Can these be removed or modified? Observe areas of tile, marble, and mirrored panels. If these features are to be removed, what is behind or below them? How big are any closets or cupboards, and could incorporating these into the main space significantly enlarge or otherwise impact the room? Apply the same thinking to architectural woodwork: baseboards, cornices, chair rails, paneling, and trim surrounding doors and windows. These elements contribute to the room's sense of proportion and scale, and may hide electrical conduits, wiring, and other unexpected infrastructure. Level changes, platforms, and steps impact accessibility and ease of access; the latter will also require railings and attentiveness to the riser height and tread depth. How are the stair and rail detailed?

Floors

What are the floors made of, and what is their condition? What type of subfloor lies underneath, and what state is it in? Even the subtle sheen and feel of a floor underfoot can convey a strong impression of luxury, modernity, or utilitarianism, thereby influencing the sense of an entire room. Take note of the following elements:

- Material
- Pattern
- Color
- Condition

Wall Finish and Condition

How are the walls finished? Are painted walls smooth and ready to accept a new coat? If they have been painted many times, the surface might be rough or bumpy, requiring sanding or skim coating. Are there cracks and, if so, what caused them? If there are existing wallcoverings, be sure to look below for signs of recurrent water damage. An assessment of the walls' condition will help determine what treatments can be applied, and how the walls must be prepared. For instance, fine paper wallcoverings require a smooth-as-glass substrate, and the process of creating an even, blemish-free surface is extremely costly and labor-intensive.

Ceiling

Document any treatments, textures, surfaces, and drops—from ceiling coves and tin tiles to acoustical elements such as a popcorn ceiling. If a ceiling is to be coated with a high-gloss paint or sheathed in gold leaf or wallpaper, then it must first be carefully plastered and sanded to a glass-like finish. Also note whether downlights or electrical conduits can be recessed into the existing ceiling. Many apartments have concrete ceilings that can't be channeled into, meaning new recessed lighting will require a dropped Sheetrock ceiling.

Columns and Beams

Columns can be either freestanding or attached to the walls (thus creating bump-outs). Are they structural or removable? Can freestanding columns be made smaller? Are there beams in the ceiling or along the tops of walls, or headers over the windows? Because beams are almost always permanent, they affect the room's overall appearance and limit many aspects of the design. Note the height from the floor to the lowest point of the ceiling—often the underside of a soffit or ceiling beams.

Heating, Ventilation, and Air-Conditioning

Where are the HVAC mechanical systems routed from, and how does the system operate? Will it require an upgrade? Are there radiators, heat pumps, baseboard heaters, vents, radiant subfloor heating, air-supply diffusers, or returns? (Behind many of these are ducts.) Do any exposed pipes need to be hidden inside walls or columns?

Sensors and Controls

Is there a thermostat or other sensors or controls? Or a security or whole-house system? Is it a "smart home"?

Hardware

Look closely at hardware style, color, condition, and materials. Hardware is like jewelry, and its finish should ideally coordinate with everything in a room. Will doorknobs, hinges, or switch plates need to be replaced, refinished, or upgraded? Bear in mind that good-quality hardware can eat up a surprisingly large chunk of the budget.

Electrical

Where are the electrical outlets located, and how much overall power is coming into the home? Does the wiring meet the current code? Where are the light switches, and do they control any outlets? It is important to note which switches control which fixtures or outlets, and the existence of any special outlets equipped with surge protectors or dedicated to appliances.

Cable/Internet

Observe phone, cable, and data receptacles. Where do the cable and Internet come into the room, and where are they routed to? This can impact placement of major furnishings such as media cabinets.

Lighting Locations

Where are ceiling lights or wall sconces located? Can the placement of any fixtures be changed, and what would that require? For instance, if the ceiling is structural concrete or intersected by steel beams—and thus cannot be channeled— how might new wiring be concealed?

Fireplaces

Is there a fireplace? If so, is it functional, and will it have to remain? Can it be moved, changed, or restyled?

Water Sources

Identify the location of all plumbing supply sources and drains, and the closest ones to each room. This information will affect the location of key elements, from a bathroom tub to a living room wet bar.

ELEMENTS OF AN INTERIOR

- Focal point: a painting, sculpture, or other artwork
- Lines: axes and circulation paths
- Planes
  » Vertical: walls
  » Horizontal: floor and ceiling
- Volume: the shape of the space
- Apertures/openings: windows, doorways, skylights
- Sources of light
  » Natural
  » Artificial

An abundance of windows, both interior and exterior, offer intriguing sight lines in a double-height, open-plan living room by David Scott.

DOCUMENTING THE SPACE

The site survey also includes thoroughly measuring and photographing every aspect of the space—for example, the span of each wall, the distance between the overhead light switch and the doorway, the height of the windowsills, and the placement of radiators. It is important to photograph the room from every angle, with long shots of each wall and of the ceiling, and close-ups of all problem areas and details. These images, along with the measured drawings, become a visual reference during the design process.

This step is like a second date, an opportunity to get more deeply acquainted with the personality of a room—its wonderful qualities and unseen challenges. Through observing, photographing, and measuring a space, one gets to know it intimately.

Site measurements are used to generate two types of drawings:

PLANS

The floor plan is a bird's-eye view of the space: an outline of a room, bordered by the walls. The ceiling plane is depicted the same way, but looking up instead of down: its edges traced, with any changes in height noted, including dropped soffits and coves. These plans are used to document all horizontal dimensions. Bear in mind that floor plans only depict a room at the level of the floor plane or a tiny bit higher. But rooms change as they go up: conditions at 12 inches are different from those at a height of 36 or even 72 inches. Thus it is important to take measurements at several heights, noting any relevant details, peculiarities, or discrepancies.

ELEVATIONS

The second type of drawing is a vertical view. Elevations are representations of each wall as seen from afar. The height of the room and of any interior elements, such as windows and built-in shelving, is marked on the elevations. Create one for each wall.

How to Measure

Surveying a room ideally requires two people: one to operate the tape measure (or laser-measure tool), another to jot down the dimensions and any notes. Start with rough sketches of the room and mark all the distances as they are tallied; these preliminary drawings need not be to scale. Then methodically transpose all the measurements into scale drawings (usually ¼ inch equals 1 foot) by using drafting tools or graph paper and a scale ruler.

An existing floor plan from the previous owner's architect or the developer can also be used for checking measurements—but only as a starting point. "Inherited" plans must always be carefully checked for accuracy, and professionally site-measured and redrawn as necessary. Often, an architect's plans are modified as the space is constructed, and these changes aren't documented anywhere. (Plans revised to reflect the final, completed design are called as-built drawings, and are rarely commissioned.)

FLOOR PLAN

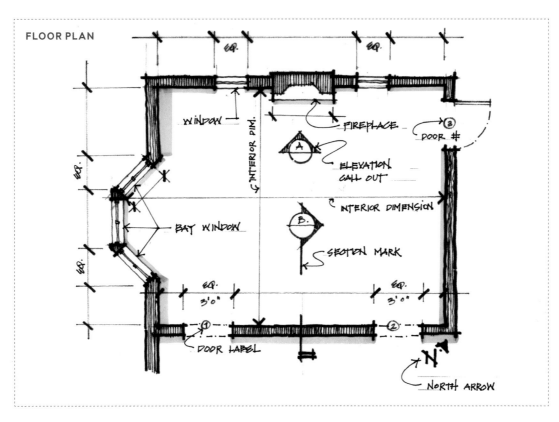

WINDOW
INTERIOR PLM.
FIREPLACE
DOOR #
ELEVATION CALL OUT
INTERIOR DIMENSION
BAY WINDOW
SECTION MARK
EQ. 3'0"
EQ. 3'0"
DOOR LABEL
NORTH ARROW

ELEVATION

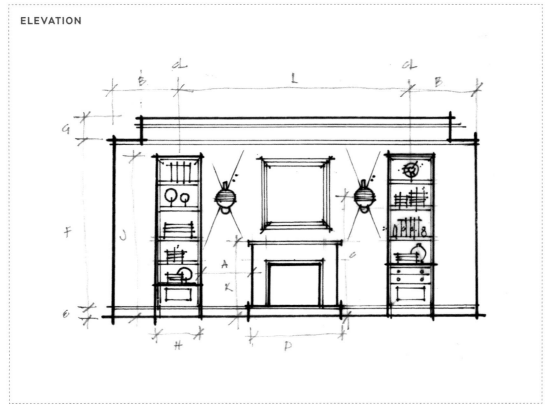

STEP 1

Create the base drawings on ¼-inch graph paper:

- Roughly draw the floor plan of the room, indicating door openings and columns.
- Draw each wall in elevation, showing approximate locations of windows, doors, significant architectural features, switches, outlets, receptacles, thermostats, and other controls or special items.
- Using another sheet of graph paper, draw a plan of the ceiling. (The technical term used on construction documents is "reflected ceiling plan.") Note the location of chandeliers, track or recessed lighting, ceiling fans, and beams, dropped ceilings, coves, soffits, or skylights. Also mark placement of smoke detectors and alarms as well as sprinkler heads.

STEP 2

Choose one corner of the room as the starting point, from which all measurements will radiate—both vertically and horizontally. From this point (referred to as 0'-0"), take the overall dimensions of the room across the length and width of the floor. Mark these on the sketched floor plan.

STEP 3

Beginning again at 0'-0", move clockwise around the room's perimeter. Note every element encountered—from radiators to windows—jotting down its distance from the nearest perpendicular wall and from the next closest element on the floor plan. Pay particular attention to the following details:

- Mark the location of outlets, cable and telephone receptacles, thermostats, dimmers, switches, and other controls. Measure these elements to their *centerline,* not an outside edge. Designers denote these electrical and mechanical elements with special symbols, which are also helpful for the layperson to know when decoding floor plans. Also note which controls are dedicated to appliances or have special configurations.
- Note if any outlets or receptacles are controlled by wall switches (these are usually found in bedrooms, often to operate nightstand table lamps). Do this by drawing an arrow from the switch to the corresponding outlet.
- Note the location of any wall sconces (to their centerlines) on both the floor plan and the elevation drawings.
- Measure any speakers on the corresponding wall elevation.
- Windows, doorways, and other openings are measured to and from their *inside* edges—as in, the actual opening—ignoring any moldings or frames.

STEP 4

On the ceiling plan sketch, measure distances from walls to all ceiling fixtures, including chandeliers, track lighting, and recessed lights. If the ceiling is very high, it may be necessary to estimate the locations and sizes. Again, it's essential to note which switches or dimmers control which ceiling fixtures.

Some measurements should be taken twice to ensure accuracy, such as the distance from the corner of a room to a window opening, and the width of the opening itself. Be exacting. Thoroughness is important, since it is often impractical (and sometimes impossible) to return to the project site or a client's home in order to double-check details. Inaccuracies can compromise the correct sizing and location of furniture and much more.

Once generated, the site-condition drawings and measurements—as well as notes from the survey—are constantly referenced by the designer, contractors, and homeowner as design decisions are made over the next few months or years. Measured drawings will show if the size of the doorway or the scale of the room can fit a particular sofa, for instance, or help determine where the seams of wall-to-wall carpeting or upholstered wall fabrics should be placed. Indeed, careful measuring requires anticipating problem areas for elements that haven't even been designed yet.

HOW TO MEASURE DOORS AND WINDOWS

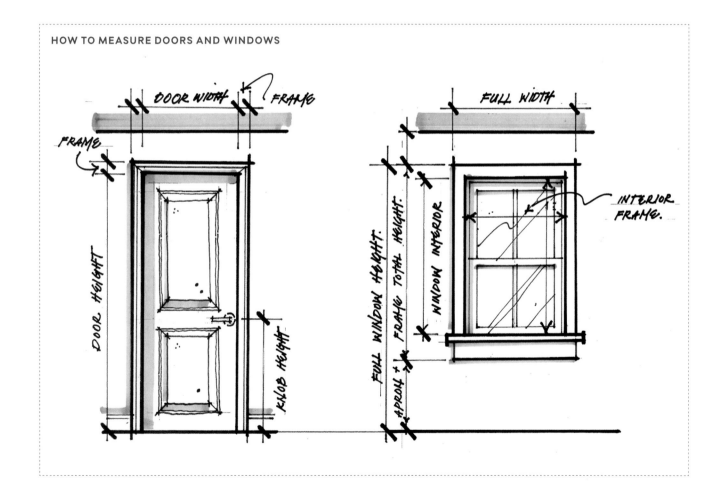

INVENTORYING BELONGINGS

After sizing up the space to be designed, it's necessary to take an inventory of any furniture and major accessories—sofas, dining tables, beds, mirrors, lamps, etc.—that will be reused in the new scheme. For a small room or a second home being outfitted practically from scratch, this task is straightforward; obviously, if the project entails buying all-new furnishings or the scope is simply to refinish a sideboard, an inventory may not be necessary. But for a suite of rooms or an entire abode for which many of the homeowner's existing possessions are being reused, the process can be quite involved and will require a methodical and organized approach.

Every piece should be itemized, measured, and photographed, and information about its characteristics and condition compiled. Make specific notes about color, material (for example: wood, brass, plastic laminate), and other pertinent details. Don't forget area rugs, table lamps, accessories, and artworks (including paintings, pedestals, and sculptures). If the project in question is a new kitchen or a library renovation, the inventorying process may be more involved. You needn't log every book in the library (or bottle in the wine cellar), but tally the approximate number of books the room will house so you will know how many linear feet of shelving are needed.

The documentary photograph should capture all sides, including the back. Use the chart on the following page as a guide for how to itemize the existing pieces.

ABOVE: Built-in bookshelves grace a library Phillip Thomas designed in the apartment of a young family. **OPPOSITE:** A curve-backed sofa—mirrored by similarly sinuous furnishings—anchors a sitting area by Amanda Poole Parisi, Hong Molitor-Xu, and Jamie Drake of Drake/Anderson.

Visual Inventory of Furnishings by Room

CATEGORY	ITEM	QUANTITY	MEASUREMENTS
SEATING	*Example:* Side chairs	2	33 in. long x 32 in. deep
	Example: Sofa	1	108 in. long x 38 in. deep
TABLES			
CABINETS			
CABINET CONTENTS			
ARTWORK			
ACCESSORIES			
MISC.			

CONDITION	COURSE OF ACTION	PHOTO
Sound; fabric is worn	Keep and reupholster	
Good	Keep	

HOW TO MEASURE FURNITURE

Understanding how to measure furniture correctly and accurately is helpful not only when inventorying but also when buying new pieces. Always tally the largest dimension first.

Upholstered Pieces

The seat cushions of most upholstered pieces are 24 inches deep, but otherwise dimensions vary wildly. What's important to measure is the height of the piece and its footprint: the overall length and width, inclusive of the arms and the back. It is the design and fullness of the *outer* elements—the back cushions, the back support, and the arms—that account for a seat's bulk and overall size. Seat backs usually angle slightly: measure the sofa or chair from the most extended point of its back to the very front edge of the seat or arm—whichever extends the farthest. If the chair has roll arms, for example, then measure the width across the widest point, from the arms' outer edges.

Tables and Desks

Jot down the height, width, and length, along with the exact placement of the legs. For desks, make a note about handedness: is the kneewell centered, or is there a return or an L-shaped surface that would require a specific placement or orientation within the room?

Case Goods (Bookshelves, Cabinets, etc.)

Measure height, width, length, and then depth. Note any moldings that extend beyond the base or the top edge. Indicate the material and if the back is finished (or built of a different material or finish than the front or outside). Note if cabinets can be placed flat against a wall.

Keeping Track

Collate the information in a digital or physical binder, with a section devoted to each room. (Professional designers often use software designed for the purpose, but even a notebook will suffice; the point is for the documentation to be thorough, not high tech.) Each furnishing should have its own page that includes the photograph, description, and dimensions plus an actual fabric sample if applicable (and possible). This careful record will be used over and over, throughout the entire design process—and especially during construction, delivery, and installation. Later, as new furnishings are specified, a tear sheet for each—listing the same information—should be added to this binder.

MEASURING UPHOLSTERED PIECES

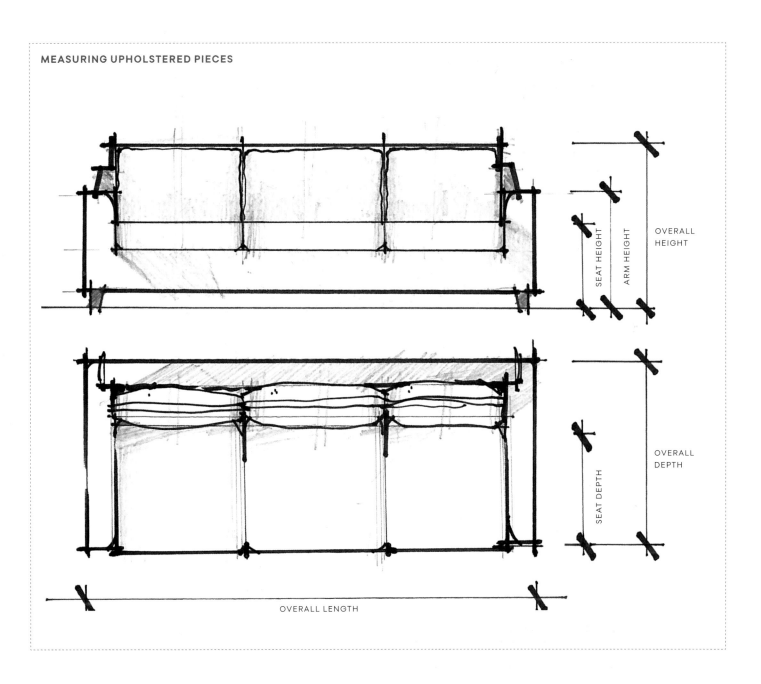

SEAT HEIGHT

ARM HEIGHT

OVERALL HEIGHT

SEAT DEPTH

OVERALL DEPTH

OVERALL LENGTH

FINDING INSPIRATION

Inspiration is the engine of creativity. The time to start gathering ideas, influences, and images to guide the interior is early in the design process. This act entails keeping an open mind, looking at a vast pool of potential material, culling the most relevant, and then organizing them in one place: a manila folder, a mood board, a digital bulletin board, or the like.

Inspiration for a design project can be found anywhere: in photography books, at a museum, or in the indigenous materials and unique color sensibility of a particular culture. References need not be highbrow or esoteric. "I've found inspira-tion in magazine ads and vintage furnishings," says Allison Caccoma. "Even a conch shell—with its lovely spectrum of beiges and pinks—once sparked the color scheme of a room."

A single source image often sparks the vision of an entire home or the treatment of a specific element. The pleating style of a favorite dress might inform a lampshade detail. Or a photograph of Diana Vreeland's iconic red-on-red living room by Billy Baldwin might kick-start the palette of a den. In other instances, inspiration is in the aggregate—a collection of visuals. A scrapbook curated over the years seems a disparate collage until a closer look reveals an underlying theme, motif, or mood.

For design professionals and enthusiasts, inspiration gathering is a continuous, ongoing endeavor. Ideas are constantly being discovered and filed away for future use. A designer will often tap into this mental or physical repository when embarking on a new interior. Once the project parameters and the character of the raw space are understood, ideas begin to germinate. These eureka moments are not whims; they are inevitably born of a lifetime of looking and think-ing, and of making mental and visual connections. Design inspiration is not arbitrary or passive; it is deliberate and purposeful—and very much related to the particular challenge under study at the time. Those new to the process, who may feel intimidated by the notion of finding inspiration, can take heart in the fact that simply immersing oneself in the particularities of the project will yield ideas to illuminate potential paths.

COMMON SOURCES OF INSPIRATION

- A poem or imagery from literature
- Nature
- Historical references
- A textile (vintage fabric, a rug)
- A painting, a sculpture, or other artwork
- Fashion
- A cultural motif
- A favorite color
- A childhood memory
- A period room from a museum or a historic property
- Iconic spaces from the annals of decorating

Mark D. Sikes took inspiration from Italian style icon Marella Agnelli—in particular her St. Moritz ski house by Renzo Mongiardino—in designing a red-on-red dining room.

CHOOSING
A CONCEPT

The concept is the vision for the project, a sort of mission statement. It not only provides cohesion but also helps elevate the design above mere decoration. This unifying idea will inform every element of the interior—from the molding profile to the shape of the coffee table. For instance, the concept of "flow" might suggest a floor plan of spaces that transition seamlessly (without doors or changes in flooring material), a palette of beachy hues, smooth fabrics with little pattern, and softly edged furniture. If the design has been well executed, the concept is apparent the moment one steps inside the space.

Because the concept will—and should—affect every decision and detail, the designer establishes it early in the design process. Often a strong idea emerges while the designer digests and analyzes the minutiae of the project brief and the unique characteristics of the space. A beautiful setting leads to the idea of bringing the outdoors in. Or a high-rise building's urban view suggests a grid-like spatial organization, rectilinear and boxy furnishings, and a palette of exposed brick, limestone, and azure blue. A source of inspiration could be the springboard: a favorite paint color may be the starting point, but a particular *attribute* that color conveys (peace and protection) is what generates the overarching idea.

Though it might seem a bit abstract, a concept is an extremely practical tool: a benchmark that every design decision can be checked against. Shopping for a sofa, you fall in love with a buttoned-up Chesterfield and a plush U-shaped sectional, both of which serve the desired functionality—but which one better upholds the concept of "nesting"? The stronger the concept, the easier it is to make choices along the way.

When working with a client, a designer will create a written statement that articulates the concept. Even for amateurs, this exercise of putting words on paper can be extremely helpful. That being said, when it comes to explaining concept, a picture is worth a thousand words.

THE BEST CONCEPT IS SUCCINCT YET FERTILE, SPECIFIC YET EXPANSIVE ENOUGH TO BE APPLIED TO EVERYTHING FROM FURNITURE AND FINISHES TO MILLWORK AND HARDWARE.

In designing a bedroom for a holiday-themed decorator's show house in New York, Harry Heissmann chose the concept of Christmas—in terms of mood rather than color or iconography. "In particular the fascination and awe, the dreamy feeling that kids have when they wake up on Christmas morning." That accounts for the trippy collision of patterning and other eclectic details. A dramatic black-on-white scheme upholds the concept while setting the decor apart from vibrantly colored neighboring rooms. "Although it's just two colors, there are so many different whites here—some warm, some cool—that they each seem to take on a different tint: blue, green, yellow, beige."

THE BIG PICTURE

Everyone has a unique sense of style and an opinion about what constitutes a well-designed space. Some feel most content in the cozy confines of a French country decor, while others find minimalist trappings calm and centering. Some people covet the intimacy of small-scale rooms; and yet others prefer living in airy, open-plan environments.

But while aesthetic preferences are highly individual, certain spatial attributes are universally (if subconsciously) appealing, engendering comfort and well-being on a neurological level. Views of nature, ample (but not glaring) daylight, and good indoor air quality are coveted traits. Being able to control one's environment—from the temperature to the illumination level—is another important criterion. Spaces should also be easy and intuitive to use and maneuver through. These features apply to any abode, from a modernist urban townhouse to a Mediterranean-style beach villa.

They are also backed up by science. Environmental psychologists, geographers, ergonomists, and efficiency experts are among the specialists who have plumbed the complex relationship between person and place. (Interior design students spend much time in school learning about the nuances of these interdisciplinary studies, which are collectively called environment-behavior research.)

There is an evolutionary basis for our spatial preferences. Because human beings evolved by adapting to the fight for survival in the wild, the kinds of spaces we subconsciously favor feature traits that helped our ancestors foil predators and find sustenance; today, they inspire calm and relaxation. Humans have an innate fondness for natural environments replete with water, greenery, sunlight, and flowers—which signaled the presence of food and water. (The term for this love of nature is "biophilia.") Accordingly, they are essential to consider while both sizing up and designing a space.

Keep the following qualities in mind for any project—whether building a new home, renovating an existing one, choosing a new fabric scheme, or simply rearranging a conversation area in a living room.

LONG SIGHT LINES OR VIEWS

Strategic placement of doors, windows, and walls can help manipulate interior and exterior views of expansive spaces. If the project is new construction or a renovation, locate portals to allow long interior views.

PLACES OF REFUGE

Spaces enclosed on three sides with a long view out are especially comforting. This effect can be achieved through furniture arrangements or by designing a built-in seating nook, for instance.

OPPOSITE: A den by David Scott inspires calm on many levels. The room enjoys ample daylight, filtered through glass walls screened by floor-to-ceiling sheers—which also serve to give the room a sense of privacy. A cozy corner sectional is positioned to take in the views of surrounding nature through full-height window walls beyond.

DAYLIGHT

Site a new home to maximize natural illumination. Specify large, mullion-free windows and treatments that allow ample light penetration. Remove interior walls to allow an influx of sunshine. Opportunities to capture dappled or changing light also invite tranquillity.

THE SIGHT OR SOUND OF RUNNING WATER

Orient a home or windows to enjoy views of a lake, a river, or a beach. When that is not an option, consider an indoor or outdoor water feature, such as a fountain.

FLOWERS OR FLORAL AND LEAF PATTERNS

Choose wallcoverings, upholstery fabrics, carpets, and textiles with an eye for natural motifs. Plants and floral arrangements encourage repose.

COMPLEX PATTERNS AND VISUAL VARIETY

An interior should have a balance of restfulness and interest. There should be plenty of variety—of materials, motifs, and treatments—for the eye to take in.

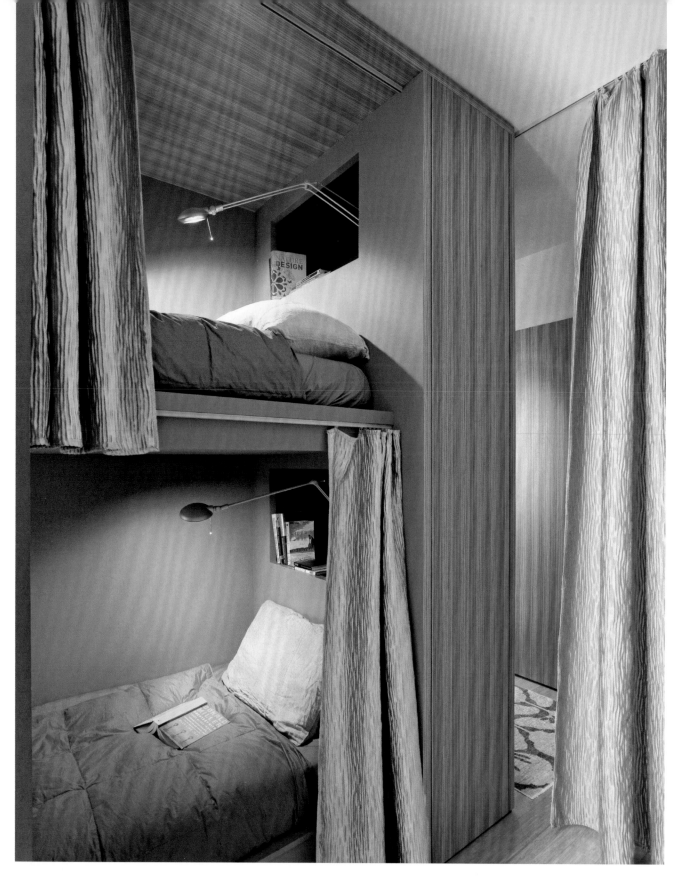

Bunk beds in a sleeping berth by Hutker Architects are enclosed
in shimmery metallic curtains for privacy in close quarters.

Reducing Environmental Stressors

Common to all environmental theories is the notion that every interior is compromised by ubiquitous stressors such as glare and noise that must be alleviated or controlled by using window treatments, light dimmers (called rheostats), white-noise machines, and similar devices.

PROBLEM/CHALLENGE	SOLUTION
POOR INDOOR AIR QUALITY	- Windows that open easily - Low-VOC finishes and materials - Easy-to-clean surfaces - Hard surfaces and low-pile textiles - Air filtration system
THERMAL COMFORT	- Zoned thermostats - Insulated walls and windows
NOISE	- Soft flooring - Abundant fabrics (from upholstered walls to window treatments) - Use of high-texture materials - Acoustical treatments - White-noise machines
INADEQUATE DAYLIGHT	- Light colors - Reflective surfaces
GLARE	- Window shades, blinds, or sheers - Dark and/or textured finishes
CLAUSTROPHOBIA/ CROWDING	- Increased light levels and brightness - Rectangular and well-proportioned spaces - Use of artwork and plants
PRIVACY	- Windows properly treated - Interior doors - Enclosed or shaded-from-view areas for changing, bathing, etc.

DESIGN ELEMENTS & PRINCIPLES

Mapping out the floor plan of an apartment; conceiving the interior of a room; rearranging a seating area; composing a tablescape for an entry—all these actions require application of the basic principles and elements of design. The best way to understand how they are used is to see them in action:

Scale

A sense of scale derives from the relationship between one element and another: between table and chair, person and room. Furnishings should be properly scaled to the size of the room they inhabit, while rooms themselves should relate to the human body. Here, two strong elements play off each other: the square painting and the angular console, both set against a stark white wall for contrast. The console and the painting also have the same visual weight, creating balance, or equilibrium.

Proportion

This principle concerns the relationship of parts to the whole. Base and crown moldings should be in proportion to the overall dimensions of a room, for instance; a table base should not overwhelm (or be disproportionate to) the top. This graceful lamp exemplifies good proportion: the width of the shade is roughly equal to the height of the

base. The pairing of lamp and artwork also uses the element of **line**—in this case, a gently meandering curve evocative of a branch.

Balance

A sense of equilibrium derives from mirror-like symmetry or carefully calibrated asymmetry, whereby opposing elements are differently arranged yet have the same visual weight. A designer plays with balance to create peacefulness (via equilibrium) or excitement (via disequilibrium). In this vignette, two male heads from different eras, rendered in different materials, commingle with an antique painting to create a male portrait–themed tableau. Contrasting with the round heads, the spiky fish skeleton at rear serves as both visual and narrative counterweight.

Repetition

Repeated elements—whether arrayed randomly, in a rhythmic sequence, or set in a grid—bring visual order and emphasis to a space. Here, an abundance of circles—the portal-like window and shutter, the chair seat and base—creates a graphic jolt. This is also a good example of **contrast:** the circles appear even stronger because the surrounding elements are so linear.

SCALE

PROPORTION

BALANCE

REPETITION

Alignment

This term describes when various features—whether artworks or architectural elements—line up along their edges or centerlines. The mirror's width matches that of the chest of drawers below, instating alignment, while wall-mounted accessories create a vertical column to one side.

Form

Each shelf boasts a strong, rounded form that lures the eye along a curving path or line, from the trio of white vases to the blue-glazed vessel, down to the clock and then the tiny framed artwork below—before resting on the curved chair back.

Color

A controlled color palette distinguishes this seating area: ivory and orange with hints of inky blue-black. Complementary hues of orange and blue are used in a variety of tints and shades (even the ivory is tinged faintly with orange), making for an extremely cohesive decor.

Texture

At first glance, this tablescape suggests a focus on symmetry, established by the pair of lamps anchoring either end of the console, and the framed artworks that mirror one another. But a closer look reveals that items were chosen with texture in mind: an abundance of smooth, polished surfaces contrasts with the more organic forms of the artwork and floral arrangement.

ANALYZING
THE SPACE

A designer begins the conceptualization phase by analyzing the architectural character of the room or space according to the elements of proportion and scale, axis and alignment, rhythm and repetition. While the initial site survey simply observed and documented these characteristics, during this next step, the goal is to determine how to celebrate, modify, minimize, or hide various architectural features and attributes. If a space feels a bit cramped, what can be done to make it seem more expansive? Is there a way to distract attention from the odd placement of the fireplace? The views are stellar, but the window moldings are kind of dowdy—what sort of treatments might be best? Can a work-around be found for that unusual soffit?

While a layperson may undertake this step on-site, observing and contemplating the space while standing in it, designers use architectural drawings—plans and elevations—to begin designing. Two-dimensional documentation allows them to notice certain spatial attributes, relationships, or patterns that are not always as apparent in person. Floor plans reveal the logic—and sometimes the illogic—of a room. Although nondesigners may find it difficult at first to understand a physical environment through drawings, it is still important to prepare them. The act of translating a 3-D space to a 2-D plan trains the brain to start "seeing" space on paper in the same way a professional would, and understanding its nuances and potential.

Here are some questions to ask about design elements and principles when analyzing a space:

Balance and Alignment

- Is the room symmetrically balanced? If not, could the addition of a built-in somewhere rectify the problem? Can an architectural feature be adjusted—a column removed or a new one added—to instate balance?
- Do the doorways or openings appear to be balanced on the walls? Could they be enlarged, or could balance be established through the strategic placement of built-ins?
- Is there a major fixed element such as a fireplace? Is it perfectly centered on its wall, or is it offset?

Windows and Doors

- Where are the openings: windows, doors, and other apertures? Should they be moved, enlarged, or possibly sealed up (to gain wall space or improve circulation, for instance)?
- What do the doors and windows look like, and how do they operate? Will their function complicate the design of any treatments?
- How are the windows placed, both on the wall and in relationship to one another? Might this complicate the mounting (and design) of any curtains or shades?
- Is there a pattern to the windows: squares, rectangles, etc.? Is just one size or type of window used repeatedly, or is there variation?
- Do the windows read as a continuous gesture, a series of slots in the walls, holes punched through walls, or frames for a view?

Paths and Focal Points

- Is there a sense of spatial hierarchy—i.e., is one area clearly emphasized by the architecture (or otherwise important)?
- Where are the room's key focal points—the features that the eye naturally gravitates to (a built-in, a window, a fireplace)?

Spatial Flow and Axis

- Where are the doorways located? Do they determine paths of foot traffic? Ill-placed doors can create awkward circulation patterns, make a space feel like a throughway, and limit where large furnishings can be placed. Is there room to anchor a sofa against the wall, or should it be floated so as not to block entry into the space?
- Is there a preferred path of circulation through the space, or a procession of some kind?
- What is the logical flow of foot traffic through the room? What are the dominant and the secondary paths?
- Is one area of the space an obvious destination?
- Does the room have a central axis or strong centerline? Does it have a secondary axis?

Walls and Floors

- Are the walls thick or the standard 4 inches? The construction will dictate how easily they can be drilled into.
- What are the building materials, and what roles do they play in the design?

- What is the flooring material? Does the way in which the wood (or other material) is laid or patterned express a direction?

Siting and Natural Light

- How is the house sited and oriented? What direction does the room face?
- Where does light enter? This will inform the need for artificial illumination and window treatments, the choice of finishes, and the placement of furnishings.

Indoor/Outdoor Connection

- Is there a view through windows or doorways? A subpar vista may need to be screened or softened, perhaps with sheer curtain panels. For a stellar view, choose minimalist treatments that keep the focus on the outdoors.
- What is the relationship between the interior and the adjacent exterior spaces?

Unique Design Details

- Note the height or detail of the base, crown, and door moldings. Are there applied moldings or panelized walls that create a rhythm or focal points in the room?
- Dropped soffits, beams, and columns—either decorative or enclosing pipes or structural elements—can require intervention to hide, disguise, or integrate them.

Once these characteristics—the good and the bad—are understood, the design process can begin in earnest. The first step is to correct (or distract from) any architectural deficiencies: odd columns, exposed pipes, surfaces that aren't aligned, and poorly proportioned windows. It might be necessary to take out an awkward level change, tear out built-in bookcases, close off a doorway into a room, or add a transom above a door. Think about where recessed lighting might make sense, where new electrical outlets or switches should be placed, and where bays could be built to accommodate cabinets. An architect, a general contractor, or a carpenter is often needed for this step.

If construction isn't possible or the architectural shell can't be modified—as is the case with most rentals—then problems are typically solved through decorative means. Strategic use of paint or wallpaper can smooth over a clunky collision of columns and beams. If a room is on the small side, then pay special attention to the windows: use high-mounted draperies with a valance above to create the illusion of more headroom. And while it may sound counterintuitive, using over-scale furniture in a diminutive space can make it seem larger.

To suit the gravitas of a grand-scaled living room, Matthew Patrick Smyth deployed a mix of classic and modern pieces and large-scale artworks and mirrors; multiple conversation areas help create intimacy in loft-like space.

LAYING OUT THE SPACE

Drawings and diagrams are the primary tools designers use to understand the space and begin to articulate ideas about how it should be laid out. A designer thinks through her pen or pencil, whether dashing off casual freehand sketches, drafting adjacency diagrams (often in the form of "bubbles" of different activities) to understand the relationships between activity zones, or laying tracing paper over floor plans to explore possible furniture arrangements. Sketching equals visualization; even the simplest line or gesture can spark ideation. Amateurs too can use doodles and rough drawings to begin the creative process and test out concepts and solutions.

Carefully measured plans and elevations, either professional or amateur, are the starting point; sketch over them to viscerally understand the character of the space. One or more dominant characteristics will begin to emerge. The existing architectural elements—columns, walls, openings, beams—along with the location of mechanical systems, plumbing, major entrances, views, and focal points, will guide the design; so will the formal properties of the building itself. As lines are drawn, they typically suggest forms and patterns that in turn give rise to concepts. Plan and program will start coalescing into a form.

Activity Areas

Consider the desired uses of the room. For a family with young children, a kitchen may need to include a play zone, a counter with stools, a television area, and a desk with a phone in addition to the usual food prep and cooking spots. Even a small room tends to incorporate at least two or three activity areas; think of a snug bedroom with zones for sleeping, dressing, and reading. Which zones should be adjacent? Where should they overlap?

And approximately how much square footage should be allocated to each activity? At this stage—prior to having a proper furniture plan—designers work with estimates. Ultimately, the size of furniture is what determines the overall footprint of an activity area or grouping (see pages 68–69, Standard Furniture Dimensions). For example, if a dining room is to seat six at a table, then estimate the space required by a typical table, six chairs, and the circulation around them (an additional 24–36 inches).

Think about how foot traffic will flow given the placement of doorways and the location of architectural features that typically guide circulation patterns. A rough layout should start to become clear.

OPPOSITE: Ellen Fisher developed a series of diagrams to think through the redesign of a residential floor plan, including ones highlighting circulation patterns and lines of symmetry.

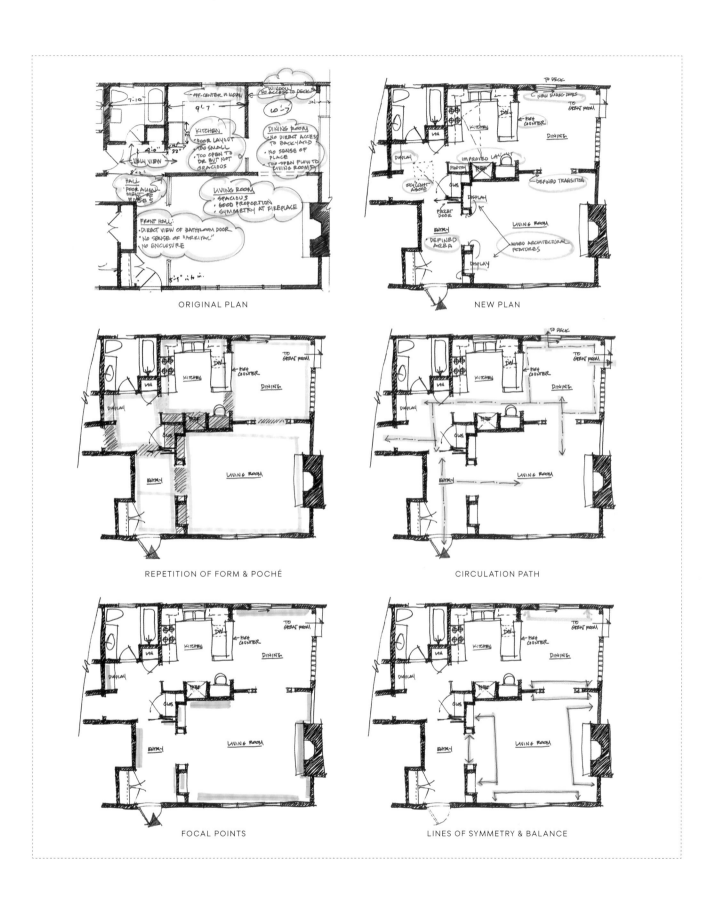

ORIGINAL PLAN

NEW PLAN

REPETITION OF FORM & POCHÉ

CIRCULATION PATH

FOCAL POINTS

LINES OF SYMMETRY & BALANCE

Standard Furniture Dimensions

ITEM		WIDTH	LENGTH	HEIGHT	SEAT HEIGHT
SEATING					
SOFA	Two-seater (loveseat)	40"	55–70"	28–38"	16–18"
	Three-seater	40"	80–105"	28–38"	16–18"
	Sectional	40"	100–164"	28–38"	16–18"
	Chaise	42–52"	68–74"	28–36"	16–18"
CHAIR	Occasional chair	16"	17–18"	32–42"	18"
	Wing chair	35–42"	27–32"	38–44"	16–18"
	Slipper chair	27–32"	25–30"	28–44"	14–18"
	Club chair	32–42"	28–35"	24–34"	16–18"
OTTOMAN	Rectangular	16–24"	18–40"	16–18"	
	Square	24–29"	11–18"	16–18"	
TABLES					
DINING ROOM	Rectangular for 6	36–42"	48–78"	29–30"	
	Rectangular for 8	42–44"	60–84"	29–30"	
	Square for 4	36–48"	28–30"	28–30"	
	Square for 6	48–60"	28–30"		
	Oval for 6	36–42"	60–72"	29–30"	
	Oval for for 8	36–44"	72–84"	29–30"	
	Circular for 4	42–54"	28–30"	29–30"	
	Circular for 6	54–66"	28–30"	29–30"	
COFFEE/ COCKTAIL	Rectangular	18–40"	52–60"	14–20"	
	Square	38–44"	16–20"	14–20"	
	Oval	30–34"	40–60"	14–20"	

ITEM		WIDTH	LENGTH	HEIGHT
SIDE	Rectangular	14–18"	18–22"	24–26"
	Round	18–22"	18–22"	24–26"
	Bunching	8–14"	12–20"	18–26"
OTHER	Console	15"	48–55"	30"
	Sofa table	17–22"	42–48"	29–31"
	Pedestal	27–45"	27–45"	28–30"
	Nightstand	16–20"	18–27"	25–28"
CASE GOODS				
	Sideboard	16–18"	63–84"	25–36"
	TV stand	18–24"	36–60"	21–30"
	Bookcase	11–14"	24–36"	36–96"
	Bookshelf	10–13"	12–36"	30–84"
	Armoire	18–30"	34–56"	54–94"
	Breakfront	19"	24–48"	76"
DESKS				
	Standard	24–36"	48–72"	29–30"
	Laptop stand	18"	16–24"	27–43"
	Secretary	16–24"	32–48"	72–84"
BEDS				
	Crib/toddler	28"	52"	
	Twin	39"	75"	
	Full	54"	75"	
	Queen	60"	80"	
	King	76"	80"	
	California king	72"	84"	
MISC.				
	Piano	58"	58–95"	39"

Furniture Plans

The furniture layout is the first limiting factor in developing a design from idea to reality. Interior designers generally move quickly to this stage, using their knowledge of human behavior and of standard ways that typical furnishings work together. "There are no secret untapped floor plans; it's all about common sense," says designer Matthew Patrick Smyth. "Keep it simple."

For laypeople, however, this step may require more patience and experimentation. All rooms are designed to accommodate at least one logical furniture arrangement; toying with ideas will help uncover this inherent potential. Freely explore a range of possible layouts. A large living area might offer many variations based on the location of important focal points, such as a bay window or a fireplace. At this stage, think outside the box and try anything in order to surprise. "We often generate numerous furniture plans during the design-development process," says Elizabeth Pyne. "Some are wacky and crazy, but it's important to go through the exercise and be as open-minded and creative as possible; a furniture plan is not a formula."

That being said, all rooms designed for real life—living areas and otherwise—need the same elements to facilitate functions such as conversation, reading, and entertaining:

- A focal point
- An entry point
- Logical circulation
- Good lighting
- Appropriate seating (which, in the case of a tiny bedroom, may mean none at all)
- Functional needs addressed (a dining room will need a table and service area, for instance)

After developing rough sketches, determine which pieces or groupings can realistically fit given standard furniture sizes. In the 1950s, industrial designer Henry Dreyfuss undertook a large-scale study to determine the average dimensions of American men, women, and children. His research ultimately led to the standardization of commonly manufactured household furniture, meaning that it is possible to know the typical size of various elements.

Designers and amateurs alike often use these measurements to make paper furniture templates, moving them around the floor plan like piecing together a puzzle. This exercise will ultimately reveal the best plan—one that fulfills all the functional, aesthetic, and conceptual goals. Over time, a designer will finesse the furniture plan a bit as furnishings are specified and their exact dimensions become known.

OPPOSITE: In designing a New York apartment, Amy Lau generated a number of furniture plans. Variations were made to test out the ideal placement of the family and dining rooms—and to maximize the enjoyment of views. The progression of such a plan should also include architectural changes that could provide more flexibility in the furniture layout, such as the removal of a fireplace.

WORKING FURNITURE PLANS

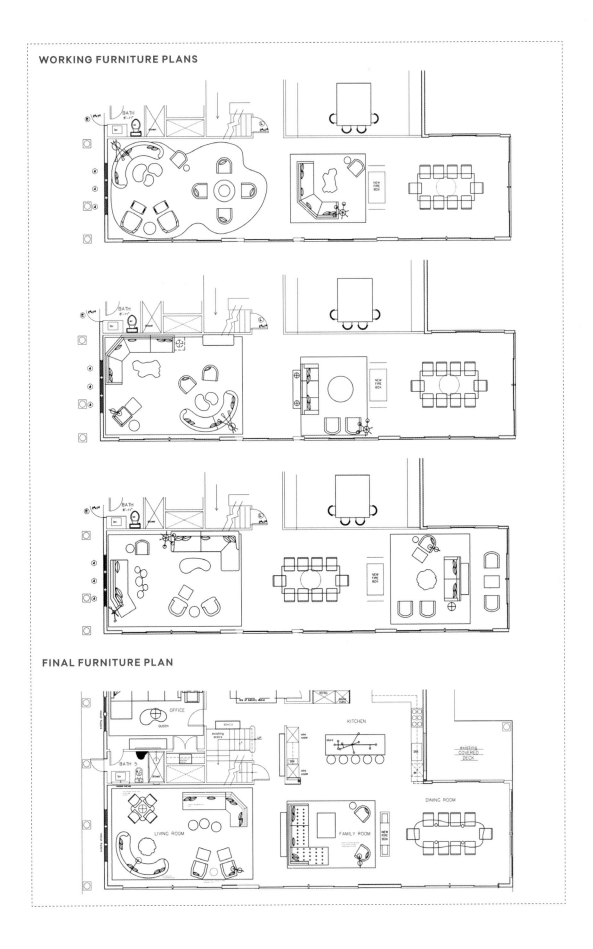

FINAL FURNITURE PLAN

CREATING
THE SCHEME

A furniture plan is like a roadmap; use it as a guide to generate the checklist of elements that will need to be purchased, ordered, and specified. The plan for a small family room might designate an L-shaped sectional, coffee and side tables (the latter with lamps), an 8-by-10-foot area rug, and a full-height shelving unit (freestanding or built-in) to house books and the TV. The ground-floor space gets ample sunshine and is exposed to the neighbors, so windows will require treatments for privacy and glare. Decisions about color, material, finish, size, and more need to be made concerning each interior element—down to the most granular detail. Paint color is deliberated over and chosen, its glossiness determined, and aspects of its application method communicated to the contractor. The model of the sofa is selected, the fabric and upholstery details resolved—including how the pattern will be oriented and applied to the cushions. The lampshade size and pleating style are debated, as well as the precise curvature of the bespoke armatures.

Such decisions must be made with cohesiveness in mind. The primary purpose of a design scheme is to unify: to integrate disparate elements, activities, and rooms into a cohesive spatial experience, all relating back to an original concept or goal. All elements, large and small, should work in concert. "The effect you want is that everything goes together—but subtly," says Elizabeth Pyne.

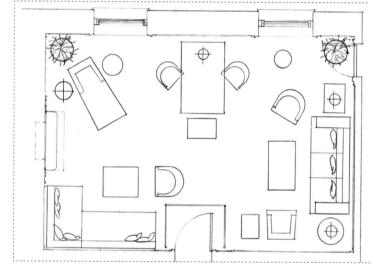

OPPOSITE + ABOVE: A series of images and documents offers insight into Alexa Hampton's working process in conceiving a salon. Photographs taken of the site helped her generate a concept and scheme, sketched out casually with ballpoint pen in her notebook. From there, she and her design team generated a furniture plan and specified all interior elements. The result is faithful to her initial intent.

CREATING A PALETTE

Keeping the design concept in mind helps ensure a consistent sensibility throughout. So does establishing a palette of color, textures, and materials. The palette is often kick-started by the inspiration images that the client or the designer has collected. Or a homeowner has inherited a lovely Persian rug that he wants to design his living room around, using and expanding upon the carpet's featured hues and motifs.

In this way, a palette arises from—and nearly simultaneously with—the concept. A designer might evoke relaxation by using hues of sea and sand, or choose a hard-edged assemblage of industrial metals, concrete, and distressed wood to set an urbane, modern tone. A room envisioned as a neutral, gallery-like container for art might inspire a white-on-white scheme, with character and interest achieved through an assemblage of textures: smooth satin-wool, nubby chenille, glossy paint, and frosted glass.

In using and applying the palette to an interior, context is everything. No piece can be considered in isolation. A working scheme or palette assembles all the materials, from fabrics to woods to metal accents to paints. The work of the designer is to observe and analyze them under different light sources, in different proportions and orientations, to ensure that they come together as a layered, complete whole.

OPPOSITE + ABOVE: Architect Terry Kleinberg curated an urbane mélange of glass and wood in devising a palette for a New York kitchen and adjacent dining area.

COORDINATING THE COLOR SCHEME

Color is the fundamental element of every palette, and yet complicated to use masterfully and in accordance with the principles of balance and proportion. Color has a strategic value, helping a designer manipulate the architecture and inherent character of a space. Color also has an emotional, symbolic content. Color speaks: It can soothe and calm, create tension or energy, depending on the desired effect.

A scheme should generally have a proportional distribution of colors—in varying tones—across the walls, floor, ceiling, furnishings, and accessories. Based on the concept and the inspiration images, determine:

- A **dominant hue,** to be used for roughly 50 percent of all the fabrics or materials. The color can be solid, textured, or appear in prints.
- A **secondary hue** or two, accounting for about 30 percent of the scheme.
- The rest of the scheme should incorporate an **accent color,** which can be brighter or more dramatic. Metal, wood, foliage, or another natural material can also act as accent or secondary color.

It can be overwhelming to pull together a color scheme at first. Interior designers learn how to use color by mixing paint pigments and understanding the science behind how the eye "reads" hues in context and across the different elements in a room. Accordingly, an excellent starting point is a favorite painting that, regardless of image depicted, has the right chromatic feeling for the room you want to create. After all,

painters study for years to become expert at telling a story with color: the proportions used, the texture, and even the patterning. A Vincent van Gogh tablescape, when meticulously analyzed for hue, value, chroma, and proportion of color, can be re-created as a French-inspired dining room with yellow walls and accents of rich blue, warm white, a shade of orange, and black.

As you develop a color scheme, ask yourself the following questions:

- Is it balanced?
- Are the colors distributed correctly across the room? Some designers apply the principle of **tonal distribution** to the rooms they create: mimicking a natural landscape, the lightest color is applied to the ceiling, like the sky; a middle tone or medium color is used for the largest area (the walls and furnishings); and the very darkest color is used for the floor, as in the earth.
- Are there enough neutrals? These paler colors can most successfully be applied over the largest percentage of surface, such as walls, curtains, and even floors, where a highly chromatic color might be overpowering. A scheme conceived to last for many decades should use neutrals for the more permanent items, and bright or colorful accents on those accessories that can easily be changed (pillows, lampshades, and even artwork).
- Does the overall color and materials scheme hold together?

Color Harmonies

Rules about color are solid guidelines for beginners, but there are no recognized formulas that can be followed like a recipe in order to achieve a specific goal. Indeed, color experts know their topic so well that they can play with and break the so-called rules. That being said, most interior schemes fall into one of the following categories, and its strength or delicacy will vary in accordance with the intensity, vibrancy, or paleness of the basic hue. Note that the rules below are based on dyes or pigments used in or on *solid* things, like fabric or wood; different theories and rules apply to color used in illumination.

MONOCHROMATIC

In this type of scheme, just one color is used, but in a range of values from light to dark—"all the tonal and chromatic values of a single color," explains expert Ethel Rompilla. Value is the relative strength or paleness of a hue; for instance, dark blue, royal blue, and baby blue are different values of blue. Interior designers typically use at least five or six different values, supplemented by neutrals. "A one-color room would read as flat, but once you start introducing a range of values, the space gains a sense of richness," says Rompilla. The more closely monochromatic the color scheme, the more varied the decor needs to be in terms of pattern and texture. Monochromatic rooms have an inherent ambience of unity and focus. Beige rooms are peaceful, but monochromatic schemes can also communicate power and drama: One of the most famous examples was an all-red room created by designer Billy Baldwin for editor Diana Vreeland.

ANALOGOUS

A room that follows an analogous scheme utilizes colors that are adjacent on the color wheel: blue-violet, blue, and blue-green, for example. An analogous scheme is inherently unified but needs a jolt from the other side of the color wheel. A screen porch at the seaside might feature a scheme of navy, sky blue, and deep aqua, spiked with rich red-orange coral or pale-yellow straw baskets to enhance the overall design.

COMPLEMENTARY

A complementary scheme pairs colors on the opposite side of the color wheel: red and green, blue and orange, yellow and violet, for example. Complementary schemes can be jarring if the two hues are used at full value. But when a red/green scheme is interpreted as burgundy plus hunter or pale pink plus leaf green, then the room takes on depth and delight. When devising a complementary scheme, achieve subtlety by playing with value and tints (the color plus white) or shades (the color plus black).

SPLIT COMPLEMENTARY

In this scenario, one color is paired with the two that sit across from it on the color wheel, adjacent to each other: violet with yellow-orange and yellow-green, for example. Again, hues in a split complementary scheme work best when used as tints or shades. A split complementary scheme is rich and nuanced and one of the most interesting to live in.

Essential Elements

Every room needs color harmony—but also a bit of tension, in the following forms:

CONTRAST

Contrast is an essential means to create tension and frisson. In a room, you see colors not in isolation but against others. Some element of contrast is necessary for definition and emphasis—but not so much that the effect is jarring. One note of caution: in a high-contrast environment, outlines will be much more distinct. Be sure to use a variety of shapes and profiles.

MIDDLE VALUES

It's very important to have middle values of the color palette in a room. The middle range is the glue that holds together a palette, keeping it from becoming too garish or high-contrast. A medium value is a bridge within a color scheme, making white look less stark and dark look less murky.

NEUTRALS

An interior needs neutrals; you can't just pile color on color. Neutral means nearly achromatic, not a distinguishable color: taupe, ecru, cool (not warm) brown, certain navies. In a home that's relatively open in plan, with rooms that flow into one another without boundaries (such as doors and full-height walls), neutrals are essential to express or support the concept of flow and unity.

Variables Affecting Color's Appearance

Colors do not stand alone, and understanding their interaction is very important. For example, certain hues are more visible during the day or night. And dark colors give the impression of advancing or jumping forward, while light colors recede. "There's a push/pull effect that a good designer can exploit," says Rompilla. "For instance, if you have an alcove, painting it one value darker than the rest of the room will push it back even more." Instead of crimson, use wine.

NATURAL OR ARTIFICIAL LIGHT

The presence or absence of light, either natural or artificial, will change a color dramatically. What looks pale tan in sunlight may read as rosy peach under incandescent illumination. That's why it's important to check fabric, material, and paint samples in different types of lighting when possible: LED, incandescent, and day light all have differing color "temperatures," ranging from warm and golden to cool and bluish white.

LEARNING ABOUT HOW THE EYE PERCEIVES COLOR WILL ALLOW YOU TO MANIPULATE THE MEDIUM IN ORDER TO ACHIEVE A DESIRED EFFECT.

SURROUNDING COLORS AND MATERIALS

Even wood has color: Think about the red-orange of mahogany versus the yellow-orange of maple. Or the difference between brass and nickel. Every room is layered in the floor plan and in elevations. The fabric on an upholstered chair will look different depending on whether the chair sits on a rug that's predominantly blue-violet or mainly red, and whether the rug itself rests on dark-stained wood parquet or a light warm-gray concrete floor. The paint is another contextual layer.

AFTERIMAGE

A related concept is called afterimage: If you stare at a red block and then shift your gaze, green—which is opposite on the color wheel—will emerge. So when placing a red sofa against a gray or beige wall, bear in mind that that green will "appear" in the color scheme. One way to work with vibrant colors is to use them in floating furniture arrangements and away from reflective vertical or horizontal surfaces.

REFLECTED COLOR

That same red sofa will also throw off a soft reddish color onto whatever is around it, especially the lighter surfaces. You can create a rosy glow in a white-painted room by using large pieces of furniture in warm tones, or even by using a golden-color floor.

ANALOGOUS

SPLIT COMPLEMENTARY

ABOVE: In a Cullman & Kravis design, a pale yellow-cream is the background for an analogous scheme of yellow, yellow-orange, and orange. **RIGHT:** Saturated yellow-green is balanced with red and violet accents. **OPPOSITE, ABOVE:** This stately room is a monochromatic scheme of varying tints and shades of yellow-orange. **OPPOSITE, BELOW:** Addie Havemeyer mixed different values of orange with subtle blue accents in a complementary scheme for a living area.

MONOCHROMATIC

COMPLEMENTARY

STYLE & LIFESTYLE

Whereas functional needs are relatively straightforward to define, style can prove harder to pin down. While some people can summarize their aesthetic—French country with a boho twist, midcentury-meets-mod—most find it hard to articulate their preferences in such a digestible sound bite. And why should they? Although rooms can often be identified by their ostensible style—Georgian, French provincial—most are a hybrid of features and sensibilities. The best interiors have off-notes and are elevated by a certain frisson, in which disparate elements play off one another to create visual interest.

From Casual to Formal

Rather than get overly hung up on style, begin by determining the homeowners' *lifestyle*—namely, where their behavior and habits fall on the spectrum from casual to formal. What level of relaxation will they seek, both for inhabitants and for guests? Will people be encouraged to put their feet up on the upholstered furniture or eat in front of the TV? If the space is being designed for an active family with three rambunctious young children, they will likely embrace a relaxed way of living. Or if the project is the townhouse of a sixty-something professor who has colleagues over for cocktails, he probably favors a more formal decor—regardless of whether he loves Louis XVI or '70s sleek.

Depending on their intended function, various rooms within a home may lean a bit more formal or casual. Perhaps the living room is devoted to entertaining. A space reserved for such an intention can include precious materials like silk and a palette of lighter colors that would stain and wear more readily in a relaxed, kick-up-your-feet environment. Seating in a formal space should be designed or specified for comfort in an upright position—no sleeping on the sofa here! But the den is a room where shoes go on the coffee table and snacks are eaten in the easy chair. Here, a good choice is hard-wearing fabrics and floor coverings, possibly textured or patterned to hide crumbs and dirt. And the seating can be a bit softer and larger in scale to support repose and sprawling. The point is that the same concept, aesthetic, and color scheme can be applied throughout the home by using different materials, details, finishes, and treatments.

From Traditional to Modern

Even those who don't know where they reside on the aesthetic continuum are able to identify whether they favor traditional or modern decor—or if they fall somewhere in the middle. Their stylistic leanings will inform many decisions about the interior architecture and the layout of the room, not to mention the specification of certain elements. A lover of art moderne can fall in love with Shaker, or see the lines of rococo in art deco . . . which might lead her to choose between an antique console and a pared-down modern interpretation. Different lines, different profile, same spirit.

Sometimes the architecture of the room will suggest a traditional or modern scheme. On other occasions a room's envelope can require moderate modifications or even a full-scale overhaul to implement the intended design vision. If the architecture of the space is resolutely traditional or modern, it can act as a foil for a scheme that's the opposite, inspiring a design concept along the lines of "the new, nested within the old."

TRADITIONAL

A traditional room is culture-specific, with references to historical design: French, English, Scandinavian, Chinese, for example. Traditional should not be confused with *period* design, in which the architectural envelope, furnishings, and materials all belong to the same era and locale. Proportion, scale, alignment, and balance are the key design principles at work in a traditional room. Unlike modern spaces, which are often open plan, a traditional room is defined and enclosed by walls. Sensitively scaled, highly detailed, and visually textured, it is characterized by the following elements:

- An emphasized point of entry
- An architectural focal point, such as a fireplace
- A full complement of trims and moldings
- Symmetrical balance

If the architectural envelope is lacking in character, then the room's elements should be manipulated to create the requisite definition, balance, and focus.

MODERN

The hallmark of a modern interior—whether contemporary in style or just minimalist in execution—is simplicity of form, color, and shape. With fewer supporting elements than are found in traditional rooms, the furnishings or groupings must act as visual anchors. Stripping away extraneous flourishes creates a blank slate—a white box into which furnishings are set like sculptures, drawing attention and inviting appreciation. The following key design principles at play in a modern interior support the freedom to make a bold design statement:

- Contrast
- Asymmetric composition
- An emphasis on form and line

ECLECTIC

Eclectic spaces allow for a wide range of elements and sensibilities. The design of the interior architecture and the selection and placement of furnishings can take a distinctly personal turn, crossing stylistic, historic, and cultural lines to conjure a unique environment. Instead of using a given period of decorative-arts history or a specific cultural tradition as a recipe for choosing a scheme, eclecticism is very much reliant on a concept to unify diverse elements. Choose floors, walls, ceilings, finishes, and architectural woodwork to express the overarching idea.

TRANSITIONAL

Similar to eclecticism is what the design industry calls transitional style. While eclectic interiors combine design from many periods and geographical regions, transitional furnishings are chosen from within just one general culture, but span the range from traditional to contemporary.

FORMAL AND MODERN

FORMAL AND TRADITIONAL

ABOVE: In a townhouse by Joan Dineen, sunshine filters in through a skylight and full-height window wall. Muted tones and dark sheers temper the ample sunshine. **RIGHT:** A grand salon by Geoffrey Bradfield is formal indeed, with pale tones and delicate fabrics. **OPPOSITE, ABOVE:** Stefan Steil treated furniture like sculptures—with ample breathing room to highlight their profiles—in this modern-minded living room. **OPPOSITE, BELOW:** For a historic townhouse, Kati Curtis chose furnishings with traditional lines and detailing—but a certain casualness befitting the inhabitants' relaxed lifestyle.

CASUAL AND MODERN

CASUAL AND TRADITIONAL

Designing a Traditional versus a Modern Living Space

While most rooms fall somewhere in the middle of these poles, understanding what defines each extreme can be educational.

	TRADITIONAL	MODERN
WALLS	Ideal is a chair rail at about 27 inches above the finished floor (the exact measurement varies depending on the height of the space). Set wood panels or applied molding below and an applied molding above (optional). Treat walls to a solid paint color or a special decorative finish, such as lacquer or Venetian plaster (a troweled-on mix of plaster and marble dust that imbues a luminous sheen). Alternatively, they could be wallpapered, upholstered, or covered with paper-backed fabric. Wood paneling is suitable too, whether stained, waxed, or painted.	Paint alone is the ideal covering, in a single color for cohesion. Interesting modern textures or wallpaper patterns are also nice to consider. In a modern interior, the distinction between window, wall, and door is minimized or even blurred. Sometimes they read as a continuous gesture; consider a full-height window wall with integrated sliding door.
FLOORS	Choose oak, mahogany, cherry, walnut, or maple—preferably parquet with a wood border pattern. Area rugs should be special and perhaps custom or one of a kind. Wool, silk, and linen are wonderful traditional choices, as are Oriental or Chinese designs.	The same wood varieties as for traditional floors are all suitable, ideally arrayed in a simple pattern (or none at all) and featuring minimal variegation. Other common materials for modern interiors include concrete, stone or tile (in a regular pattern), and poured or troweled terrazzo or synthetic stone. Area rugs should be simple in color and pattern or contrast greatly (in age, cultural origin, or texture) with their surroundings. Wool, silk, and linen can confer modernity, or choose a rug fabricated of an unusual material such as recycled textiles.
CEILINGS	Detail with applied moldings or a recessed cove (in which the ceiling steps up in the middle). Ornamental rosettes are a nice touch.	Keep the ceilings as simple and as smooth as possible; perhaps paint them with a high-gloss finish.

	TRADITIONAL	MODERN
MOLDINGS	The various junctures where walls, floor, and ceiling meet should be gracefully trimmed with properly proportioned moldings. Large rooms with high ceilings need large crown moldings (also called cornices) and tall and gracefully detailed baseboards (aka skirt moldings). Smaller rooms should likewise feature elegant millwork details, although they should be more daintily scaled and have cleaner profiles.	Specify a simple flat base molding or a ¾-inch reveal (i.e., a gap) where the floor meets the walls. Avoid crown and window moldings.
OPENINGS	Doorways and windows need wide, substantial wood trim. Doorways should also be embellished by plinth blocks (a sort of base molding for door trim) and ideally feature mitered (or angled) joints.	Leave openings untrimmed—no wood moldings. The thickness or weight of the frames should be in keeping with the overall design intention.
WINDOWS	Where possible, windows should have sills and aprons (a base/molding below the sill), solid-metal hardware, and glass panels framed by mullions.	Keep the design spare. Windows may be deeply inset but will have no mullions and no trim. Opt for solid round knobs or simple unadorned pulls.
WINDOW TREATMENTS	Dress with shades, overdrapes (i.e., the primary curtain panels), and casements (a sheer underlayer). Consider special trims or contrasting lining as well as tiebacks (either fabric or passementerie). A top treatment, such as a valance or a hard cornice, is an agreeable option. Decorative hardware—including rods, finials, brackets, rings, and holdbacks—makes a classy finishing touch.	Treat architecturally. Leave windows untreated, or choose simple mesh shades or unfussy panels with minimal, clean-lined hardware and top treatments, using plain fabrics in solid colors. Keep any drapery rods as spare as possible; better yet, install a hidden or recessed ceiling track.
LIGHTING	As with any room, traditional spaces need as much light as possible. Given the stridently modern look of architectural lighting, any such fixtures need to be rendered as inconspicuous as possible. Appropriate decorative lighting includes chandeliers, sconces, and table lamps.	Architectural lighting can take the form of recessed downlights, monopoints, or track lighting. Sconces, table lamps, and other decorative lighting fixtures should be clean-lined and match the furnishings of the room in form, shape, material, and style.
COLORS	Warm and varied, emphasizing either pale hues or jewel tones, or with exuberance, as in floral chintzes.	Kept to a minimum, or used as a statement to play against a neutral palette.

	TRADITIONAL	MODERN
SEATING ARRANGEMENTS	Whether traditional or modern, a living area is meant for conversation and entertaining. Those activities will require at least one major seating grouping, ideally anchored by a large sofa (84-plus inches), with two club or pull-up chairs, a coffee table, and two end tables—all set on an area rug that defines this island of conviviality. Hang a large or important work of art, such as a painting or a tapestry, above the sofa.	Likewise needs at least one major seating grouping, anchored by a large sofa (84-plus inches), with two club or pull-up chairs and a coffee table (or other large central surface). End tables are optional. In lieu of table lamps, consider a large floor lamp that arcs over the sofa to illuminate the coffee table. When space permits, float the major furniture grouping in the center of a room to free up wall space for large artwork.
SECONDARY SEATING AREAS	Similar in layout to the main grouping but smaller in size—cozy enough for two or three people to chat or share a drink. Group a sofa and two chairs; two loveseats; or a chaise, a loveseat, and an ottoman (or a single chair). Accompany groupings with the requisite tables and surfaces to hold drinks, books, or small plates.	Supplementary groupings provide opportunities to create vignettes, either to draw attention to a beautiful view or to emphasize a particularly striking piece of furniture (or special acquisition): an Eames lounge, a Le Corbusier pony skin chaise, a Giacometti floor lamp, or a pair of Marcel Wanders chairs. Leave enough visual "white space" to appreciate them as works of art.
FURNITURE SELECTION	An array of fully upholstered seating (two- and three-seat sofas, club chairs, slipper chairs, tub or barrel chairs) accompanied by mobile occasional chairs with exposed-wood frames and upholstered seats. Round out the mix with fabric-covered ottomans (or poufs) and wood benches (or stools). Common surfaces include wooden or skirted side tables, coffee or "cigarette" tables, bunching or stacking tables, desks, console tables, and sofa tables. Cabinets include secretaries, hutches, linen presses, chests, and wall-mounted consoles.	Showcase at least one or two iconic modernist pieces amid other furnishings that are less special yet stylistically sympathetic (or even neutral). Tables or cabinets of every form have a place; the same applies to seating, case goods, and decorative objects. The materials palette and detailing are what differentiate a modern room from a traditional one: wood, lacquer, glass, metal, plastic, and even corrugated cardboard are all suitable.
FABRICS	Textures and patterns know no bounds in traditional interiors; mix scales and motifs freely. A traditional interior often features a large, complex floral (or similar) print that provides the color and pattern direction for an entire room, from paint to upholstery, draperies, and carpets.	Texture—versus pattern or color—should be the main attribute. A monochromatic scheme is favored, as is minimal pattern (a small motif that reads as a solid when viewed from a short distance is acceptable). Same-colored fabrics might exhibit a range of textures, from smooth to rough. Brilliantly colored and patterned modern textiles, such as those by Jack Lenor Larsen, are themselves hallmarks of the era to be used as decorative accents.

	TRADITIONAL	MODERN
ACCESSORIES	From decorative screens (made of fabric or lacquered wood) to curated assemblages of ceramics, objets d'art, photographs, and globes. Use such collections to embellish étagères, bookcases, mantelpieces, tables, and wall-mounted shelves or brackets.	Ceramics, handmade glass, and fine or craft art are great choices. Appreciation of the maker's hand is a facet of the modern vocabulary, rooted in the movement's Arts and Crafts origins. Today's more expansive view of modernism leaves room to appreciate more industrial works, exemplified by the ceramics of Russel Wright and Eva Zeisel.
BUILT-INS	Built-ins provide an opportunity to add elaborate millwork. Design them like freestanding furniture, using fine veneers, elegant detailing, and beautiful decorative hardware.	Attaining a gallery-like atmosphere in which to exhibit carefully curated furnishings depends on clutter control. Design niches and soffits to accommodate cabinets exactly (a task that demands careful calculation and exact measurements and drawings). Built-in cabinets are often designed to be flush with adjacent surfaces and to appear integral to the architecture. It is very elegant to showcase collections and individual objects in a display unit customized for that purpose. Wall-hung cabinets or consoles and simple shelves with integral lighting also have their place in modern interiors.
HARDWARE	Choose surface-mounted hardware that's ornamental and/or historically detailed. Opt for brass, bronze, or copper (for a more country look) coloration in a polished, satin, antiqued, or rusticated finish.	Sleek, minimally detailed flush-mount versions in silver tones, such as stainless steel and nickel, or black coloration—preferably in polished, satin, or rubbed finish—are de rigueur.
DOOR AND CABINET HINGES	Use decorative flanges.	Minimally embellished and geometric designs are best.

ORGANIZING & KEEPING TRACK

The staffer in a design firm who is responsible for and oversees every aspect of an individual project is called the project manager. She works directly with the GC and any other contractors, as well as with the workrooms and vendors. To organize and structure the long and complex ordering and realization process, she relies on various record-keeping and tracking systems. She also generates myriad documents and drawings, which are used to communicate the design intent to both clients and professional collaborators, such as architects and contractors.

"FOR A DESIGNER, A LIFETIME GOES INTO DESIGNING A SPACE FAST—A LIFETIME OF DEVELOPING RESOURCES AND TASTE, OF EDUCATION ABOUT HISTORY, DESIGN, ARTS, AND CULTURE. THAT KNOWLEDGE IS ONE OF THE GREAT VALUES OF THE PROFESSION."

—Jim Druckman, president and CEO of the New York Design Center

SPREADSHEETS AND LISTS

To kick-start the specification process, the designer creates an initial inventory (or list) of items to be purchased and labor to be contracted. Interior designers refer to lists as "schedules"; for example, the finish schedule itemizes elements ranging from wall paints to flooring, noting location, manufacturer, and spec number or color. Schedules for hardware, doors, and windows are also generated. These schedules are incorporated into what's known as the interior design intent drawings—similar to construction drawings but minus the structural notations and anything else outside the designer's professional, legal purview.

OPPOSITE: A pillow schedule by Amy Lau itemizing the chosen fabrics, trims, and detailing for each design.

THROW PILLOW SCHEDULE

Room / Pillow Location	Qty	Size/Description	Yardages	Face Fabric	Back Fabric	Fabricator	Fabric Status	Labor Status
ROOM # 2 | FAMILY LIVING ROOM								
A. Rudin Tufted Sofa # 2736 (Furniture item A in Room Description Package)	4	**(4)** 16" x 16" Knife Edge *No welting*	**Fromental:** 1 sq. yd. (TBC) **Lee Jofa:** Please advise *to confirm yardages*	**Fromental** Item # 7119S3 Custom Embroidered Velvet Width: 55" Repeat: None (custom)	**Lee Jofa** Item # 960033-110 "Queen Victoria Antique Velvet" Color: Mauve Width: 54" Repeat: None		**Fromental:** Strike-Off approved **Lee Jofa:** No CFA being issued - color guaranteed	
Vintage Pearsall Wave Sofa (Furniture item K in Room Description Package)	6	**(6)** 18" x18" Knife Edge *No welting*	**Fromental:** 1.5 Sq. Yd. (TBC) **Jim Thompson:** 5 yards (TBC) *to confirm yardages*	**Fromental** Item # 7119S1 Custom Embroidered Velvet Width: 55" Repeat: None (custom)	**Jim Thompson** Item #139706 "New Khmer" Color: Autumn Fern Width: 54" Repeat: None		**Fromental:** Strike-Off approved **Jim Thompson:** CFA #139706 approved	
Edward Wormley Swivel Chairs (Furniture item C in Room Description Package)	2	**(2)** 16" x 12" Knife Edge *No welting*	*to confirm yardage*	**Scalamdre** Item # 26832-002 Sophie Onde Campagna Damask Width: 51" Repeat: V: 14" | H: 12.75"			CFA Approved	
Kagan Barrel Swivel Chair (Furniture item F in Room Description Package)	1	**(1)** 16" x12" Knife Edge *No Welting*	*to confirm yardage*	**Pierre Frey** Item # F29290001 Atlas, Sable Width: 55" Repeat: 14.6"			Need CFA	
Vintage Carlo Di Carli Chair (Furniture item J in Room Description Package)	1	**(1)** 14" x14" Knife Edge *No Welting*	*to confirm yardage*	**Pollack** Item # 130-27-06 Retablo, Wisteria Width: 54" Repeat: None			Need CFA	

NUMBERED FURNITURE PLAN

Each item depicted on the furniture plan is assigned a unique digit, prefixed according to genre—CH denoting chairs, for example. These numbers are cross-referenced in various places: in the designer's tracking spreadsheet, on the purchase order to the vendor, and on the piece itself (or its packaging) when the vendor readies it for delivery. The numbered furniture plan not only facilitates the ordering process but also forms a map during the installation, showing the correct room location and exact placement of elements as they arrive on-site.

INTERIOR DESIGN INTENT DRAWINGS

Interior designers are not legally allowed to create drawings that show construction or structural changes, which is the purview of architects and engineers. But interior designers do create drawings that show the nonstructural design work: lighting, electrical and plumbing elements, and specification of paint and other finishes. The homeowner reviews and approves them in writing before work begins. The interior design intent drawings also stipulate what's termed "boilerplate" (i.e., the required quality of materials and workmanship, which form a sort of standards guide for the GC). For example, these standards will specify the brand of paint to be used and how that paint is to be applied: the type of primer, the number of (and degree of sanding between) coats of paint, and characteristics of the finish. Often, these intent drawings are given to the architect to incorporate into a comprehensive set of construction documents for reference by tradespeople on the job site.

CONSTRUCTION DOCUMENTS

Produced by the project's architect, if one is involved, these document sets include detailed computer-generated drawings and written notes that fully explain the demolition, new construction, and any other structural work the project entails. (A full set can be up to 50 pages for a 5,000-square-foot house!) If building department approval is required, the architect will prepare the necessary drawings.

FIELD MEASUREMENTS

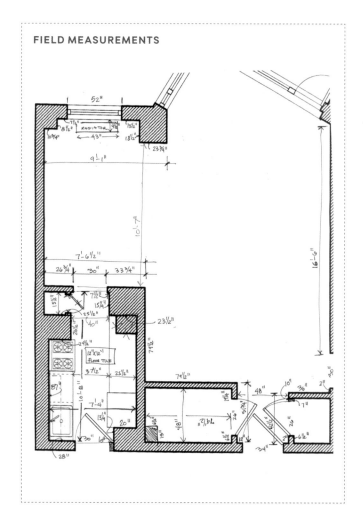

DEMOLITION/NEW CONSTRUCTION PLAN

EXISTING
TERRACE

EXISTING
ALCOVE

EXISTING
LIVING ROOM

EXISTING
BEDROOM

EXISTING
KITCHEN

EXISTING
BATHROOM

REMOVE PARTITIONS, DOOR,
SUSPENDED CEILINGS &
CLOSET FITTINGS.

REMOVE ALL CLOSET
FITTINGS.

REMOVE & DISCARD
FIXTURES, FITTINGS AND
TILE.

FURNITURE PLAN

TERRACE

BEDROOM

LIVING ROOM

KITCHEN

ENTRY

AFTER

OPPOSITE + ABOVE: Field measurements, a construction plan, and a furniture plan chart the design path Terry Kleinberg took in realizing a space-efficient New York apartment.

Furniture, lighting, and accessories specified from a mix of sources create a layered decor in a breakfast room by Kati Curtis.

SPECIFYING & PURCHASING

Once a detailed design scheme is solidified and the requisite drawings completed, the purchasing process begins in earnest. A designer will initiate custom orders, revisit furniture and fabric showrooms with specific needs in mind, contact workrooms, peruse auction catalogs for unusual items, and commission artisans to create custom items.

Retail stores, vintage and antiques shops, and even art galleries that sell limited-edition furnishings are among the resources a layperson can access to complete this step. Retail buyers can pursue a semicustom route too, thanks to consumer-friendly purveyors that offer pieces in a wide array of sizes, colors, finishes, and fabrics. And while high-end upholstery shops and curtain makers typically cater strictly to designers—that is, "to the trade" only—some are willing to work directly with end users. In fact, many trade-only vendors have shifted their business models and now sell to laypeople directly (or through a buying program that helps them navigate the customization process). However, a truly custom piece or element is best done under the aegis of an interior designer.

For designer and homeowner alike, there are ample sources at both ends of the spectrum:

RETAIL SOURCES

The most accessible option: everything is on display, ready to be tested and tried on for size. Many retail shops have in-stock programs so pieces can be purchased and delivered within a few days (if not carried out of the store right then and there). Some offer in-house design services to help customers make better-informed decisions about sizing, fabrics, and finishes. The disadvantage of many retail stores is that choices are usually limited. Designers shop retail for many reasons: to take advantage of the wide range of price points and the availability of items, to make the most of a given budget, or to buy certain items that are too exorbitant to customize. For instance, a custom leather-upholstered sofa or club chair can cost over $15,000 (animal hides being very expensive), whereas leather furniture purchased from a retail store is often high quality and much more reasonably priced.

ANTIQUES AND VINTAGE STORES

History, patina, character, provenance—all are attributes of vintage items. "Antique items are a win-win," explains Kati Curtis. "They give spaces a more collected feel and are a sustainable choice." Giving pre-owned items a new home is the highest level of green design: reuse. Antiques have the advantage of being immediately available, although many shops are willing to store pieces for a few months if necessary. An added bonus is that items made decades ago are daintier in scale than contemporary versions—a boon for smaller spaces. There is one drawback: even with online access to inventories, finding just the right piece can prove to be something of a treasure hunt if a particular design (or specific dimensions) is needed. Vintage destinations reward not only patience but also quick decision making.

TRADE SHOWROOMS

Designer showrooms are often located in buildings dedicated to providing professionals with one-stop shopping for products and resources. Under one roof, an interior designer has access to numerous fabric houses, furniture makers, distributors of lighting, stone and tile purveyors, manufacturers of bathroom fixtures, and more. Some showrooms are devoted to a single brand; others carry multiple lines. All offer ample opportunities to customize, because pieces in their catalogs are typically built to order. "Everything can be tweaked—from dimensions to aspects of the construction—and the designer can choose from a curated selection of finishes," says Dennis Miller, president of an eponymous multiline showroom. Plus, many trade centers or showroom buildings offer retail consumers the opportunity to work with professional designers.

CUSTOM WORKROOMS

When a designer wants to envision a piece completely from scratch, she turns to a custom workroom. Not only are bespoke products one of a kind, but they are designed to the exact dimensions and configuration of the space they'll inhabit—and to the client's preferences as well. A workroom can even size a club chair for a smaller stature and adjust the filling for the most comfortable "sit" for that person. Similarly, draperies and carpets can be designed for a specific setting, color scheme, or architectural challenge.

Strategic Sourcing

Kati Curtis used the full spectrum of resources in the master bedroom of a New York townhouse, pictured opposite:

1 CUSTOM
The velvet-upholstered tufted headboard and footboard are custom creations by Cisco Brothers, a trade-only workshop in Los Angeles with an eco-friendly bent.

2 ANTIQUE
The Oriental carpet and crystal chandelier are both vintage.

3 TRADE
The dresser and nightstand are from Noir, a to-the-trade resource that also sells its products through a handful of consumer-friendly retailers. Curtis often takes advantage of the label's "quick ship" program—a great way to get special pieces without the long lead time typical of custom items.

4 RETAIL
British brand Timorous Beasties designed the wallpaper, available through both trade and retail resources and also purchasable on the company's website.

How a Designer Makes Purchases for a Client

When a typical consumer buys a dining room table, he visits a retail store, selects the model he likes, and then places an order with a salesperson, paying in full at the time of his order. For a designer who handles a purchase on a client's behalf, the process unfolds a bit differently. She generates either a sales order (SO) or a purchase order (PO); see pages 444 and 447 for a sample of each.

- When a designer requests from the client one inclusive payment for the cost of the item *plus* the attendant purchasing fee, as well as any applicable sales tax, it is called a sales order. The SO itemizes everything to be purchased but specifies only the *total* amount—which includes the designer's coordination fee—for all items. Unlike a purchase order, a sales order does not list individual costs. Sales orders entail less paperwork than purchase orders but are not as transparent. The client submits a check covering the full requested payment to the designer, who is then responsible for creating and processing POs to any vendors on the client's behalf, along with required payments and deposits.
- When a designer creates a purchase order, it is given to the client for approval and accompanied by a request for payment to be made directly payable to the vendor/workroom. The client reviews the PO, approves it, and writes a check—usually a 50 percent deposit—to the vendor. The designer then submits the PO and payment to the vendor. The designer bills the client separately for the related sales tax and design fee (or purchasing coordination fee).

Project Management and Purchasing Coordination

The project manager oversees the purchasing process, functioning as the liaison between the design team and all vendors. She follows a careful sequence of steps from specifying individual items to getting quotes to ordering. She maintains and monitors a spreadsheet and comprehensive order file, tracking every item from inception to installation. (For a complete breakdown of the steps, see page 441.) The timeline is similar but much more succinct for a homeowner who is tackling the selection and purchasing of items on his own—and likely not accessing trade-only resources:

1. Create a spreadsheet listing every element specified, with columns for ordering information, lead time, and price/quote. Key each item with a reference number to the furniture plan.
2. Obtain quotes and verify that items are available/in stock. Check lead times.
3. Review the spreadsheet to make sure the overall cost is within the projected budget.
4. Order each item. Start with those that have the longest lead time.
5. Monitor progress, scheduling deliveries as needed and ensuring that everything is going as planned.

PRICING AND DESIGNER DISCOUNTS

Vendors and workrooms sometimes (but not always) offer designers a discount. Showrooms that cater exclusively to the trade will extend a discount to designers ranging from 15 to 40 percent off the *list* price (i.e., the retail price to nonprofessionals). The price offered to the designer is called the *net* price.

The trade discount is a courtesy that allows the designer to set her own price for any item, according to the contract between her and the client. A designer has the option of purchasing an item and then reselling it to her client at any price she desires—including with no markup at all. However, the method used to calculate any fee for purchasing and reselling *must* be stated in the initial contract between designer and client. (See page 443 for more.)

LEAD TIMES

Time management is a critical aspect of the ordering process. Custom pieces have lengthy lead times: typically twelve to sixteen weeks from order placement to delivery. When a vendor quotes a lead time, it's best to get an actual estimated delivery date. You may hear "twelve weeks" and mentally calculate mid-May, when the actual date is in June. Always rely on the calendar—don't guess. And check for updates regularly.

Creating a custom item involves many steps. The actual hands-on fabrication is just one part of the process; be sure to budget adequate time for processing orders and receiving and approving fabric and finish samples. Indecision can draw out the process; the clock is ticking while a client deliberates over wood stains for the coffee table. In addition, many people want to receive new pieces in time for important holidays or events, and these are just the seasons when the trucking industry slows down.

Paperwork, coordination, and shipping times also factor into the schedule. Once a piece is finished and the balance has been paid, delivery to the customer can still take a few weeks.

A NOTE ABOUT PAYMENT

Retail items, fabrics, and wallpaper are generally paid for up front in full. For furniture and custom orders, vendors typically require a 50 percent deposit. The percentage is calculated on the net price and does not include sales tax and delivery. The balance is billed when the piece is ready, and includes the remaining 50 percent, *plus* shipping and freight, *plus* tax (based on the full amount, including shipping and delivery). Estimate shipping charges at about 15 percent of the piece's cost. Sales tax is collected on interior design services (even those performed by an architect) in some states.

Be sure to inquire about the vendor's payment procedures. Some will accept credit cards; others take only cash, check, or wire transfer. Credit cards are often accepted for the deposit but not the balance. Vendors do this to protect themselves from clients who dispute a charge in an effort to return a nonrefundable item. While even orders from design showrooms can sometimes be returned (but not without incurring a hefty restocking charge), custom orders can't be canceled or refunded.

LEAD TIME

A "lead time" is the time to delivery from the placement of the order with the vendor.

COLLABORATING WITH CONTRACTORS & WORKROOMS

When the scope of an interior design project involves more than just furnishings, the homeowner or designer will need to collaborate with various tradespeople: a decorative painter to stencil the foyer walls, an audiovisual consultant to wire the media room, a millworker to craft a built-in desk for the kids' room. Even a project that seems simple can warrant the services of multiple specialists. For instance, renovation of a pint-size powder room may require a carpenter, a plumber, an electrician, a tile installer, a painter, and possibly a wallpaper hanger.

Intricate projects need a general contractor to help coordinate tasks and ensure their completion in a timely and efficient manner. A licensed GC is a must for any major new construction or renovation project. A building site functions like an organism: every part—and every decision—is interrelated. Interior construction is a messy and complicated process that calls for an expert trained to see the big picture: the full scope and sequencing of work, from demolition through finished space. "There are so many moving parts; everything needs to be coordinated *perfectly*," says Chip Brian of Best & Company. Key to a successful outcome is the GC's ability to anticipate problems, deal with the unexpected, and work harmoniously with the various professions and personalities involved.

Hand-stitching custom window treatments is a fine art at Jonas, an upholstery workroom in New York.

The GC's Role

The GC is typically hired after all interior elements have been determined, and the designer and architect have completed the construction documents. Here are some of a general contractor's responsibilities:

- Provides a detailed proposal (called a bid) for the project based on the interior design intent drawings and construction drawings
- Creates a detailed schedule for the work to take place
- Assumes overall responsibility for the job-site safety; maintains liability and other insurance; meets building and other construction and delivery restrictions
- Hires, manages, and coordinates subcontractors (commonly called subs)
- Oversees all aspects of construction, including:
  - » Demolition
  - » Rough carpentry (framing)
  - » Finish carpentry (millwork)
  - » Drywall installation
  - » Electrical work
  - » Plumbing
  - » Painting and skim coating
  - » Plasterwork
  - » Tile and stone installation
  - » Wood flooring installation
  - » HVAC
  - » Wallcovering installation
  - » Site protection and cleanliness
- Schedules and processes all of the payments from the client

- Ensures that tradespeople work in sequence and aligns their schedules with the purchase and delivery of all materials, fixtures, equipment, lighting, and special finishes, such as tile
- Works with the designer to resolve questions or field issues
- Maintains a safe, clean, and orderly site; arranges for Dumpsters and debris removal
- Supervises the progress, quality, and completion of the work

Even when a GC is involved in the project, the designer or homeowner often directly contracts tradespeople such as drapery installers, audiovisual or security consultants, and decorative painters. However, designers sometimes have good reason for managing certain tasks that typically fall under the GC's purview—and are willing to take on the liability that that will entail. "I usually hire the painter myself, so I can better control the final outcome," says designer Katie Ridder. "When a project involves a specialty finish or wallpapering, I want to ensure the walls are up to my own exacting standards."

Note that painters, flooring installers, plumbers, and many other tradespeople charge the same price whether dealing with a designer or a consumer. If the designer or homeowner hires a subcontractor directly, the GC is likely to charge a fee of at least 10 percent of the value of the service to coordinate the sub's work with the overall schedule.

The Designer's Role in Project Management

Construction takes care—and time. It is executed by people, not machines, and is thus subject to human error. Projects require all kinds of obstacles that need resolution. Nevertheless, the client wants his project completed as soon as possible and expects flawless results. The primary role of the designer is to be an ally for the client and serve as a communications conduit between the GC and the client. The designer also ensures the contractor is paid on time and that the work meets the specifications. Here is a list of tasks a designer should expect to undertake when collaborating with tradespeople and contractors:

- Completing the interior design intent drawings and working with the architect to generate construction drawings.
- Identifying prospective GCs. Finding reputable contractors through word-of-mouth references, local building departments, shelter publications, the National Association of the Remodeling Industry, and design-trade organizations. Scoping out construction signs and trucks parked in upscale neighborhoods is another way to identify companies vetted by others.
- Creating a bid sheet specifying exactly how proposals should be formatted, which aids comparison of submissions. Unless all bidders structure their estimates with the same categories, in the same order, it is tricky and complicated to discern discrepancies between them. "Bid sets could be one page or a hundred pages—which itself is telling," says Chip

Brian: a truncated bid set could mean that not a lot of thought went into it. All bids should specifically reference the interior design intent and/or architect's documents by job name, date, and numbers.

- Assessing bids from prospective contractors. The designer scrutinizes the submissions to determine how they differ. Because the quality of materials and workmanship should be clearly spelled out in the construction documents or specifications, labor costs and the percentage of overhead are the two main areas where bids differ. Keep in mind that some GCs or subs are able to buy materials at a lower price based on their supplier relationships. Other GCs may have a talent for finding good subs who charge less for their labor.

  The lowest bid is not always the best. In fact, a bid significantly lower than others indicates that the bidder has overlooked some element of the design or hasn't accounted for sufficient profit to cover the cost of completing the project. This is called *underbidding* and bodes trouble down the line. Contractors who underbid are often anxious for the job to pay off prior debts or to keep their staff employed or to grow their business because they're inexperienced. At some point, they will realize that finishing the project means losing money, so they simply disappear and move on to the next job—or try to renegotiate the contracted price.
- Negotiating bids. "In reviewing the proposals, the designer is answerable to the client on budget and responsible for getting the bid within it," explains designer Vicente Wolf. Multiple rounds of revisions can extend the bidding process for a few weeks.

- Helping the client select the GC. While the general contracting company may appoint a project manager or a job captain to supervise the site on a day-to-day basis, someone at the top is ultimately making the decisions and administering the contract. Because the designer and client will be working with the GC for many months (sometimes years) during the course of construction, it is essential for them to have a good feeling about the character and trustworthiness of the GC. Also vital is a sense that the GC will be able to resolve the inevitable disagreements and unexpected crises that occur on every project.
- Monitoring—but not actually supervising—construction on the client's behalf, verifying that the GC is performing on schedule and meeting the agreed-upon quality standards.
- Interfacing with the apartment building management, if applicable. Co-ops, condos, and rentals have strict rules governing the hours during which construction can be done, how and when materials can be brought in or out, and which entrance, loading dock, or elevator workers must use. The designer or general contractor—on *behalf* of the homeowner—must present the building permit to management before work is allowed to commence.

How to Deal with Changes

During the course of any project, situations arise that require alteration of the original scope of the work—for instance, having to accommodate unforeseen conditions such as rotten wood or hidden pipes. Other changes result from a shift in the initial decisions, such as when a client wishes to switch the specified tile or to alter the height of the backsplash after work has been completed to prepare for its installation. Any deviation from the original drawings or specs can delay the project and will increase its cost.

The proper procedure is for the designer (or architect) to revise the drawings and have the GC write an itemized quote—called a change order or additional work order (AWO)—for the cost of extra labor and materials, including overhead and profit. It is imperative that the client authorize and sign the change order *prior* to the contractor beginning the work, to avoid later misunderstandings. Many GCs insist on having a signed change order before proceeding with alterations, which is in everyone's best interest.

The best way to avoid unexpected costs and delays is to finalize all design decisions in advance, and to prepare a set of construction documents and specifications that is as complete and exhaustive as possible before the project is put out for bid. Leave nothing to the imagination—or open to interpretation. Anything not detailed in the accepted bid could be considered a change, and all changes come at a cost—in time, materials, and coordination and management—that's inevitably borne by the homeowner.

Record Keeping

The designer and client should work together to maintain a complete record of the project, as outlined below. A homeowner handling the project on his own, without the aid of a professional, should also keep records of every meeting, conversation, and decision.

PROJECT FILES

Create a physical or digital project binder that lists the names and contact information of all parties involved: the client, the designer, the GC, the subs, and the building staff (including the superintendent and management office employees). It should contain a copy of all contracts, requests for payment, meeting minutes, a reduced set of control drawings, all specifications and purchase orders, change orders, and records of all conversations—both formal meetings and casual chats addressing important matters.

MEETINGS

A regular schedule of job meetings—ideally weekly—is recommended. The designer, the GC, and all relevant subs should attend; the client may or may not be present. The team reviews all work completed to date, discusses upcoming or ongoing tasks, and raises any questions and concerns. Daily meetings might be called for as the project nears completion.

MEETING MINUTES

It is the designer's responsibility to take minutes, noting the date and time of every meeting (or conversation), attendees and their roles, items discussed, and actions required to be taken, by whom, and by what date. Minutes should be distributed immediately afterward: they are an important means of tracking open items.

NOTES

Maintain a record of all notes exchanged by the GC, the designer, and the client.

PHOTOGRAPHS

Regularly scheduled photography is a good way to document progress, particularly of open walls during installation of electrical, computer, audiovisual, or security-system wiring and the execution of plumbing work.

Scheduling

Because trades are carefully sequenced with little buffer between them, one small snafu or delay could set off a chain reaction that derails the entire calendar. For example, during the summer, heat and humidity extend drying times of paint and stains; a designer may find herself in a bind if the floors and walls are not fully cured when expected. Installation of wall upholstery has to be pushed back a few days, but the installer is due on another site at that time. The next available slot in his schedule is three weeks away, by which time the decorative painter will be out of commission. And so it goes. Take these road bumps in stride and be realistic: assume the work will take a month or two longer than expected. Although delay, aggravation, and the unforeseen are par for the course with construction, an inspired collaboration between a talented designer, an experienced GC, and a conscientious client can lead to superior results.

DELIVERY & INSTALLATION

The last stage in completing a project is the installation, during which the furnishings, draperies, decorative lighting, and accessories ordered months before are delivered and put into place. This step occurs after the renovation (if any)—construction, cabinetry work, and "wet" work such as tile installation—has been completed; AV systems have been installed; walls have been painted or papered; scaffolding has been dismantled; and a thorough cleaning has been executed. Only then can the installation begin: furniture is delivered, table lamps are placed and lightbulbs screwed in, dishes are stacked in the cabinets, the pantry is stocked, and clothes are hung in the closets.

Because the ideal scenario is to install items together, all at once, in the shortest amount of time, designers favor warehousing furnishings and decorative elements and delivering them to the job site in a succinct, consolidated fashion. Completed items are stored in one place and safeguarded until the big day. Before installation, the designer can inventory and inspect everything to check for problems—a chair sporting the wrong fabric, a too-dark or scratched finish, a broken or missing piece of hardware. Warehousing also allows for a more efficient delivery and installation process from the standpoint of both time and sequencing. For instance, area rugs are ideally delivered and placed in a room prior to the arrival of heavy or unwieldy upholstered furnishings and case goods—but after the painting is finished.

Coordinating carpet installers, furniture movers, drapery hangers, decorative painters, and art handlers all in one place is like piecing together a puzzle. Decisions have to be made about the sequencing of final tasks: Is it best to install the dining room chandelier and then raise it so the movers don't crash into it, or should the electrician hang it *after* the table has been placed? Should floors be finished before or after painting? (In other words, is it more likely that the floor installer will ding the just-painted walls or the painters will drip Benjamin Moore on the newly stained parquet?)

Although every project unfolds in its own way, depending on the scope and nature of the work being done, there is a point for all where the tail end of construction overlaps with the installation process. Indeed, for an interior designer, "installation" is about more than placing furniture and accessories; it means ensuring that the light fixtures are present when the electrician is on-site to wire them and the walls have been prepped just before the decorative painter is scheduled to arrive. Here is a common order of events for the installation process:

1. Install speakers and other audiovisual equipment and computer, communications, and security systems, and connect wiring.
2. Finish wood floors and then protect them with paper.
3. Paint the walls, ceiling, and any woodwork. Nicks can be touched up later, after all the furniture has been placed.
4. Install wallpaper and other wallcoverings.
5. Install coverplates, thermostats, and other interfaces.

6. Hang window treatments. Installers need room to maneuver, so this task should be scheduled for a day when no other work is occurring. That being said, the curtain installer can usually be coordinated with the electrician, since the two of them will work on different parts of a room.

7. Deliver decorative lighting, such as sconces and chandeliers, ideally at least one week in advance of the furniture's arrival. Keep fixtures covered in their protective wrappings until after furniture installation so movers don't damage them.

8. Install light fixtures. (Always install sconces, chandeliers, and pendant fixtures before the furniture to ensure proper placement.) The electrician needs elbow room, so schedule him or her for a day that won't be busy.

9. Install area rugs and carpets and then protect them with paper. Execute this step only after *all* plumbing work is complete, especially the installation of kitchen and bath fixtures.

10. Install decorative hardware. Start preparing any furnishings stored in a warehouse for delivery at this time. Mark the packaging of each item with its destination location.

11. Install all furniture. Have a comprehensive spreadsheet listing all furnishings ready as the furniture movers arrive at the job site so pieces can be checked off as they are unloaded. If there are two entrances to the site, post someone at both doors; each person has her own spreadsheet, and at the end of the day the two are cross-referenced to make sure nothing is missing. Direct the delivery-men to each item's destination. Try to work from upstairs (and downstairs) to the main level, and from inside rooms to those closest

to the door. If possible, big items should be moved into the house first. (If the delivery truck was loaded properly, then the smaller items were placed in the back, with bigger pieces in front, to be off-loaded first.)

12. Create a staging area for accessories and small goods; a dining table is ideal (remember to protect the tabletop before spreading out items). Place these items last, after the furniture is in position.

In the best of all worlds, the client vacates the premises during the furniture installation, which usually lasts a few days. The process is stressful and dramas occur: workers tromp all over just-refinished wood floors; a chair gets nicked as it's unwrapped. Items look improperly scaled or the colors don't seem correct when observed out of context. "Everything in a room interrelates, so if one piece of the puzzle is missing, the space looks off," says designer Tracey Winn Pruzan. A chandelier looks enormous without the perfectly sized dining table below; the bright chartreuse armchair reads a bit loud without the ecru wool sofa to temper it; the library lighting appears glaring before the shelves are filled with colorful tomes.

But orchestrating a consolidated installation is often not feasible. Warehousing is not an option if homeowners aren't keen to pay for storage, although vendors will often be willing to store items until closer to the big day. "Tell them to delay delivery," suggests Vicente Wolf. "And when ordering, work backward from the longest to the shortest lead time, so items arrive around the same time." Clients may be unwilling or unable to relocate for a week, and sometimes they just want to enjoy their furniture the second it's delivered—no matter if a single sofa

IN CONSTRUCTION

INSTALLATION

is the only thing in their living room for a while. And sometimes the project scope simply entails freshening up versus wholesale reinvention, so the designer inherits a space that's already partially furnished and lived in.

Things inevitably go wrong during delivery and installation. The desk is too wide to fit down the hallway—can it come in through a window? An installation is occurring at the same time in another apartment in the building, and the elevator that you can use only until 3:59 p.m. is tied up. Pieces are damaged as they come off the truck or get dirtied as they are unwrapped, and, despite all the careful attention to detail, something is defective or not the approved color. The chain of custody of a piece of furniture is long, and it is only as strong as its weakest link. Be prepared for unexpected problems, because they are unavoidable. The best preparation is to hire seasoned professionals who have both the prescience to anticipate problems and head them off and the experience to deal efficiently with issues as they occur; however, even a novice can learn as much as possible about each step of the design process by asking professionals—workroom managers, skilled tradesmen, woodworkers, salespeople, and deliverymen—to explain how they create, manage, and install their work. The adage "Knowledge is power" holds especially true in the field of interior design.

Nearly every issue encountered during a design project can be resolved with resourcefulness, industry knowledge, and common sense, to deliver a beautiful and composed space that will surpass one's wildest dreams.

OPPOSITE + BELOW: A series of photographs taken of the same space—a bedroom by Cullman & Kravis—shows the progression from construction site to final result.

FINAL

ELEMENTS
of a ROOM

Every space is composed of key elements that need to be selected: millwork, furnishings, floor coverings, window treatments, and more. The specification process entails a series of design decisions regarding the minutiae of each and every interior detail. Both style and function play an important role at each decision point. One may lead the other, but both must be taken into account. For example, when specifying curtains for a sunroom, think about what fabric would drape well and withstand everyday use. What print or motif, pleating or header would work best to support the room's overall design concept?

The budget, schedule, and technical considerations will inevitably limit the choices of furnishings and details—making it easier to choose from what can seem an overwhelming sea of possibilities. At the same time, these limitations present exciting opportunities for the creativity and unexpected (but planned) juxtapositions that are the very essence of interior design. A modest decorating scheme becomes a true design when all aspects and elements of a room are considered in context, and every detail attended to.

WOODWORK

From balustrades to boiserie, architectural wood-work, also known as millwork, gives a space a resolved and finished look. The category includes wood paneling, baseboards, moldings, chair rails, and all manner of built-in cabinetry. Such elements are instrumental in establishing a room's architectural character—whether modern or traditional, French country or Hollywood regency.

Every plane offers ample opportunity for embellishment and punctuation; even the ceiling can be a canvas for applied elements, involving beams and coffers that add depth. Trims such as base and crown moldings give a space a sense of scale. Strategic built-ins (niches, custom cabinets) tailored to the room's exact dimensions and spatial quirks can maximize square footage and functionality—not to mention hide architectural flaws.

WOODWORK IS A GREAT WAY TO INVITE THE ILLUSION OF EXPANSIVENESS; IT MAKES A ROOM APPEAR LARGER BY DRAWING THE EYE TO ITS BOUNDARIES.

OPPOSITE: Coffinier Ku made clever use of a long hallway, giving it presence—and functionality—with built-in bookcases that extend floor to ceiling.

THE OPTIONS

Woodwork features are limitless, but most are made by creatively combining three essential building blocks: moldings, paneling, and cabinetry. These elements form the basis of window and door trim, wainscoting, decorative ceiling beams, shelving—even vanities and desks. Use them to realize fireplace surrounds, emphasize niches, create room divisions, and highlight focal points.

Moldings

Moldings are shaped, decorative lengths of solid or composite wood (or, alternatively, plastic). They help "finish" a room by covering the often imperfect intersections of adjacent materials, masking the joints between interior elements and planes:

- **Base moldings** are installed where walls meet the floor.
- **Crown moldings** (also called cornices) are installed where walls meet the ceiling.
- **Case moldings** (aka casings or trim moldings) are installed where walls meet the windows and doors.

Moldings can also be used to create architectural elements such as fireplace surrounds and pilasters. Available styles range from flat stock—an unarticulated plank of wood—to highly voluptuous profiles carved using a milling machine. (Elaborate designs can also be created by assembling several moldings into one unit.)

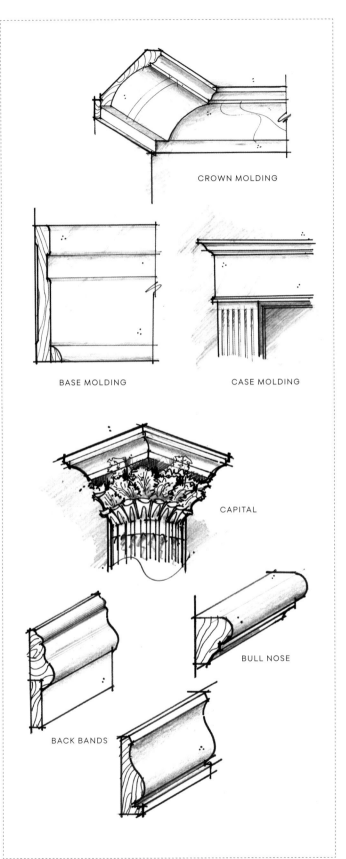

CROWN MOLDING

BASE MOLDING

CASE MOLDING

CAPITAL

BULL NOSE

BACK BANDS

There are three primary sources of moldings:

- The most affordable solution is to source a stock profile from a lumberyard or a home-improvement store. The disadvantage is that these vendors offer only limited styles and wood species.
- Specialized molding companies showcase a wide variety of designs and wood species in their catalogs (which can also be found at lumberyards). Some have the capacity to fulfill a custom order with a minimum setup charge.
- More specialized and unique moldings require fully custom fabrication and must be hand-crafted in a mill shop. These artisans can also reproduce existing moldings if an intact piece (or a detailed, accurate drawing) of the profile is available—a great option for historic renovations.

TYPES OF MOLDINGS

- Standing trim
- Running trim
- Shoe moldings
- Ogees
- Noses
- Back bands
- Capital moldings

OPPOSITE: A wood-paneled library by Hamlin Goldreyer Architects features a fireplace mantel accented with a decorative stone medallion.

Paneling

A paneled room is a cocoon, a refuge from the outside world. It provides a measure of sound insulation too, which creates a special experience. Wall paneling—also called boiserie—can look quite elaborate, but construction is straightforward: an expanse of wood framed by moldings. There are several ways to produce paneling:

- On the job site by highly skilled "finish" carpenters, specialized craftsmen who work on decorative elements (rather than hidden infrastructure, such as wall framing)
- In the shop by a custom millworker; opt for this when choosing stained premium woods
- By combining moldings with a premade panel product such as MDF or veneered plywood—a more economical, semicustom approach

LEFT: Gray-stained paneling clads a sunlit family room by Kristin Fine. **BELOW:** Cerused paneling is a warm but neutral backdrop to art in a study by David Scott. **OPPOSITE:** Built-in bookshelf detail.

Cabinetry

Also called *casework* or *millwork*, cabinetry combines function and form, providing storage while adding decorative dimension. Units are constructed just like wood furniture: built of either hardwood or veneer-faced plywood (or both). A cabinet or case good is basically a box fitted out with shelves, drawers, doors, or a combination. There are three types:

- **Stock** cabinets are fabricated in a factory and offered in only certain sizes and limited door/drawer styles, qualities, wood species, and finishes.
- **Semicustom** cabinets are also factory made, but these companies offer custom sizing and a greater variety of door/drawer styles, wood species, molding options, and finishes. (Many semicustom cabinet suppliers also provide fully custom services.)
- **Custom** cabinets are built by a millwork or woodworking shop, a route that allows greater artistic freedom to produce intricate and integrated schemes. Choose custom when exotic wood species are selected, when matching wood grain and color is important, or simply when details matter.

Cabinetry can be freestanding or anchored into the wall. Upper cabinets are those mounted high on a wall, generally above a counter or work surface, while base cabinets stand on the floor. Additional design considerations for the latter include what material to top them with, and how to shape the counter's edge.

ANATOMY OF A CABINET

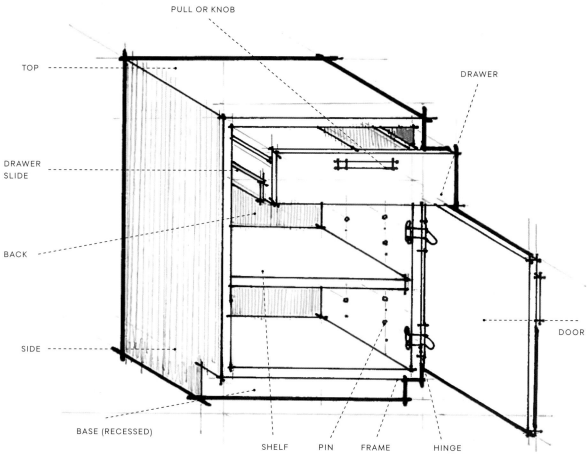

PULL OR KNOB

TOP

DRAWER

DRAWER SLIDE

BACK

SIDE

DOOR

BASE (RECESSED)

SHELF   PIN   FRAME   HINGE

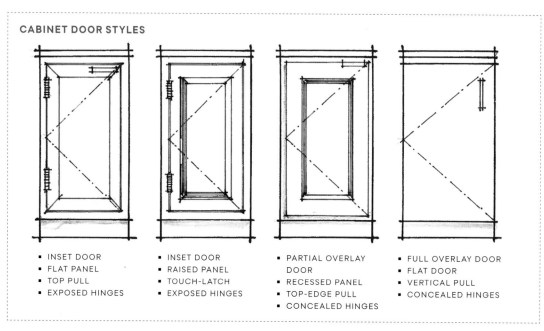

CABINET DOOR STYLES

- INSET DOOR
- FLAT PANEL
- TOP PULL
- EXPOSED HINGES

- INSET DOOR
- RAISED PANEL
- TOUCH-LATCH
- EXPOSED HINGES

- PARTIAL OVERLAY DOOR
- RECESSED PANEL
- TOP-EDGE PULL
- CONCEALED HINGES

- FULL OVERLAY DOOR
- FLAT DOOR
- VERTICAL PULL
- CONCEALED HINGES

KEY DIMENSIONS

- Standard wall cabinet depth:
  12 inches
- Standard wall cabinet height:
  12 to 48 inches
- Standard wall cabinet width:
  in 3-inch increments
- Vanity base unit depth: 20 inches
- Standard base unit depth: generally
  24 inches
- Standard base unit height:
  30 to 36 inches
- Shelves: ¾ inch thick by 36 inches
  wide

Finishing Touches

Further embellish woodwork with decorative
touches such as capitals, dentils, carvings, and
applied moldings. These elements add interest
and detail, reflecting and capturing light so their
appearance changes over the course of a day.

Rich millwork slats clad all surfaces of a kitchen
by David Scott.

1. Kristin Fine converted an oddly shaped window eave into a fanciful nook for reading, playing, and even sleeping courtesy of a custom mattress and built-in drawer below. 2. Hardware-free custom cabinetry imparts a modern look. 3. Decorative ceiling beams added to a newly built space confer a traditional touch. 4. Crown molding with coordinating ceiling embellishment. 5. Built-in beds and storage make the most of an attic space, converting it into a shipshape sleeping loft. 6 + 7. Hamlin Goldreyer designed a traditional wood-paneled library with numerous classical details, from columns to pediments, all carefully scaled to the exact dimensions of the room.

BRINGING IN THE PROS

Architectural millwork can be complex, and elements are best planned in collaboration with an interior designer and a custom woodworker or a specialized finish carpenter who will be realizing the design.

DESIGN CONSIDERATIONS

Designing a whole-house woodwork scheme entails a play of continuity and variation. Woodwork elements should relate to one another and, taken together, reinforce the overarching design concept and desired architectural character. Determine an appropriate woodwork style consistent with the spatial qualities and dimensions of each room, and in keeping with the overall style of the home. Although the scale and even the details of various elements will change slightly from room to room, they should all be of a piece.

Trims such as baseboards, crown moldings, and window and door casings are integral to every room, no matter how spare or unadorned. To create a unified design, choose one profile for each and apply throughout the home; don't switch from an art deco Ziggurat design in the hallway to a Rococo silhouette in the dining room. For example, the same casing profile might be stained in one room, painted in another, and embellished in a third. Choose or design trim elements first and then plan the other room-specific millwork to create a harmonious composition. Keep in mind that proper proportions of one element to another are essential.

A custom kitchen by Hamlin Goldreyer Architects toes the line between classic and contemporary.

CHOOSING THE MATERIAL

Millwork can be made of solid wood, composite wood (with a finish veneer or solid edges), or a synthetic material intended to be painted.

Solid Wood

There are many suitable species to choose from. The Architectural Woodwork Institute's *Architectural Woodwork Quality Standards Illustrated* features a handy table that delineates the relative costs, hardness, dimensional stability, and other qualities of forty common species.

Consider what's best suited to the particular application, visually and structurally: where the woodwork is to be installed, whether it will be exposed to moisture, and what the preferred finish is among the variables. Millwork being stained requires a species of suitable quality and beauty since the grain will show through. Woodwork to be painted requires a smooth material that "takes" the paint well.

Two other features, grain type and sawing method, can add further visual character:

- **Open-grain** (or ring-porous) wood bears a distinct pattern.
- **Close-grain** (or diffuse-porous) wood is more uniform and less variegated.
- Sawing methods describe how the planks were made. The three types—**rift-, quarter-, and plain-sawn**—are distinguished by increasing irregularity of patterning.

Careful selection and combination of wood species, sawing method, and finish can create many aesthetics. For a country look, consider a plain-sawn, open-grain wood with a clear or light finish. For a traditional library, a more refined selection of rift-sawn, close-grain wood with a dark stain is a popular option.

Composite Wood

Large expanses of solid wood are prone to warping, while manufactured wood (or veneered composite) is far more dimensionally stable. Most moldings are crafted of solid wood, but they can—and should, in the case of moisture-prone areas—be made from more affordable manufactured wood or plastic. Panels too are more typically fashioned from a composite product usually faced with veneer. Here are two common choices:

- **Finger-jointed wood** is a composite of small wood pieces glued together and then milled into a molding profile. It is less expensive than solid wood since it utilizes recycled material. But the joints will show through the finish if it is not painted properly or is subject to a fluctuating environment.
- **Plastics** such as cellular PVC can be used for moldings and panels and are frequently specified when dimensional stability is required to withstand moisture, humidity, and rot.

Veneers

The orientation and placement of veneer leaves is another variable to bear in mind when specifying panels and cabinetry. Here are a few common configurations:

- **Slip matching** places subsequent leaves side by side, producing a repeat pattern.
- **Book matching** places subsequent veneer slices adjacent to each other but in an alternating direction—every other leaf is reversed—producing a symmetrical, mirror-image pattern in which the grain appears continuous.

- **Random matching** results in a more contrasting but still pleasing pattern.
- **Diamond matching** puzzles together matching pieces across two axes, creating the titular patterns.

Veneers created from slices of the same tree log will bear a matching pattern and are sold together in a flitch (or batch). To execute a large area of paneling, such as a wall or a long tabletop, several panels of book- or slip-matched leaves are aligned side by side to form what's called an end-match pattern.

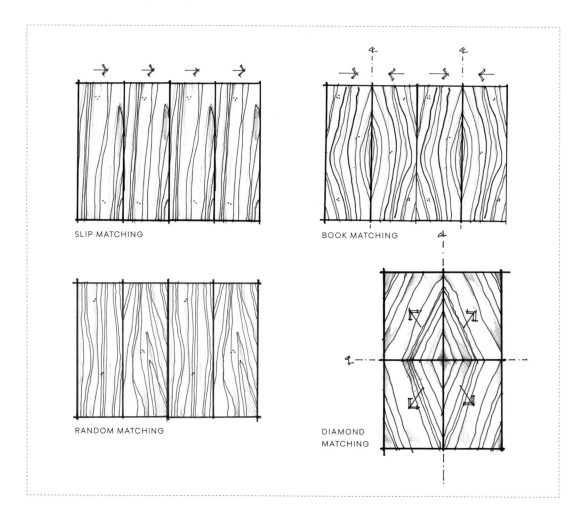

SLIP MATCHING

BOOK MATCHING

RANDOM MATCHING

DIAMOND MATCHING

Custom cabinets faced in zebrano veneer distinguish a kitchen by Joan Dineen. The veneer complements the coloration of the more classically styled woodwork in the adjacent dining room.

Material Comparison

Other common cabinetry materials include plastic laminate, melamine, and metal. Here's how they stack up to finished or painted wood.

MATERIAL	PROS	CONS
PAINTED WOOD	• Unlimited colors • Can be easily refreshed or repainted	• Can chip or fade over time
STAINED WOOD	• Offers a rich look	• Requires expensive, high-quality hardwood as base • Hard to paint over
HIGH-PRESSURE LAMINATE	• Durable finish • Waterproof	• Inexpensive and common • Black edges • Burnable • Gloss finish is delicate
LOW-PRESSURE LAMINATE (MELAMINE)	• Inexpensive	• Not durable
GLASS	• Durable	• Scratchable
STAINLESS STEEL	• Durable • Can be polished or satin finished	• Scratchable • Hard to keep clean looking

CHOOSING THE RIGHT FINISH

Paints and stains are used to finish woodwork. By adding brilliant color and shine or an antiqued patina, the right finish can emphasize the beauty of a wood cabinet or make an inexpensive composite molding look rich. Try one of these three options:

- **Transparent stains.** Used for prominent elements, including bookcases and cabinetry, where the natural beauty of the wood is the main aesthetic element. These stains have microscopic pigments that penetrate and bond with wood to dye it, creating integral coloration.

- **Semitransparent stains.** A hybrid of paint and dyes, these add color and coverage while still allowing the grain or character of the wood to show through. They don't penetrate the wood as deeply, veiling the surface somewhat.

- **Paint.** A creamy, satiny plane of consistent color is the goal. Paint should be applied only to the smoothest woods or to plastic. Traditional milk paint offers a soft look that's desirable for traditional spaces.

Custom millwork can be finished in the wood shop or on-site. Either way, the joints between moldings and panels should be pre-stained or treated with primer prior to assembly; otherwise, unfinished wood will peek through as the piece naturally expands and contracts. An experienced woodworker will know this.

THE PROCESS

Whether stock elements are purchased from a manufacturer or a custom creation is commissioned, adding cabinetry or millwork to an interior requires the following steps:

1. Take accurate measurements of the room.
2. Create a drawing at a half-inch (minimum) scale of the molding or cabinet. For the latter, include a plan, elevations of all exposed sides, and notes about any interior shelving or accessories.
3. Specify the stain or finish.
4. Specify the desired quality of construction, materials, and manufacturing standards by referencing the quality levels of the Architectural Woodwork Institute (AWI):

- **Economy** is the lowest grade; it stipulates inexpensive finishes and hardware, cheaper joinery, and thinner materials. In a residential interior, it's generally only specified for utilitarian spaces such as garages.
- **Custom** is the most widely used grade. It is the default when a grade is not specified. A cabinet constructed according to this grade will be sturdy and made of high-quality materials, with nice detailing and hardware.
- **Premium** is reserved for high-end, high-budget woodwork. A premium cabinet uses the topmost quality materials, joinery, finishes, and hardware.

BELOW: Working drawings of custom woodwork elements by David Scott. OPPOSITE: Painted board-and-batten wall paneling in a home by Kati Curtis.

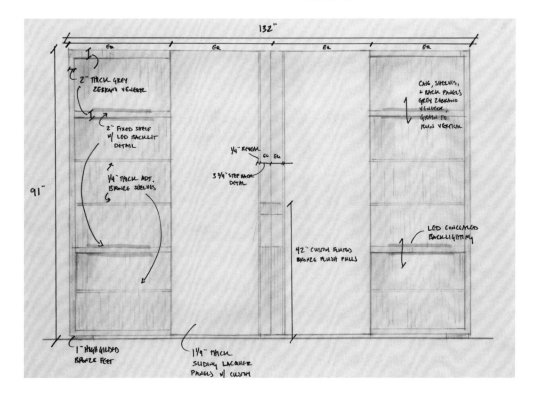

INSTALLATION CONSIDERATIONS

A combination of good design, excellent documentation, and hands-on involvement in the fabrication and installation processes is critical to success. Follow these steps:

1. **Generate drawings.** Architectural woodwork requires detailed, dimensioned drawings done in a scale that adequately conveys the appearance and finish of the interior *and* exterior of the entire piece as well as the expected quality of materials and joinery. These documents help a designer or a homeowner work out details pertaining to profile, scale, and resolution at the floors, ceilings, corners, and other interruptions. Drawings also help convey the intricacies and subtleties of the design to the fabricator.

2. **Produce technical drawings.** Based on the aforementioned renderings, a millwork shop will create detailed technical drawings (called shop drawings) at a larger scale for approval. Their magnified dimensions—usually at half or full scale—are intended to guide fabrication, helping the installer understand the design and assembly of components. Inconsistencies and conflicts are more visible in the enlarged rendering. Shop drawings are reviewed by the designer or homeowner to ensure adherence to the original intent.

3. **Specify heights.** There are no rules regarding dimensions of various millwork elements; it depends on the context. For instance, a wainscot molding can be set at 36 or 60 inches; it depends on the height of the room, the function of the wainscoting, and the intended ambience. Don't leave these essential details up to the installer to determine.

4. **Order samples.** Finished material samples should be ordered for approval, and a full-scale mock-up built from them to verify that the effect is as desired and to clarify the installation process. This should be done *prior* to fabrication of the entire job.

5. **Visit the shop.** It's a good policy to visit the millwork shop during fabrication to inspect cabinets before they are finished.

6. **Inspect the site.** During the build-out, inspecting the construction site regularly is necessary to confirm that rooms are properly readied for cabinetry installation, with all blocking in place, dimensions verified, and full adherence to the design (as depicted in the contract documents and shop drawings).

7. **Schedule the delivery.** During a full-blown renovation, cabinetry is ideally one of the last elements to arrive on the construction site. Protective wrappings can only go so far to defend against damage in an environment where workmen are trekking through the space carrying Sheetrock, tools, and tarps.

OPPOSITE: The salon of a townhouse by Joan Dineen boasts high ceilings and fairly generous proportions—matched by the thick base and crown moldings.

Drawings allow the designer to study the proportions of the raw space, and to finesse and manipulate the elements to achieve the proposed vision—which often requires painstaking scaling of elements. These drawings are keyed on the plan, elevations, and sections.

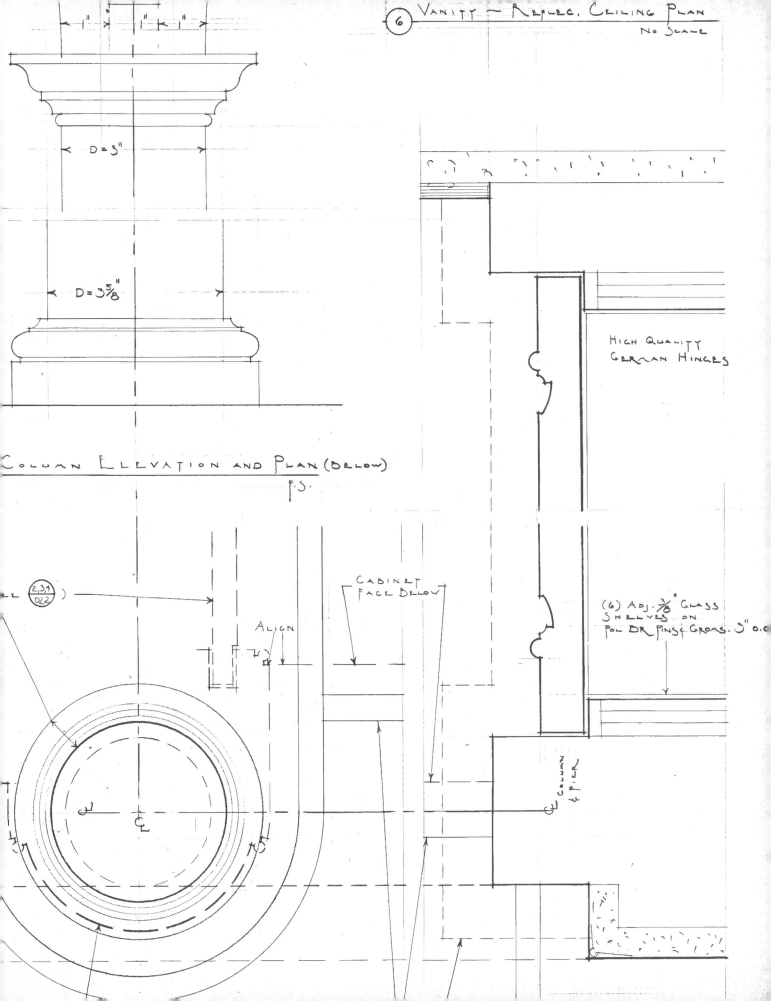

D = 3"

D = 3 5/8 "

COLUMN ELEVATION AND PLAN (BELOW)
F.S.

HIGH QUALITY
GERMAN HINGES

(2,3,1
D22)

CABINET
FACE BELOW

ALIGN

(6) ADJ. 3/8" GLASS
SHELVES ON
POL BR. PINS & GROMS. 3" O.C

CL

COLUMN & PIER

CL

ARCHITECTURAL FEATURES

All residential spaces feature doors, windows, and often something special—a fireplace, a staircase, or a designed ceiling. In most cases, the homeowner or designer is working with existing elements, but for a major renovation or ground-up construction, the designer or architect will specify or modify some or all of these features. The treatment of these architectural elements plays a major role in expressing the identity of an interior.

APERTURES

Doors, windows, skylights, and other openings serve multiple roles. Purely functional purposes include securing a home, controlling movement between spaces, modulating the influx of daylight and fresh air, and framing views. But these features also punctuate the six planes of a room, providing focus, visual rhythm, and interest.

The key design principles to consider are shape, scale, and proportion. Door and window openings must relate to the size of the wall (or other plane) they are placed in. A too-small window or one that's poorly located will throw off the balance of the entire room and challenge a good furniture layout. But architectural features can also be used or manipulated strategically—to create the illusion of loftiness, for instance. Raising the heights of a room's doorways will make a space appear much taller. When interior construction is not possible, drapery panels can confer the same effect by emphasizing the vertical line of the window moldings,

either through the design or mounting height. A meager opening is given greater importance by adding depth: use beefed-up trim or increase the thickness of the overall wall (the design term is "poché") through built-in cabinetry or shelving.

Doors

Upgrading from a plain-Jane hollow-core door to a paneled showpiece can elevate a room and transform its look and feel. Choosing the right door style is a critically important factor in expressing a design concept.

When an architect or an interior designer is involved in a new-build or renovation project, either can specify the interior doors, although it is usually the latter's purview. Decisions about the following elements need to be made—and to be itemized in the door schedule:

- **Material.** Options include metal and solid or manufactured wood; glass is another popular choice where visual privacy is not a concern. Doors can be solid- or hollow-core, the latter being lighter in weight, without the heft that equates with quality. Choose solid-core doors when the budget permits.
- **Size.** Doors come in different sizes, with a thickness of 1 to 1¾ inches and a typical height of 82 to 96 inches or more. (The taller the door, the thicker it is; more hinges are needed for heavier doors.) Standard widths range from 28 to 36 inches.

Full-height window walls in a house by Suzanne Lovell.

- **Finish.** Options include paint, laminate, solid wood, and wood veneer.

- **Operation.** Most common are swinging, sliding, and folding doors. Sliding pocket doors are great space savers when square footage is tight, but will require building out the thickness of the wall to create the pocket.

- **Fire rating.** Local building codes may require rated doors for residential applications. Be sure to check with your building department.

- **Hardware.** Although doorknobs and knockers are generally listed on the hardware schedule, the amount of hinges is typically specified in the door schedule. The number will depend on the size and weight of the door. (See "Hardware," page 143.)

Windows

A view to the outdoors is one of the most important features of a room. As people sit, work, or socialize, they need a moment to pause and mentally step away. A framed view—called a vista—is a point of release, and an invitation to enjoy a serendipitous and fleeting work of art . . . that of nature.

A window's operation informs what type of drapery or treatment is most appropriate—and what may not be feasible.

Clean-lined rail-and-stile doors by Phillip Thomas.

ANATOMY OF A DOOR

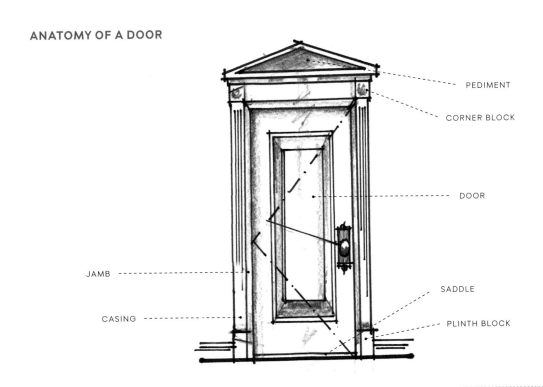

- PEDIMENT
- CORNER BLOCK
- DOOR
- JAMB
- SADDLE
- CASING
- PLINTH BLOCK

STYLES

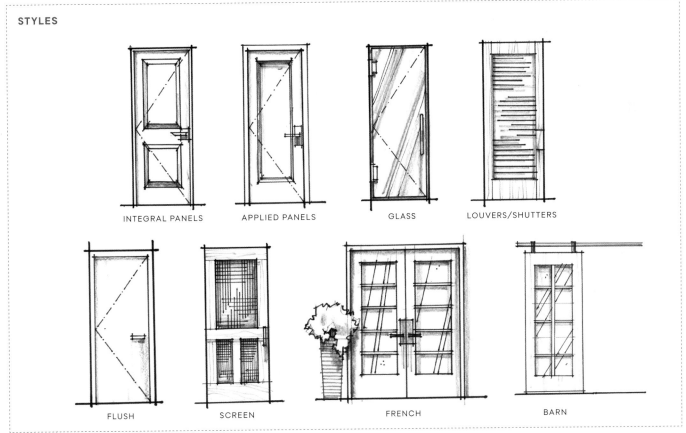

INTEGRAL PANELS

APPLIED PANELS

GLASS

LOUVERS/SHUTTERS

FLUSH

SCREEN

FRENCH

BARN

ANATOMY OF A WINDOW

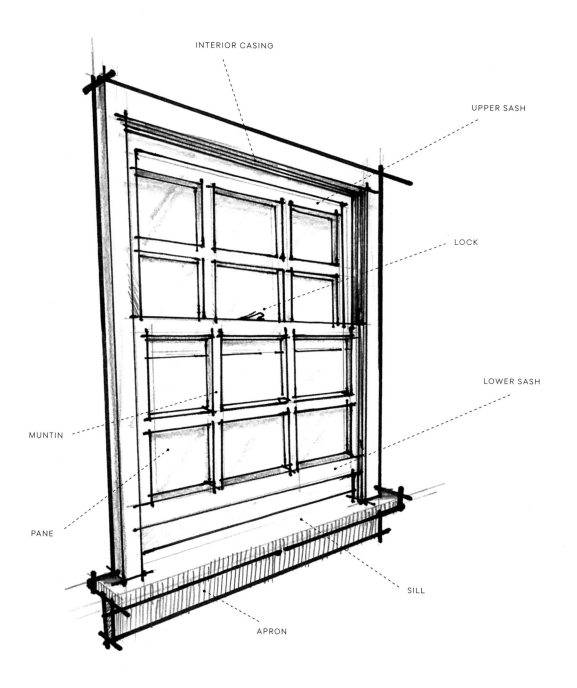

INTERIOR CASING

UPPER SASH

LOCK

LOWER SASH

MUNTIN

PANE

SILL

APRON

STYLES

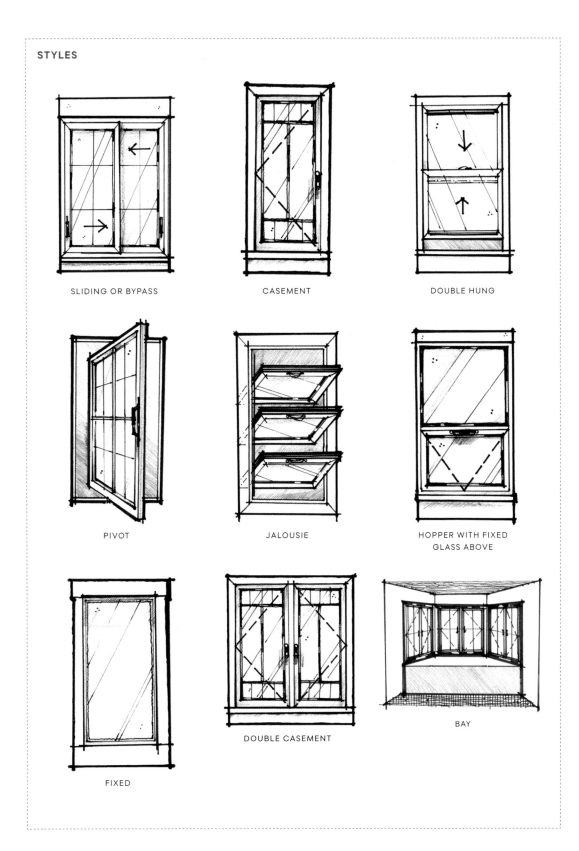

SLIDING OR BYPASS

CASEMENT

DOUBLE HUNG

PIVOT

JALOUSIE

HOPPER WITH FIXED
GLASS ABOVE

FIXED

DOUBLE CASEMENT

BAY

STAIRCASES

A staircase is a diva: a leading architectural feature that influences a room's atmosphere and expresses movement, even when awaiting use. It is a key interior component, establishing a diagonal gesture as it links levels. From tread material to railing details, each element of a stair presents a creative opportunity, a chance to make a statement.

Stairs get their character from all their parts and pieces, but most of all from the overall shape. Each stair layout has a specific design presence, irrespective of its style.

Stairs are also structural, incorporated into a building's framing and subject to stringent codes. As such, the modification of an existing staircase or the erection of a new one will require the involvement of an architect or a structural engineer.

A glass balustrade on a staircase by Phillip Thomas.

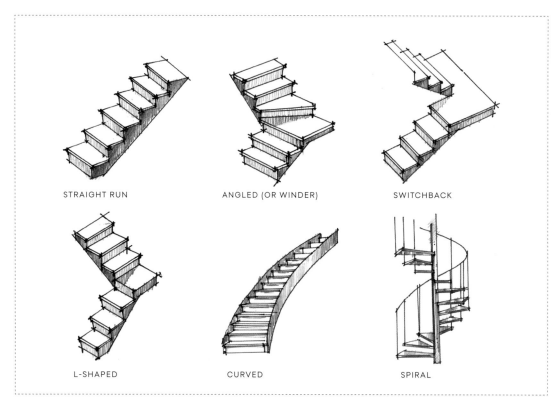

STRAIGHT RUN

ANGLED (OR WINDER)

SWITCHBACK

L-SHAPED

CURVED

SPIRAL

ANATOMY OF A STAIRCASE

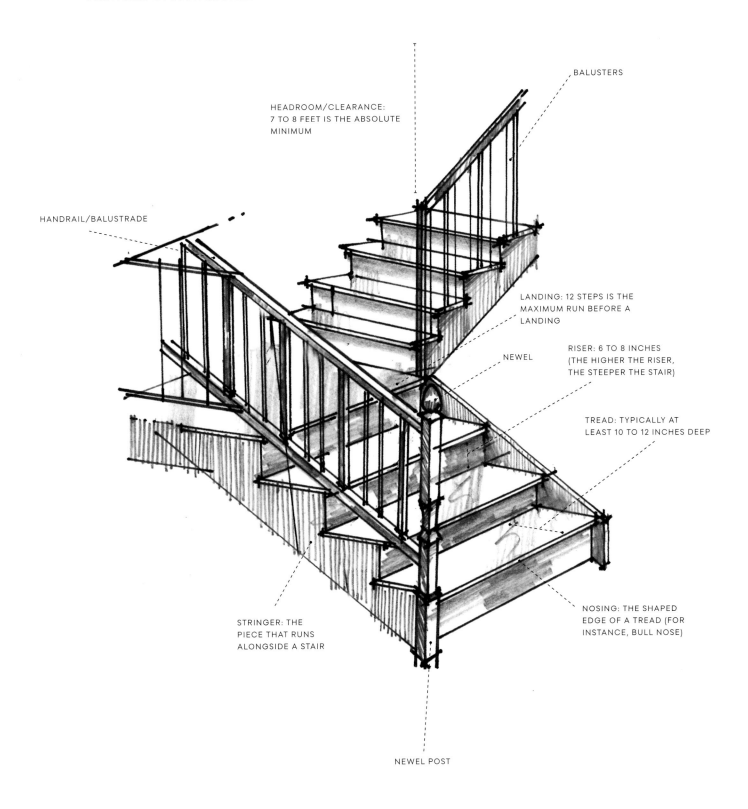

BALUSTERS

HEADROOM/CLEARANCE:
7 TO 8 FEET IS THE ABSOLUTE
MINIMUM

HANDRAIL/BALUSTRADE

LANDING: 12 STEPS IS THE
MAXIMUM RUN BEFORE A
LANDING

NEWEL

RISER: 6 TO 8 INCHES
(THE HIGHER THE RISER,
THE STEEPER THE STAIR)

TREAD: TYPICALLY AT
LEAST 10 TO 12 INCHES DEEP

STRINGER: THE
PIECE THAT RUNS
ALONGSIDE A STAIR

NOSING: THE SHAPED
EDGE OF A TREAD (FOR
INSTANCE, BULL NOSE)

NEWEL POST

FIREPLACES

Fireplaces bring visual and physical warmth to a room and can serve as its primary focal point, anchoring a conversation area or seating group. A freestanding fireplace complete with hearth and chimney can also act as a spatial divider, demarcating discrete zones within an undifferentiated open space.

A fireplace is essentially a boxy void set into a wall. The void itself is called the firebox. Installed in front and just below is the hearth, a stone or tiled area to protect the floor (and room) from sparks. This fireproof element is a code requirement, and can be set into the floor or cantilevered off the wall. A mantel and decorative surround are optional; their existence lends grandeur. But in a minimalist or modern interior, the firebox is often left unadorned; its size, shape, and placement *are* the design statement, turning a simple opening into a key focal point.

Some rooms have absolutely no character, and need it desperately. While building a real fireplace in an existing home is often out of the question, inserting a faux fireplace is always an option to anchor a room or provide a focal point. This usually involves bumping out a wall about 18 inches to create a faux chimney and recessed firebox, framed with a decorative mantel. The firebox can be used to hold real wood logs or even decorative arrangements of candles or flowers.

There are several types of fireplaces:

- **Wood-burning.** These are the most traditional type and require a source of fresh air. Smoke needs to be vented directly to the outside.
- **Gas-fueled.** They must connect to a gas supply and ignite automatically (often via remote control) like a stovetop; the ceramic faux logs look quite real when surrounded by flames. Gas-fueled fireplaces can be retrofitted into existing fireboxes and must be vented through a chimney or directly to the outside via a duct through an exterior wall. There are also ventless gas fireplaces engineered to fit against walls or recess into cavities; they work by drawing fresh air from the room, warming it, and then recirculating it.
- **Zero-clearance.** These prefabricated, gas-fueled models feature a metal firebox enclosed in glass doors. Combustible materials can be located at close range.
- **Freestanding fireplace.** Often serving as a sculptural element in a room, these require a fireproof surface behind and below, as well as proper venting to the outside.

OPPOSITE, LEFT: A fireplace by Matthew Patrick Smyth.
OPPOSITE, RIGHT: A marble fireplace surround.

ANATOMY OF A FIREPLACE

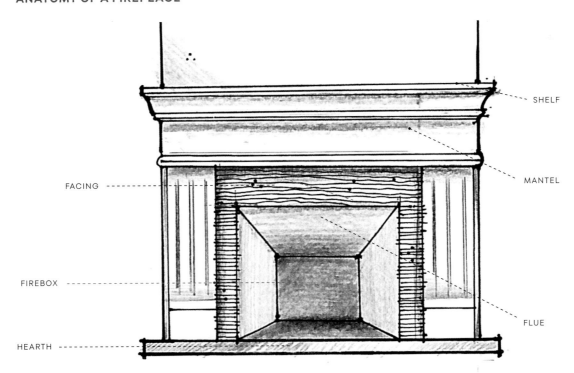

SHELF

MANTEL

FACING

FLUE

FIREBOX

HEARTH

HARDWARE

Hardware is one of the more function-driven features of an interior. Devices such as latches, hinges, and doorknobs make a space *work:* they enable the opening of cabinets and windows, abet movement through rooms, and help secure a home, among other roles. But hardware can—and should—also perform a decorative purpose in a residential setting, especially more visible and oft-used elements like cabinetry pulls. In addition to coordinating with surrounding furnishings and finishes—from textiles to lighting—hardware can serve as the jewelry of a room, adding richness and sparkle, a sense of sophistication and artistry. Striking just the right note to complement the overall design takes forethought and attention.

THE OPTIONS

Hardware is an integral part of every door, window, cabinet, and drawer. The average suburban home has several entry doors and six to twelve rooms, which equates to a *lot* of hardware. Even the smallest space typically features a laundry list of items. Take front doors alone, which need two knobs (or lever handles), an accompanying lockset, two or three hinges, a dead bolt, a peephole, a doorbell, a kick plate, and possibly a knocker. One door, ten or eleven pieces of hardware . . . and that tally doesn't even include the doorstop.

For a new home being built from the ground up, a designer or a homeowner will need to specify myriad hardware items. Creating a hardware schedule (or spreadsheet) that lists the following information will make the job easier:

- Each item
- Manufacturer
- Details of its style
- Item number
- Finish
- Operation
- Where it is to be installed

If the project is a renovation or simply a decorative refresh, the scope of work may be narrower, with just a few key elements meriting an upgrade: front-door hardware, kitchen cabinet pulls, and interior doorknobs, for instance. Either way, many mechanisms are quite technical, so professional advice is a plus. Most salespeople at hardware stores and suppliers (as opposed to big-box retailers) will be knowledgeable and willing to help, weighing in on locking mechanisms, keying schemes, the handedness of doors and door swings, and how to coordinate finishes from different manufacturers.

OPPOSITE: Phillip Thomas chose Lucite hardware for a ladylike dressing room.

A Definitive List of Hardware

The design industry divides hardware into two categories: cabinet hardware—which includes pulls, hinges, and the like—and architectural hardware, which encompasses everything else, from doorknobs to switch plates. (Kitchen and bathroom hardware is a separate category called fittings.) Here are some items that may need to be specified in a design project:

DOOR HARDWARE

- Doorknobs, handles, pulls, levers
- Pocket door hardware
- Back plates (and push plates), key plates, rosettes, escutcheons, and handle sets
- Locks, turns, bolts, latches
- Keys
- Hinges (either decorative or concealed)
- Door knocker and peephole (for front doors)
- Doorstop

WINDOW HARDWARE

- Latches
- Levers
- General room hardware

- HVAC grilles
- Switch plates
- Electrical outlet back plates
- Carpet rods
- Artwork picture rods
- Drapery hardware, including rods, finials, and tiebacks

CABINET HARDWARE

- Handles, pulls, knobs
- Hinges
- Catches
- Locks

CLOSET INTERIOR HARDWARE AND ACCESSORIES

- Clothes poles and mounts
- Hooks
- Accessory racks

Whether a design project entails assessing a space and gauging the condition (and presence) of existing elements or embarking on a wholesale build-out, the above list is an invaluable aid. Use it to generate a hardware schedule.

A suite of door and cabinet hardware—including door knob and lever—that David Scott designed for SA Baxter.

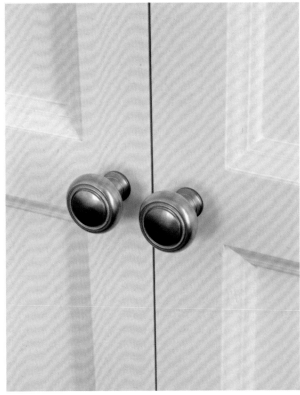

LEFT: Lucite drawer pulls offer a modern look. **ABOVE:** Round pulls in a warm brushed-bronze finish have a subtle chisel detail that reads a bit traditional.

A dressing area's custom cabinetry, by Cullman & Kravis, is serviced by delicate brass pulls.

DESIGN CONSIDERATIONS

Style, material, and finish are the paramount attributes to contemplate when specifying hardware. But it's just as necessary to think about the relative size of the hardware vis-à-vis the room and the architectural element to which it is affixed. Also consider the details of its operation: Are the knobs and hinges for a left- or right-hand operating door, for instance? How does the lockset work? Is a master key needed? Finally, consider easy-to-use lever handles or pulls to ensure aging-in-place accessibility.

Style

Hardware should match the style of the surrounding interior, whether the decor is country French or midcentury modern. A sleek design is a nice fit in an assertively contemporary abode, whereas a more traditional space will demand that the shape, finish, and decoration of a lever or an escutcheon relate to the details of the overall room. Historic doors need period-appropriate hardware. Bear in mind that a door's two knobs can differ in style depending on what room they face into: the door between a bedroom and master bath may feature a unique finish on each side.

Material

Not to be overlooked is the tactile aspect of hardware: a knob or a pull should be pleasing, firm, and reassuring in the hand. Solid brass and steel feel heavier and more substantial than lightweight aluminum, and thus communicate value. Hardware is often constructed of one material and plated with another; note that the plated finish will wear off over time. Doorknobs, drapery-rod finials, and cabinet pulls may also incorporate special treatments such as porcelain, glass, or semiprecious stone.

Finish

Base your choice on what degree of abuse the hardware will undergo and what room it's to be installed in. A front doorknob needs a more hard-wearing finish than decorative hardware in a less used location does. Drapery rods and finials—seen but rarely touched—can feature a more delicate finish. A highly polished finish will show dust, fingerprints, and scratches and takes more housekeeping to look good, while a satin or brushed finish is less fragile and more low-maintenance. Choose from the following options:

- Brass: durable
- Bronze: durable
- Chrome: expensive and fragile
- Copper: interesting and trendy
- Gold: expensive and soft
- Nickel: elegant and fragile
- Silver: expensive and soft
- Stainless steel: durable but somewhat commercial and industrial looking

Sizing

Select hardware that's properly sized and pro-portioned for the room and the architectural element it is affixed to. A heavy, oversize door requires hardware of a similar scale and heft, whereas a small pull will suffice for a slim built-in cabinet. Think about the thickness of the door or panel and whether it's solid- or hollow-core; a tall door will need more hinges or a single, con-tinuous piano hinge (panels will warp without hinges to stabilize them).

Operation

Every door has a "hand," meaning where the hinges are located relative to the doorjamb, and how it is pulled in or pushed in. Be sure to select the proper handedness, which is identified on the floor plan in a new-build or renovation project.

Be sure to coordinate door hardware with other finishes in a room, especially in a small bathroom where elements are in close proximity.

HANDEDNESS

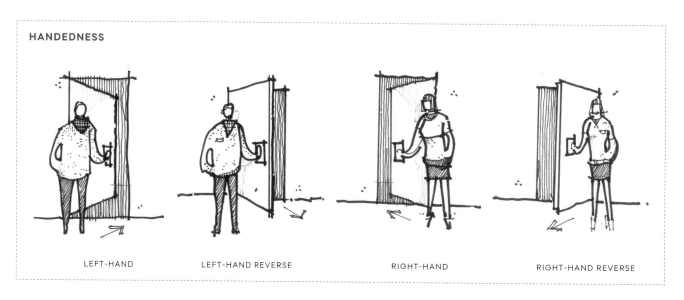

LEFT-HAND   LEFT-HAND REVERSE   RIGHT-HAND   RIGHT-HAND REVERSE

INSTALLATION CONSIDERATIONS

Architectural hardware is selected by whoever is overseeing the interior design. If the homeowner is tackling the project himself, then the onus will fall on him. If an architect and an interior designer are both involved, the latter generally takes the lead on specification and oversees the detailed hardware schedule or list (to match the more general architectural hardware schedule). A master bedroom remodel might just entail new door and closet hardware, while a whole-house renovation will be infinitely more complex. For very large or complicated projects, a hardware consultant is imperative to ensure no essential element is overlooked. In most instances, the general contractor (if one is involved) actually *places* the hardware order.

Because hardware is small in size and not necessarily the first detail that comes to mind when envisioning an interior, it often gets overlooked—especially by a homeowner or a designer who hasn't previously tackled such a project. But it is essential to address and document these components—every hinge, lock, and pull—early in the design stage for a few reasons:

- Hardware must be properly budgeted for, especially if the project is new construction or if all-new hardware is required. Given the sheer quantity of hardware needed in a home, even the most cost-conscious option is expensive.

- Hardware needs to be incorporated into the construction (or design intent) drawings and priced as part of the general contractor's bid, since he or she will be placing the order.

- Lead times for custom orders or special finishes such as nickel and satin can be long: four months or more (compared with the typical four weeks for standard products). For a substantial project or one with uncommon finishes, the maker will provide a sample, possibly requiring some back-and-forth before approval. Note that custom hardware is *very* expensive so it is best reserved for projects with a large budget or unique needs, such as a historic renovation.

- When commissioning custom cabinetry, arrange for the hardware to be delivered to the woodworker in advance. That way, it can be installed in the shop after the pieces are fabricated but prior to delivery.

CHOOSING THE RIGHT HARDWARE DESIGN TAKES TIME, ATTENTION, AND CARE BUT ADDS IMMEASURABLE VALUE.

FLOORING

People are highly sensitive to the most subtle aspects of their environment, subconsciously noting all kinds of information through the incredibly sensitive nerve endings in the soles of the feet. The design of a floor conveys the essential character of a space not only through visual appearance but also through the feel of textures, transitions, and temperature. Whether buttery leather or superslick glass tile, the choice of flooring material speaks volumes.

Unlike wall paint and upholstery fabrics, materials such as wood planks and marble mosaics are relatively permanent and not easily changed or modified: they are laid over and generally adhered to a subfloor, which is part of the building structure. Tearing up a floor and installing a new one is a major renovation project, one that may require a GC, a designer, an architect, or all three. Even retiling a small laundry nook is a big effort not to be taken lightly. Of course, some materials can be given a relatively straightforward makeover: a tiled floor can be regrouted in a new color; wood floors painted or sanded down and refinished. But in cases where an overhaul is not possible, the homeowner will need to work with the existing flooring and design the room or space around it.

THE OPTIONS

Flooring ranges from poured concrete to carpeting, with a wide variety in between. Options are divided into three categories:

- **Hard flooring** includes wood, ceramic, porcelain, stone, glass, and concrete. Properly installed and maintained, these durable and long-lasting materials offer many creative options.
- **Resilient flooring** refers to cork and linoleum as well as rubber and vinyl. These materials are softer underfoot and kinder on joints, boast acoustical properties, and are easy to maintain. Courtesy of their flexibility and ability to conform to uneven surfaces, resilients are a good alternative to hard flooring when a nonlevel subfloor presents a difficult installation.
- **"Soft flooring"** is the term for wall-to-wall carpet or broadloom, which is installed atop an existing hard material. In many cases, wall-to-wall is laid directly over the subfloor. (For more on wall-to-wall carpeting, see page 248.)

OPPOSITE: A wood floor by Cullman & Kravis stenciled in a graphic pattern.

As with all design elements, selection depends on aesthetic preferences and performance expectations. Floors are subject to more wear and tear than any other interior feature, which tends to limit choices. Here are a few questions to ask:

- What is the desired style? Almost all materials are offered in a range of looks, but glass and concrete lean modern, wood is the most traditional, and stone can go in many directions.
- What is the end use of the space? Steer clear of marble or limestone in a heavily used mudroom. In a playroom where kids will be playing, go for resilient cork or wall-to-wall.
- How much foot traffic will the flooring receive? Wood floors with three coats of urethane will stand up better than a soft white marble in a heavily trafficked foyer. Cork or vinyl is easy to maintain.
- How will the flooring be maintained, and by whom? No finish lasts forever, and the tasks of waxing or mopping can be challenging.
- Is sustainability important? Think about where the flooring material comes from: Is it local or shipped from a great distance? Are the forestry or quarry sources sustainable?
- Is accessibility an issue? Soft flooring is difficult to navigate in a wheelchair but definitely safer in a fall.
- Is the budget tight? Surprisingly, some marble or stone tiles are similar in price to carpet, although the installation can raise the cost. Opt for soft flooring in synthetic fibers.

OPPOSITE: The installation pattern of a wood floor plays off the slightly angled interior wall of corridor. **TOP:** Stone flooring with a rustic tumbled edge. **LEFT:** Two walls of glass enfold an eat-in kitchen by Hamlin Goldreyer. When open, the room is exposed to the elements, which guided the choice of porcelain flooring.

Wood

From plainspoken wood strips to centuries-old oak parquet salvaged from a French château, no other material can match the warmth of wood. The material connotes value, permanence, and tradition. However, wood is not a universally appropriate flooring option. It is affected by moisture and dampness and will expand, contract, and shift. Wood cannot be used in locations where it might be exposed to standing water or excess humidity, such as bathrooms (unless the homeowner is vigilant about upkeep). Wood floors are finished with a varnish, which often shows wear patterns over time. There are many decisions to make:

SOLID VERSUS ENGINEERED

Wood comes in solid and engineered (composite) varieties. Both types are offered in strip, plank, and parquet-tile formats. The key difference is that engineered wood is constructed of dimensionally stable plywood, topped with a ¼-inch layer of hardwood veneer. The laminated structure renders it less vulnerable than solid wood to the effects of water and moisture, plus it can be installed over radiant heat. But since the hardwood surface is so thin, engineered wood can only be refinished once or twice. Solid wood is more expensive, but it can be refinished many times, which means it has a far longer life span.

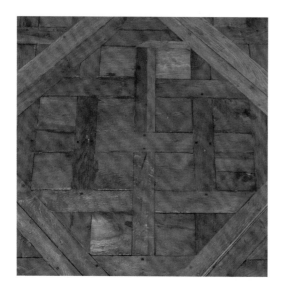

ABOVE: Parquet de Versailles is the most intricate and large-scale pattern. Made of oak finished to a luster, it connotes nobility and has a timeless beauty.
RIGHT: Diamond checkerboard parquet flooring.

SPECIES

Common varieties used for flooring include oak, maple, ash, walnut, mahogany, and bamboo. Soft woods, such as pine and fir, are less hard-wearing, although lovely. When choosing a species, consider the color (which can often be altered by using a stain or a finish) and the presentation of the grain (some woods feature more assertive figuring). Also note the tightness of the grain, which is an indicator of the wood's hardness and thus durability. For example, tight-grained maple—used for bowling alleys and butcher blocks—is extremely resistant to wear and scratches.

FORMAT

The primary choice is between parquet and either strip or plank wood, although wood mosaics and end-grain blocks are also available (if far less common):

- **Strip.** Narrow wood strips are between ⅜ and ¾ inch thick and offered in widths up to 2¼ inches. Within any given batch will be a random mix of lengths, from 12 to 84 inches.
- **Plank.** More generously proportioned planks are ¾ inch thick and range from 2¼ to 8 inches wide. They likewise come in random lengths, from 12 to 84 inches.
- **Parquet.** Parquet flooring is typically square, and manufactured in 12-, 16-, and 24-inch formats. There are also beautiful custom parquets crafted of hand-cut and -fitted tesserae of oak, mahogany, or maple. The most famous patterns are parquet de Versailles and double or triple herringbone. The ubiquitous

8-inch prefab tile sold at big-box retailers is a cost-conscious alternative that's well suited to rental apartments and high-traffic, low-maintenance spaces, such as playrooms.

NATURAL VERSUS STAINED

A well-chosen stain color can enhance the wood's richness and depth—or totally transform its natural tone and character. Stain can stylistically elevate even the plainest pine floor. A nice effect is to leave the wood unstained and exploit its inherent coloration as a design element, using different species (rather than different stain colors) to create a border or tesserated patterning. Dark ebony or walnut contrasts beautifully with maple or mahogany, for instance.

FINISHES AND SEALANTS

Choose a finish that either celebrates the wood's inherent character or reinvents its look. Whether stained or left au naturel, all wood flooring needs a finish to protect it from wear. Most common is polyurethane, a nonpenetrating coat that's clear, tough, durable, and available in four sheens: high gloss, semigloss, satin, and matte. The finish is applied either at the project site or in the factory prior to installation. Specify a low-VOC finish so as not to compromise indoor air quality. Work with your contractor to determine the proper product for your needs. (See chart on the following page.)

Wood Finishes and Sealants

FINISH	PROS/ATTRIBUTES	CONSIDERATIONS
OIL-MODIFIED URETHANE (OMU)	• Moisture-resistant • Durable • Fast drying	• Yellows over time • Dries in 8 hours—but needs 24 hours to cure
WATER-BASED URETHANE	• Clear • Nonyellowing • Dries in 2 to 6 hours	• More expensive than OMU
MOISTURE-CURED URETHANE	• The most durable and moisture-resistant polyurethane finish • Comes in nonyellowing formulas	• Has a very strong odor • Must be professionally applied • Not recommended for residential applications
VARNISH	• Vinyl-alkyd base	• No longer in wide use • Obscures the wood's natural depth
PENETRATING STAIN	• Formulated to both color and seal the wood • Semitransparent color	• Offered in limited colorways
PASTE WAX	• Is spread in thin coats over a stained or sealed floor • Easy to apply • The least expensive finish • Fast drying • Durable	• Needs regular buffing
PAINT	• Can be used on any wood floor • Durable • Repairable	• Obscures the natural grain pattern (although the texture will be visible)
BLEACHED	• A white stain is applied to a bleached-wood floor, allowing the grain to show through • Any wood can be bleached	• Dangerous to execute • Can warp wood • Over time the natural oils will eventually darken the original creamy white
CERUSED (OR LIMED)	• Used mainly as a furniture finish but a nice option for floors as well • White wood filler is applied over stained, sealed wood and then scraped off, leaving behind a white residue in the grain pattern; a wax finish is then applied	• Works best for an open-grain wood such as oak

Ceramic Tile

Courtesy of its durability, ceramic tile—which ranges from traditional unglazed terra-cotta to contemporary-leaning porcelain—is a popular choice in bathrooms, entries, and sunrooms. But the genre is equally well suited to other areas of the home. Porcelain designed to mimic wood-plank flooring is a sturdy and pleasing choice in a family room or an open-plan kitchen/dining area. However, ceramic is quite hard underfoot and a bit loud acoustically if the room doesn't have enough soft finishes to dampen sound. And while the material's cool touch is welcome in sunnier climes, it can feel downright cold on bare feet unless paired with subfloor radiant heating.

The category spans the gamut, both aesthetically and performancewise. What type of clay a tile is composed of, whether it was baked in a kiln or formed under high pressure, and whether it features a glaze or other finish will dictate end use. Be sure to scrutinize the manufacturer's technical information sheet.

TYPES OF CERAMIC MATERIALS

Most ceramic varieties are only suitable for light- or moderate-traffic areas, whereas sturdier porcelain can be used pretty much anywhere. Each clay base has different attributes and relative virtues:

- **Terra-cotta.** Literally "baked earth" in Italian—and looks it, with its characteristic reddish color. Available glazed or unglazed, terra-cotta is strong and waterproof.
- **White clay.** The pure-white body allows the glazing to have true coloration. Highly decorative tiles usually have a white body.

- **Red clay.** This is less expensive than white-body tile, but the red tint may affect the color of the glaze. Traditional Saltillo tiles, though beautiful, are not durable and crack easily.
- **Quarry tile.** Features integral or "full body" coloration: the color (typically red or gray) extends all the way through the tile, so cracks and chips won't show. Extremely durable, quarry tile is sold in 6- or 8-inch squares.
- **Porcelain.** The specific clay mix used to manufacture porcelain results in a dense, impervious, and superstrong tile that's smooth and suitable for high-traffic areas. Many porcelains feature full-body coloration.

FINISH

Glazed tiles are slippery underfoot and often show wear patterns over time. In general, unglazed tiles are best for floors, whereas glazed tiles should be relegated to walls. (The manufacturer will typically specify appropriate use.) For wet areas, choose an antislip finish or a textured ceramic; some even have a surface treatment that mimics rough stone.

FORMAT

Size and shape range from coin-size penny rounds to large-format porcelain slabs up to 3 meters long. When making a choice, bear in mind that the larger the tile, the more likely it is to crack—meaning a perfectly level subfloor is mandatory. (Smaller tiles on uneven surfaces crack at the grout line, which is an easier fix.) In a shower, use the smallest possible tiles in order to accommodate the slight angling of the floor (for drainage) and to create a less slippery grid.

GROUT

Grout is a necessary component of most tile installations. (The exception is when the tile has precisely cut rectified edges that can be installed "butt joined," or flush, with no gap in between modules.) When designing with tile, specify the desired thickness of the grout joint (the spacing between tiles) and the grout color (either earth-toned or tinted). Grout stains easily and catches dirt, so it must always be sealed; minimize its use if possible.

Glass

Made of earthen material and fired in a kiln, glass is technically a ceramic. The key difference is the rich coloration and how glass catches and embodies light. Glass tiles come in brilliant hues—iridescent, translucent, and opaque. The most common size is 1 to 4 inches square, but micromosaics and large-slab versions (up to 24 inches) also exist. Although glass is quite durable, it's best to use it in low-traffic areas such as bathrooms and swimming pools. The key to its enduring beauty is to follow the vendor-recommended installation method.

Stone

Stone floors are emblematic of luxury. The range of veining can evoke the pattern of rippling water, and colors range from violet to wheat. In general, marble is softer, less durable, and more stainable than granite, slate, or schist. All will require a protective coat of sealant.

FORMAT

Stone comes in slab or tile format—the latter is most common for floors. Tiles range from small inch-square mosaics to 12-by-24-inch rectangles. Another option is to custom-cut stone into shapes to create parquet.

COLOR

A multitude of hues and patterns—including blues, yellows, golds, greens, and burgundies—is available. A visit to a stone yard reveals an overwhelming number of possibilities and choices—all naturally exquisite, and some quite surprising.

Concrete

Concrete is malleable and moldable in its semisolid state but tough once dried and cured, which makes it a great option for hardworking spaces and for when an industrial look is desired. Some notable points about the material:

- Concrete flooring can be poured or installed in tile format.
- Poured concrete floors can be left natural, colored with pigment, or stained (using an acid stain, a dye, or a staining agent).
- Texture is a big part of a concrete floor: choose rough or polished, uniform or variegated. Etch the surface or imprint it with a texture.
- Concrete must be sealed (top to bottom) or waxed every six to nine months. Mold can grow in porous concrete if it's left unsealed.

Types of Stone Used for Flooring

Each type of marble or granite varies in its appearance, hardness, and degree of absorbency.

STONE	APPEARANCE	PROS	CONSIDERATIONS
MARBLE	Comes in solid colors, including pure white and black	Beautiful and venerable, with lovely veining	<ul><li>Absorbent and stainable</li><li>Soft, so will show scratches</li><li>Should only be installed in areas where no harsh cleaners or acetone-based sprays will be used</li><li>Best for low-traffic floors</li></ul>
TRAVERTINE	Rustic in look, with a beige or walnut hue	Commonly available	<ul><li>Highly absorbent and easily stained; requires sealing</li><li>Wears easily</li><li>Specify either its natural open-pore state, or filled-pore to create a more even (and cleanable) surface</li></ul>
GRANITE	Available in interesting varieties	Extremely durable and great for flooring in high-traffic areas	<ul><li>Few choices of solid colors</li><li>Can read rather busy courtesy of its highly variegated coloration</li></ul>
FLAGSTONE, BLUESTONE	Tends to be quite neutral, ranging in tone from gray to reddish to green-blue	Durable and suitable for indoor or outdoor use	<ul><li>Few color choices available</li><li>Cannot be polished</li><li>Flagstone can't be installed butt-joined</li></ul>
LIMESTONE	Comes in pale, solid colors	Acquires a beautiful patina over time	<ul><li>Highly stainable</li><li>Soft and easy to scratch</li><li>Hard to clean</li><li>Best for low-traffic floors</li></ul>
SLATE	Available in a wide range of colors	Inexpensive and comes in tile or slab formats	<ul><li>Wildly varied</li><li>Sold only in boxes of tiles, not slabs</li><li>Cannot be smoothed</li><li>Highly breakable</li></ul>
QUARTZITE	Pure white, such as marble	Stain-resistant, naturally dense, and extremely durable	<ul><li>Expensive</li></ul>
SCHIST	Gray toned	Durable and stain-resistant	<ul><li>Great for bathrooms</li></ul>

Resilients

Resilients are soft and durable underfoot. Usually made of naturally recurring or recycled materials, resilient flooring is also one of the most eco-friendly choices. (The exception is vinyl, a man-made synthetic.) Options include:

CORK

By far the most popular sustainable flooring material, cork comes unstained or pre-stained in colors ranging from neutrals to bolds, in tiles and planks. It provides sound and thermal insulation as well as cushioning and comfort underfoot. It even thwarts mold and mildew growth. The crush-resistant material can be laid over an uneven surface without cracking (and is often used as an underlayment for other flooring). Cork needs to be waxed every six to twelve months and resealed every five years, as well as maintained through regular buffing.

VINYL

Typically selected for its durability, low cost, ease of maintenance, imperviousness to water, and the efficiency of its installation, vinyl comes in the form of sheets or composition tile (VCT)—the latter is most common in residential installations. Vinyl does off-gas, so it may compromise indoor air quality; check the manufacturer's directions.

RUBBER

Likewise impervious and incredibly durable, rubber has more give underfoot than vinyl. (It's pricier too.) Rubber is sold in tiles or sheets and comes in myriad surface textures, such as ribbing, raised dots, and squares.

LEATHER

Floor tiles are cut from hides of thick saddle leather. While expensive, the durable material is cushiony and softens sound; it brings a beautiful patina to a room. Its wonderful aroma is quite nice in a closet and other snug confines. Leather darkens over time and requires regular waxing and buffing.

LINOLEUM

Made of linseed oil and other natural additives, linoleum offers many benefits: it is sustainable, biodegradable, antimicrobial, nonallergenic, and water-resistant. The material comes in sheets, is very flexible, and can be custom-cut on-site to create inset patterns. It is a particularly good choice in high-use playrooms and in places where rigid stone or tile would crack because the subfloor is uneven or too flexible.

1: Large-format porcelain tile. **2**: A shapely mosaic of glass and marble in a bathroom. **3**: Pale stone flooring imparts a beachy look.

DESIGN CONSIDERATIONS

Hard and resilient flooring is typically installed in modules (tiles) that are adjoined to create an overall design. Think about how best to attain the desired pattern and effect, and plan ahead.

Directionality

Courtesy of its shape, motif, and grain patterning, hard flooring typically creates a directional effect within the room—that is, an implied sense of direction. Flooring should therefore be installed in a manner that reinforces the main and secondary axes as well as the focal point of the room. In most cases, plank or strip flooring should be run perpendicular to the path of circulation, and tiles laid so that the installation pattern or motif centers on the doorway or main entry path. Collaborate with the installer to determine the starting and focal points of the

pattern or grid *before* ordering any material, as this affects the amount of material required— and therefore the price of the job. An interior designer will always specify details of directionality and be present during installation to verify adherence to the design intent drawings.

Borders

In the most refined installations, a border helps mitigate the irregularity of a room's perimeter created by doorways, radiators, and fireplaces. The border, generally about 12 inches, outlines a rectilinear shape and is sized to fit a specific number of full tiles (or the full pattern of the flooring). In other cases, this element simply allows for the central design to be regular on all sides. Borders are also utilized in transition areas such as deep passageways or doorways. Although not mandatory, borders are highly desirable; they confer a finished look and allow the flooring to change orientation.

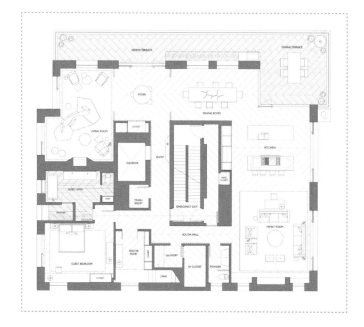

In designing a New York apartment, Dufner Heighes created a plan that denotes where each of the diagonally oriented oak floor planks should fall. The angles intersect at the entry's pedestal table.

GRID   BRICK   ASHLAR   CHECKERBOARD

SINGLE HERRINGBONE   DOUBLE HERRINGBONE   TRIPLE HERRINGBONE   SPECIAL INSET

Choosing an Installation Pattern

With tiles of any material—ceramic, stone, leather, wood parquet—it will be necessary to choose an installation pattern such as the following:

- **Grid.** Orderly, rational, and stable, the grid is the basis for most patterns. It's sometime set on the diagonal.
- **Brick.** This classic has a more dynamic sense of movement than the grid.
- **Ashlar.** This random pattern mixes tiles of various sizes.
- **Herringbone.** Timeless and elegant, the classic herringbone comes in single, double, and triple versions.
- **Checkerboard.** In wood, the checkerboard is the basis for parquet patterns; in stone, it is usually black and white, bordered in black. Depending on the material, it can be formal or playful.
- **Special inset.** A foyer or an intersection provides a perfect opportunity for some type of decorative inset.

Grout Joints

The grout joint emphasizes the grid (or other tile pattern), giving the room a sense of scale and cohesiveness. Common widths are $\frac{1}{8}$ and $\frac{1}{4}$ inch; more prominent "finger joints" measure $\frac{3}{4}$ inch. The wider the grout joint, the more rustic the look; however, keep in mind that grout will stain, and large lines will have a strong visual effect on the floor's overall appearance.

Transitions Between Materials

Transitions between different types of flooring require special attention. Flooring materials usually have different thicknesses, so when there is a transition between materials, the general contractor should calibrate or adjust the subfloor to ensure a perfectly level result. If this cannot be managed, then the installer should recommend other solutions. Typical methods include building slight ramps in the subfloor or bridging the gap with surface-mounted transition strips or saddles.

1: Bleached-wood planks create directionality in a corridor. 2: Subtle borders help a single herringbone flooring pattern transition from room to room. 3: Leather tiles segue seamlessly into carpeting with a narrow transition strip.

SLAB STONE

Designers often visit a stone yard to select individual slabs for a project. These very large, flat pieces of solid stone are generally 4 to 5 feet wide, 8 feet long, and ¾ inch thick. They have rough edges, although the surface may have been somewhat polished to show off the veining and color (making it easier to choose). In the stone yard, five to ten slabs cut from the same block will be arranged on their side. The pattern, color, and veining will be consistent from one to the other, with imperfections. These sets of slabs can all be used together in one room—for instance, in a bathroom, where the floor and walls are all intended to match. (An alternative to rough or uncut slabs is dimension stone, which comes ready to install. It can be bought at a stone yard or a supply house.)

Stone used for interior applications is almost always prefinished. Its surface treatment plays an important role in establishing spatial character. An intriguing effect is to mix tiles of the same stone, treated to different finishes, in the same area.

The following are a few popular options:

- **Honed.** This smooth, matte finish is not slippery.
- **Thermal (or flame).** Rough and highly textured, this finish is usually applied to granite.
- **Polished.** Polishing results in a surface that's reflective and smooth but slippery.
- **Tumbled.** A distressed finish is created by literally "tumbling" the stone in a drum with abrasives. Edges and surfaces are softened to create a faux-aged appearance.

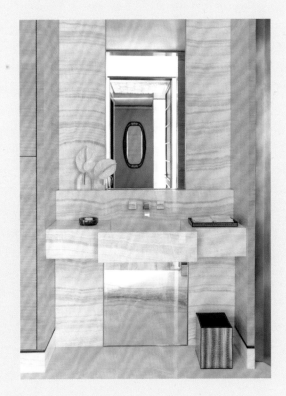

A bathroom vanity by Phillip Thomas appears carved from the slab of striated stone behind it.

INSTALLATION CONSIDERATIONS

A beautiful result depends on a perfectly prepared subfloor that's sound and level. Each kind of flooring requires a particular preparation and installation method:

- **Tile** is typically installed over a mortar bed. A thicker bed allows the installer to level and adjust the slabs or tiles to account for any unevenness in the subfloor, and thus preventing cracking. It is best to install stone in a thickset "mud" base, but ceramic tile can often be installed thinset (that is, a thinner cement layer).
- **Wood** floors, including parquet, are either glued to a plywood subfloor or "floated"—that is, fitted together via a tongue-and-groove connection rather than nails to allow expansion, contraction, and movement due to moisture.

- **Resilient** tiles often come with an adhesive already on them so they can be attached directly to the subfloor; others need to be glued in place. According to manufacturer's instructions, some resilients can be laid directly on top of existing flooring, but this is not advised.

Once a stone or tile floor is adhered to the subfloor, it's permanent: changes cannot be easily made. Therefore, the installer will often "dry lay" in advance, setting out tiles or slabs on the subfloor—prior to applying mortar—in order to map out the perfect balance of coloration and veining, and to place the less desirable pieces in unobtrusive areas.

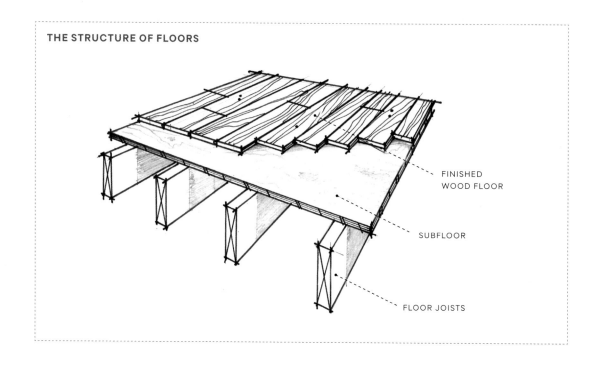

THE STRUCTURE OF FLOORS

FINISHED WOOD FLOOR

SUBFLOOR

FLOOR JOISTS

ORDERING & SAMPLING

Expect product variation. Materials—whether man-made or natural—will have variegation, either organically or between dye lots. Get a sample for review, and allow a bit of back-and-forth and resampling before signing off.

- Tile from quarries comes in boxes, and the patterning will be unpredictable, even within one box or when sourced from the same section of a particular quarry.
- Factory-made tile is uniform, available in large quantities, and very consistent from batch to batch. Each box of tile will be designated with a lot number that corresponds to its batch. Lots can vary within a very restricted range, but the color change may still be jarring. To avoid this problem, order at least 10 percent overage so that the most extreme variants can be discarded. (Let the installer provide the quantity estimate.)
- Check dye lots of any materials, including resilients, very carefully.
- Wood is a natural material and there may be a wide color variation—this is part of its beauty. If consistent color is very important, then order extra wood and hand-select the pieces to be installed. Keep in mind that some woods, such as maple and cherry, will also darken and change over time.

Parquet flooring in an apartment by Stefan Steil.

PAINT

The most common interior finish is paint applied to walls, trim, moldings, doors, cabinetry, ceilings, even floors. A well-chosen paint treatment can make a room or space look brighter, bigger, better proportioned, more intimate—or just more atmospheric.

THE OPTIONS

A paint job requires many decisions to be made, from color palette to the type and sheen of paint.

The Medium

Paint is composed of pigment suspended in a viscous medium that helps spread the pigment evenly onto a surface and then evaporates as the paint dries (so that just the pigment remains). Each medium has certain advantages, limitations, and applications for which it's best suited. Two are most common:

- **Acrylic paint** dries fast and is ideal for large surfaces, such as walls, but is less appropriate for cabinetry or trim
- **Oil-based products** are preferred for decorative treatments such as glazing, because they offer a long window of workability before drying, but are not an ideal choice for walls or ceilings

Dark red walls impart a sense of sophistication and luxury in a sitting room by William T. Georgis.

Bright red paint drenches a dining room by Addie Havemeyer Designs; even the recessed niche is treated to the color.

Finish Type

Interior wall and ceiling paint comes in several levels of sheen, from fully matte to a reflective high gloss. The finish will affect both the performance of the surface and the perception of its color. Shiny or glossy paint makes a surface smoother and easier to clean, but any textural imperfections in the wall underneath will be more noticeable. When choosing a color or a palette, keep in mind that surface reflectivity makes hues look brighter or more saturated.

- **Flat** paint is the most common and easiest to apply; it doesn't have the same innate interest as a glossier paint, but it is the go-to finish for most walls and ceilings.
- **Eggshell** is perfect for most wall surfaces: it has a little sheen and is more cleanable than flat finishes.
- **Pearl** is the finish to use when semigloss is too shiny, but the walls need to be easily wiped down: bathrooms, playrooms, and kitchens are great candidates.
- **Semigloss** adds a reflective sparkle and is easily cleaned. Use semigloss paints on trim, moldings, and doors.
- **High gloss** is great for trim and for ultrasmooth, specially prepared surfaces. High-gloss paints are also used for lacquer treatments, in which layered coats imbue flat surfaces with a sense of depth and dimension.

Chemical Makeup

For many years, paints and stains incorporated chemical vehicles that emitted unhealthy levels of volatile organic compounds (VOCs), which negatively affect human respiratory and nervous systems. These VOCs escaped from the product as it dried and lingered for many weeks, affecting surrounding air quality. Manufacturers have since reworked their formulas to greatly reduce or eradicate VOCs, creating paints that are far less noxious, yet still as effective in their coverage as their more chemically laden counterparts. Always specify no- or low-VOC products.

Richard Mishaan dressed up a bedroom bereft of architectural character with bold painted stripes for a dynamic visual statement.

CHOOSING THE RIGHT COLOR

Color is relative: context and setting are everything when picking a palette. Hues look different based on what others are adjacent or within view, whether outside a window or through a doorway into a contiguous space. The brain subconsciously registers all colors in an environment, from fabrics to natural woods. Even viewing angle alters perception. This is why the exact same paint color seems to shift a bit from room to room. The intensity and character of natural and artificial illumination within the space also affect a color's appearance.

It is ideal to make final color selections while actually standing in the space where they'll be applied. Here are a few guidelines:

GET A BIG SWATCH

When paint goes up on the wall, in elevation, it reads differently than it does on a small swatch. "It's a fallacy that you can pick the right hue from a little swatch," says Ethel Rompilla, a color expert and a professor at the New York School of Interior Design. "Put any color up on the wall and it gets exponentially brighter. It's important to get a big sample on a board and move it around the room." A 2-foot square of cardboard, Masonite, or plywood can do the trick. Color consultant and fine paints creator Donald Kaufman advocates a test patch that's 5 feet wide and the full height of the room (not framed on four sides by swaths of white primer), on a wall opposite windows.

A stenciled wall pattern creates a lively backdrop to traditional wood furniture. Note the buff-colored ceiling.

WAIT FOR THE PAINT TO FULLY DRY

Pale paint colors will look darker dry than wet, while deep colors will appear lighter after they've had time to cure.

THINK ABOUT LIGHT

"Light—and thus color—changes from the top of the wall to the bottom, and as the conditions shift from day lighting to artificial illumination," says designer Ellie Cullman. "And with few exceptions, walls are painted before decorative lighting is installed, which changes the look. Plus, you're seeing the color without the surrounding furniture and fabrics. A color will look warmer when the lights go in, and in context. You have to account for that difference."

Review the color at various times of day and under many lighting conditions, even over the course of a few days. A color is ever changing, so think hard about how it appears under the most common conditions.

Think of Surrounding Surfaces

Many people fear using darker or more saturated colors on walls lest the room read as gloomy or overwhelming; however, this is a limiting viewpoint. Contrast is the key to using rich hues. Never consider wall colors in isolation; instead, think of their relationship to the surrounding environment. The four walls of a room are balanced by the two other planes—ceiling and floor—as well as by the moldings, doors, windows, views, and light. The colors and patterns of the furnishings and drapery also provide a counterpoint. If the walls are dark but the floor is a glossy-finished natural oak and the ceiling and moldings are white or pale-hued, the proportion of dark to light creates a sense of balance. The contrast between rich hues and paler accents imparts liveliness and gives the dark colors an energy. This is a good time to play with texture, using a satin or glossy light-color paint for moldings and cabinetry, and a matte or textured finish for dark walls or medium-tone ceiling.

As a rule of thumb, it is better to select wall colors that have a gray undertone or are not overly vibrant or saturated. This holds true for even the lightest colors. Such hues will be more subtle over large areas and are thus more livable. Some paint manufacturers label these "historic" colors.

Account for Differences in Materials

If you want paint colors to match those in a rug or a fabric, be sure to account for the variation between the materials: paint and textile, pigment and fiber. The identical red used on a china plate and in a carpet can look entirely different, an effect that's called metamerism. Designers train their eye to account for this discrepancy, but novices can play it safe by picking a paint color that blends with the other finishes in a room scheme rather than attempting to exactly match. However, if perfectly matching colors is the goal, then the feat will require lots of close looking, under different light conditions and various locations within the room.

CEILING COLOR

People often default to white ceilings, but even a very pale shade—nearly white with just a faint tint of the wall's hue—will add depth and resolution to a room. It will also create a noticeable contrast with adjacent crown moldings, making more of a statement. Although flat paint is usually preferable for ceilings, a glossier finish can add reflectivity, movement, and luminosity to a space. A shiny ceiling recedes yet still has presence. If flat is your preference, consider the most common variety, Ceiling White: every manufacturer has a version.

In a den by Drake/Anderson's Caleb Anderson, dark-painted walls exude drama and form a gallery-like backdrop for fine furnishings, including a Louis XV–style desk. OPPOSITE: Lacquered walls in a living room by Phillip Thomas.

DECORATIVE PAINTING & FINISHES

An artisan can create a special effect that will transform a simple space into something spectacular. Decorative treatments are usually applied directly to walls or objects, but sometimes artists apply murals or paint effects to canvas or composite panels in the studio and later install them on-site. For something more unique than a continuous swath of color, consider the following decorative treatments:

- Stenciling
- Murals and scenic painting
- Metal leaf
- Venetian plaster
- Strié
- Glazing
- Ragging
- Stippling
- Marbleizing
- Sponging
- Lacquer

Special finishes are often painstaking and labor-intensive to execute, so be sure to budget adequate time: even a tiny room with a lot of windows and few large wall surfaces can take five or six days to complete. Always get a 12-inch-square (minimum) sample for approval prior to execution. If a mural has been commissioned, the artist should provide for approval a maquette (or small model or painting) to scale.

Hand stenciling imparts a crafted touch in a bedroom by Cullman & Kravis.

A sampling of decorative-paint treatments from Dean Barger Studios.
1: Double strié cross-drag 2: Faux marble 3: Venetian stucco 4: Strié drag
5: Stipple glaze 6: Faux tortoise shell 7: Stipple glaze with stencil pattern
8: Faux horn 9: Moon gold

INSTALLATION CONSIDERATIONS

To what substrate is the paint being applied? This can make all the difference when choosing a painted finish or technique. Common surfaces include plaster, gypsum wallboard (also called drywall or its trademarked name, Sheetrock), stucco, various woods, and cast-resin moldings. In very rare instances, paint can even be applied over an existing wallcovering or wallpaper, although this is not advised. Each substrate has a unique texture or grain that repels or absorbs paint to varying degrees. Proper surface preparation will cover and eliminate any such variegation and seal the surface to ensure adhesion of new coats.

HIRE GOOD LABOR

There is only one guarantee for a good outcome: hire an expert painter—the best you can afford. Most of the cost of paint work is labor. The highest-quality paint job takes the longest to execute, which will be reflected in the painter's price. Don't choose the lowest bidder unless absolute necessary. A master painter has seen it all and understands the nuances of every step, from surface preparation and materials to techniques and tools. If so empowered, a master painter will act not only as a contractor but also as a consultant, advising on matters ranging from application to maintenance.

CHOOSE A GOOD PAINT

The cost of paint does not always correlate to its quality; the most expensive product is not necessarily the best. Choose paints that emit few or no VOCs and are made with healthier pigments and bases, and make your selection on the basis of *durability*. The cost of paint runs a wide gamut, but look for "name" brands that promise to cover in one coat. The painting contractor usually provides the paint and materials based on the designer's or client's specification. Ask these questions before buying:

- How fragile or tough will the paint be over time, in terms of abrasion and resistance to staining and dirt?
- How many coats of paint will it take to cover the previous color?
- How much will the color fade, and how long will it last?

PROPERLY PREPARE SURFACES

Superior execution demands superior preparation of the surface being painted; any imperfections will show right through the paint, especially if the finish is glossy. The more time and effort spent properly sanding, patching, skim-coating, priming, and otherwise readying a surface for application, the smoother and more refined the final appearance will be. The amount of preparation will also affect the cost of the work.

OPPOSITE: Joan Dineen enlisted decorative painter Eva Buchmiller to create a mural for the stairwell of a New York townhouse.

WALLCOVERINGS

Wallpaper was originally designed to enhance the architectural character of a room by simulating hand-painted murals or elaborate millwork details such as boiserie. Today, wallcoverings remain an effective way to bring color, pattern, texture, scale, narrative, and architectural interest to a room. As such, they are a great vehicle for reinforcing the design concept. Since any wallcovering is more decorative than simple paint, it adds a layer of finish to a room as well as emphasizing the sense of enclosure. Materials such as cork and paper-backed fabric also serve functional purposes, among them improved acoustics and insulation. True to its name, a wallcovering plays an equally important role in hiding imperfect walls and protecting surfaces from damage.

A wallcovering is most commonly applied to all four walls of a room, but there are some other suitable applications:

- A single accent or focal wall
- A niche or an alcove
- Wainscoting
- A ceiling
- A folding screen
- A backing for a bookcase or built-in shelving
- A faux headboard

OPPOSITE: A hand-painted scenic wallpaper in a bedroom by Cullman & Kravis. The designers collaborated with Gracie to place the birds in prominent locations where they wouldn't be hidden by other elements of the decor.

THE OPTIONS

Wallcoverings range from the finest, most delicate European papers to the toughest vinyls; from natural fibers, such as linen and grass cloth, to eco-friendly, digitally printed synthetics. Material options abound: wood veneer, cork, mica, beading, leather, and much more. Stylistically, the genre is limited only by imagination: there are traditional toiles and op-art Mylars, stately florals and masculine flannels, imitation gold leaf and oil-stained kraft papers. Every conceivable pattern exists in printed or woven wallcoverings, and there is an appropriate option for any interior surface.

Paper

Wallpaper is just that: a paper product that comes in rolls and is adhered to surfaces with paste. The category encompasses myriad styles, including unique designs made via silk-screening and hand- or digital printing. Some of the most beautiful papers are crafted by artisans using subtle base papers overlaid with abstract patterns. Note that 100 percent paper is extremely delicate and tears easily when wet or damp.

In residential applications, washable wallpaper—which has a surface coat of latex or polyvinyl chloride (PVC)—is the most commonly used covering for everyday areas. These topical treatments render the paper durable and ensure that it can be easily stripped from the wall at the end of its life cycle. (These prepasted products ease installation.)

Vinyl

Perfect for areas requiring heavy-duty protection, vinyls are washable, durable, and often highly textured to hide imperfect walls and the dings and scratches that plague busy areas. They come in a huge range of colors and patterns and in two weights (heavier type 2, which has a higher fire rating, is primarily used in commercial installations). Vinyls are often designed to simulate paper, silk, linen, and grass cloth; unlike fabric and other natural materials, however, the rolls have no selvage, meaning that the entire width can be used—the installer doesn't need to trim off the edges. (A cheesecloth-like cotton-scrim backing aids in pasting them to the wall.) One drawback is that many vinyls off-gas, so they are not suitable when air quality and environmental consciousness are concerns.

Scenics

Some of the earliest wallpapers were scenic designs: a pastoral image hand-painted over a series of paper strips installed side by side to create a mural that enfolds an entire room. This type of wallcovering is still being produced today—a well-known maker is Gracie—and is experiencing a resurgence in popularity.

Grass Cloth and Paper-Backed Textiles

This genre encompasses varied materials: hemp, sea grass, and a range of linen weaves. Some are more pliable (and thus easy to install) than others. Madagascar cloth, for example, is quite coarse. Although these papers are often chosen to imbue a space with an earthy touch, the category has expanded in recent years to include more decorative and sophisticated options. Grass cloths now come in bold colors, printed with graphic motifs, studded with nailheads, and even embroidered. Nonetheless, if you choose grass cloth or a textile, be prepared to embrace its organic quality: natural materials are prone to fading over time and typically exhibit wide variegation. The seams will also be very noticeable, which is considered part of the product's beauty.

Custom Fabric Wallcoverings

Most fabrics with dimensional stability and opacity are usable as wallcoverings when bonded to a paper backing. Because the fabric gets stretched a bit as it's pressed down onto the backing, it has to be structurally sound; otherwise, the integrity of the weave could be compromised. (For instance, open-weave silk or linen is not suitable.) The effect is one of subtle softness. "Paper-backed fabric confers a much cleaner look than traditional padded walls—while offering a texture and depth that you don't get with wallpaper," explains designer Martyn Lawrence Bullard. Companies that put paper backing on fabric can also provide surface coatings that help thwart dirt and stains or allow cleaning with a damp rag; the manufacturer can even laminate the fabric with a vinyl facing or treat it with fire-retardant chemicals. Backed fabrics will have a selvage edge that requires trimming.

Specialty and Exotic Wallcoverings

Almost any natural material that comes in sheet form can be backed with a paper or fabric lining for pasting to a vertical surface: wood veneer, raffia, cork, thin metals, mica, crushed stone, and even kraft paper. Some options retain their natural character after being dyed a bold color. Have a master installer cut sheets into smaller pieces and arrange them in a checkerboard or striped configuration like a collage.

Upholstered Walls

Upholstered walls offer an enveloping feel and great acoustics in rooms that demand a sense of intimacy, such as sleeping areas and libraries. "People consider the treatment to be quite traditional, but it can veer contemporary depending on the fabric chosen; matching it to the drapes creates a clean-lined look," says designer Timothy Corrigan. To make an upholstered wall, an installer will follow these steps:

1. Apply a wood frame to the wall.
2. Pad the frame with thin acrylic batting.
3. Stretch the fabric over the batting and staple it to the frame.
4. Trim raw borders or edges with decorative tape, ribbon, or piping, in the same or complementary material.

Wallpaper lines a bedside niche.

1: Pink-and-gray toile-print wallpaper injects a graphic yet ladylike edge to a bedroom by Amanda Parisi of Jarvis & Co. Interiors, bringing interest to an otherwise spare architectural envelope. **2.** In a living space by Alexa Hampton, a neutral but highly patterned wallpaper is accented with jewel tones. **3:** A textured velvet wallcovering in a rich jewel tone brings a soft, cozy touch to a den. Choosing a textile to match the sofa fabrics creates a monochromatic scheme.

DESIGN CONSIDERATIONS

There is an appropriate wallcovering design for every room in the home, from the most heavily used spaces to the most intimate, from a formal living room to a moisture-prone master bath. Whether aesthetics or function prompted the initial choice to use a wallcovering, both need to be taken into account before making a selection, so consider the following:

- Who uses the room: adults, children, both?
- Is this space formal or informal?
- Are there many exposed surfaces or corners that residents might touch or bump into?
- What does this room need in terms of desired atmosphere: cheerfulness, softness, closeness, welcome, intimacy, formality?
- What are the proportions of the room? Can the right wallcovering somehow modify the perception of the spatial attributes?
- What are the architectural features of the room? Can the wall treatment emphasize the room's best assets?

Bold or Neutral?

When covering large areas or entire walls, it's best to choose neutral colors or monochromatic tones—including natural textures. A neutral is also preferred when artwork is prominent, to avoid introducing a competing background. However, in modestly scaled spaces and those in which people spend little time—a powder room, for instance—vibrant motifs and geometrics can lend interest, liveliness, and drama.

BOLDLY PATTERNED WALLS NEED FEWER—OR BOLDER—DECORATIVE ACCESSORIES, SUCH AS LARGE-SCALE MIRRORS OR SCONCES.

Pattern Size

Consider the size, scale, and boldness of the pattern, the strength of contrast between motif and background, and the use of stripes. The scale of the pattern will ultimately affect the perceived scale of the room. Generally speaking, a small pattern is best for a small room, while a larger room can accommodate a large pattern. Vertical stripes will create the illusion of more headroom, while horizontals lend a widening effect.

One important dictum is that if the drapery or upholstery boasts a strong pattern, the walls should be quieter and simpler. The reverse is also true: solid or textured window treatments and upholstery fabrics can balance a visually assertive wallcovering. Of course, some of the most beautiful and classic interiors boast a large-scale print on the wallpaper, with the same pattern on the draperies and a majority of the upholstery.

Patterns are printed in vertical and horizontal intervals called repeats; the larger the repeat, the larger the pattern. The repeat size will be noted in the wallpaper book, on the spec sheet, or on the back of the sample. Larger repeats will require that more yardage be purchased.

How to Choose the Right Wallcovering

IF YOU WANT	CONSIDER	AVOID
Regularity of pattern	Digitally printed paper	Natural materials, such as grass cloth, silk, or cork, which have a lot of variegation
Consistency of color	Vinyl	Natural materials and handmade papers
To cover imperfect walls	Something heavily textured or an embossed pattern	Fine wallpaper; narrow rolls
An eco-friendly option	Natural fibers, such as grass cloth; wallpapers printed in water-based inks; cork	Vinyl
A covering appropriate for kids' spaces	Washable papers	Fine papers
To improve acoustics	Upholstered walls; cork; other soft or textured materials	
Something durable for heavy-traffic areas (mudrooms, kitchens, playrooms)	Vinyl	Grass cloth or textile papers

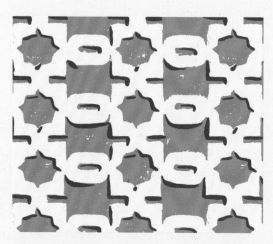

Wallpapers that NYSID alumna Inez Croom designed in the 1960s have been recently recolored and re-released by Waterhouse Wallhangings.

INSTALLATION CONSIDERATIONS

A superior installation is key to a good design. If an interior designer is overseeing the project, she may prefer to hire and supervise the paperhanger in order to exert creative control and ensure that the quality is up to her standards. Homeowners tackling this task themselves should be prepared to answer numerous questions on-site during the installation, including where seams and the focal point of the pattern should lie.

Prep the Walls

Ideally, walls should be blemish-free before any coverings are installed. (The exception is the installation of heavily textured material specifically chosen to disguise imperfect walls.) In what painters call a "level five" finish—the degree of surface perfection required when glossy paints and fine papers are to be applied—a wall is troweled with a fine skim coat of plaster and sanded until very smooth. For new construction, it will be necessary to specify a skim coat

A BRIEF HISTORY OF WALLPAPER

The earliest wallpapers were made in China around 200 BC. Hand-painted Chinese papers were first exported to Europe during the Renaissance, when international trade routes opened. Common imagery was of nature—birds, flowers, landscapes—and scenes of battle. Over subsequent centuries, Europeans put their own spin on these designs, and also expanded the genre to include paneling, leather, and tapestries. Brocades, velvets, and damasks later flourished.

In the early eighteenth century, French engraver Jean Michel Papillon invented wallpaper as we know it today. Papillon devised a printing method using carved wooden blocks to create repeating patterns that matched when separate sheets were aligned and installed together. Designs could be printed in any color desired. Later craftsmen, such as Jean-Baptiste Réveillon, Joseph Dufour, and Jean Zuber, conceived scenic papers—produced in strips or panels—depicting seascapes, town views, classical ruins, and mythological events.

Printing rollers capable of applying allover designs to long rolls of paper were developed in the 1840s. This cylinder process is still used to produce commercial wallpapers. Many time-honored methods are experiencing a resurgence today, including traditional hand-blocking, with repeating motifs made by pressing a wood block; and silk-screening, in which stencil-like frames of stretched silk are repeatedly placed on the background and inked, adding successive layers of color to create the imagery.

if desired, as it is a level above standard wall finish. If the project is a renovation, walls can be scraped and treated to a fresh skim coat in order to create a uniform base: over time, even the best-applied plaster becomes uneven due to the accumulation of dents, nail holes, poor repairs, general wear and tear, water damage, and even paint buildup.

Use a Lining

Before installing wallcovering—especially thin and delicate papers from a European heritage brand—the paperhanger often mounts a bridging material. This is typically a layer of muslin or a lining paper applied with seamless connections called butt joints. A lining paper is an extra expense, but it serves several purposes:

- To keep textural imperfections of the underlying wall from showing through
- To give a timeworn wall greater surface integrity
- To reduce the visibility of any cracks that may develop
- To protect the finish paper from being discolored by the plaster or gypsum board below
- To allow removal of the paper without tearing—a boon when rarefied, antique, or scenic wallpaper is being used (and potentially reused elsewhere)

Hide the Seams

The paperhanger should render the seams relatively invisible, double cutting the rolls and aligning them to match the repeat. How the pattern aligns vertically between rolls will influence the complexity of the installation. This will be noted on the label.

- **Random match.** The pattern will match no matter how adjoining strips are positioned— vertical stripes, for instance.
- **Straight-across match.** The design elements align when strips are hung from the same datum line.
- **Drop match.** There is a vertical distance between the matching design elements, which means the rolls must be hung in an offset fashion—and it will be necessary to order more overage.

Note that while natural materials, such as grass cloth, do not have a repeat, the seams between hung rolls are always visible—and part of their organic beauty.

RIGHT + OPPOSITE: When using wallpaper, be attentive to transitions like doorways and other architectural features.

ANATOMY OF A WALL

In older, pre-twentieth-century homes, the wooden framework of studs was covered with a fine metal lath, upon which plaster was applied directly. Today, most interior walls or partitions are built from gypsum wallboard—also known as Sheetrock or drywall—a stiff, paper-covered board made of compressed plaster powder. It's a five-step process:

1. The 4-by-8-foot sheets are nailed to the wooden or metal stud frames and joined tightly edge to edge.
2. The seams are taped and spackled with joint compound to render them invisible.
3. Screw holes are also filled with spackle.
4. A skim coat of plaster is applied if specified.
5. The wall is then sanded smooth to create a seamless, glassy surface.

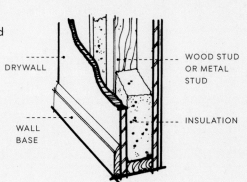

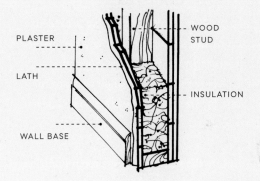

ORDERING & PURCHASING

Paper and natural wallcoverings are usually sold as single rolls, but are often *packaged* as double or triple rolls—a figure that refers to the *length* (versus three rolls packaged together). A longer roll means less waste during installation. Note that, unlike many other interior products, wallcoverings must be paid for in full when the order is placed.

Estimating Quantities

Estimating how much wallcovering is needed is not difficult, although it is always best to let the paperhanger verify the actual quantity before placing the order. To align the pattern properly, the size of the repeat has to be taken into account.

1. Measure the perimeter of the room in inches. *Do not omit the span of doors, windows, or other openings!* In order to align the pattern and have sufficient stock, include these apertures as if they weren't there.
2. Divide the total perimeter by the width of the wallcovering rolls to determine the number of "widths" needed for the room. For instance, an 8-by-10-foot room measures 432 inches, or 12 "widths" of a 36-inch-wide roll.
3. In a standard room no taller than 9 feet, allow one single roll (15 feet long per roll) for each width. Tall rooms and those with cathedral ceilings may require more rolls, but a 15-foot roll can fit almost every room.

4. If the openings in the walls are very large, and if the pattern repeat is less than 5 inches (vertical or horizontal), then the size of the openings can be deducted from the number of widths/rolls needed. But round up a bit anyway.

Overage

Always order an extra 10 percent from the same dye lot to have on hand in the event of problems requiring reinstallation or repair. Certain applications, spaces, and natural materials—plus large-scale patterns or repeats printed with a drop match—will require additional overage.

Coloration and Dye Lots

The dye lot refers to the batch in which the wallcovering was colored or printed. Rolls from the same dye lot will have consistent coloration, whereas subtle shading variations are often evident between batches—especially if the designs are handcrafted or made of variegated natural materials. Accordingly, the final product may differ slightly from the sample. Because vinyl is made in large quantities, its coloration from batch to batch is usually very consistent, whereas that of grass cloth or silk varies widely. Always specify product from the same dye lot when possible.

Common Wallcovering Widths

Single rolls of wallpaper are generally 21 to 36 inches wide and 11 yards long. But formats vary widely depending on the material, the manufacturer, and the place of origin; rolls of vinyl, for instance, come up to 50 yards long.

TYPE	ROLL WIDTH	INSTALLATION CONSIDERATIONS
ENGLISH-MADE PAPER	22 inches	Extremely delicate; can tear when wet or damp
FRENCH-MADE PAPER	18 to 22 inches	Extremely delicate; can tear when wet or damp
AMERICAN-MADE WASHABLE PAPER	Generally 36 inches (although widths of 21 and 27 inches are not uncommon)	Not available with large patterns or repeats
HAND- OR BLOCK-PRINTED PAPER	18 to 36 inches	Can't be replicated easily, resulting in variation in ink color, pattern, or printing
GRASS CLOTH AND LINEN	Usually 36 inches	Irregular; easily soiled
VINYLS DESIGNED FOR COMMERCIAL APPLICATIONS	51 or 54 inches	Commercial appearance
PAPER-BACKED FABRIC	The width of the final product will correspond to that of the fabric bolt	Not cleanable; attracts dust and dirt; expensive

Two more wallpapers designed by Inez Croom and reproduced by Waterhouse Wallhangings.

FABRICS & TEXTILES

Textiles "dress" the architecture of an interior, bringing a soft touch to the harder-edge elements. Features such as upholstered furniture, throw pillows, area rugs, and fabric shades are used to accessorize seating, cushion floors, and cover windows—and to make a fashion statement, injecting color, pattern, and texture into a room.

THE OPTIONS

Selecting the right fabric, whether to clad a sofa or top the bed, can prove an unexpectedly overwhelming task. Stylistically, there are seemingly limitless prints, colors, weave effects, and decorative embellishments to choose from. First, consider what type of fabric is appropriate:

- Plain or patterned
- Smooth or textured
- Heavy or light

How will the fabric be used? To fashion curtain panels or soft Roman shades for window treatments? Or to upholster a family room sofa or a little-used side chair? Upholstered pieces require durable, tightly woven fabrics, while the gathered nature of drapery headers calls for a lighter-weight cloth.

What special feature or character of the room or furnishing do you want to emphasize? If the ceiling height is low, vertically striped curtains are a smart option. A sumptuous solid may be best if the goal is to play up a fauteuil's curvy profile. And a print or woven pattern can lend interest to a sofa with clean lines.

Textile expert and designer Adrienne Concra suggests a beloved fabric or a preferred motif as a starting point. "It should be a crime of passion," she jokes. "But the next question is: What makes practical sense for this particular application? There will be limited answers." Each end use requires different material properties. (See chart on page 195.)

Performance expectations over time are also a factor. Textiles are highly susceptible to wear and tear and can be tricky to clean—especially after being applied to furniture. Certain fabrics age better than others; chintz, for instance, develops a soft patina over time, while chenille tends to crush. And even before they begin to fray, many textiles get irreversibly dirty and dingy; linen is notoriously quick to stain. Consider the level of abuse the fabric will endure and the source: kids, pets, moisture, or sunlight?

OPPOSITE: A lively dining room by McMillen Plus, with the same floral print used on the draperies and the chairs. The backs of the chairs are upholstered in a different fabric for a nice contrast.

Read the fabric's label to find out how it can be used. In addition to the name, style number, and color, the following information will be listed on the label:

- Fiber content (in percentages)
- Recommended applications (and disclaimers on usability)
- Any backing or finishing
- How the fabric tests for wear, light/colorfastness, flammability, etc.
- Width of a linear yard (in inches)
- Pattern repeat size
- Whether the fabric can be "railroaded" (or installed horizontally, which saves yardage)

Showrooms simplify fabric selection by presenting textiles on movable vertical panels called wings that display the full width of the bolt, showing the complete pattern. Each fabric is also presented in all available hues, or colorways. Solids are often available in dozens of colors, while prints may be offered in just two or three. The buyer is able to see a large repeat in its entirety (sometimes gathered to show how it drapes), along with coordinating solids and complementary patterns that might work well on other elements in the room—a boon for creating a complete fabric scheme.

HAND

The term "hand" refers to the tactile quality of a textile. A soft hand is welcome on upholstery and carpets; a crisp hand for curtains and tablecloths.

Fiber Type

The building blocks of a textile are fibers, which are typically spun together to form yarn that's then manufactured into cloth.

Textile fibers fall into three categories:

- **Natural.** Deriving from plants, grasses, and animal hides, natural fibers have many positive attributes. They "breathe," have a nice patina from the start, and take a wide range of colors and dyes well. (Cotton can even be grown in pale colors, eliminating the need for dyeing.) Many have a recognizable "hand," or feel, that is satisfying to the touch.
- **Synthetic.** Most synthetics derive from sludge, a by-product of refining oil. Man-made fibers are hydrophobic, meaning that moisture cannot easily penetrate them. The result is a fabric with a dry and sometimes plasticky feel that is static-prone and less cleanable. Earlier generations of synthetics were often frowned upon in higher-end residential applications, but that bias no longer holds true. Modern production methods are capable of creating fabrics that closely approximate linen, wool, and suede and are in fact preferred over their natural counterparts for certain uses. For instance, silk strands will quickly disintegrate in the sunlight, whereas look-alike polyester is durable and lasts a long time, even in tropical climates.
- **Hybrids.** Rayon and viscose are made of wood pulp, a natural product that is chemically processed into yarn.

Gary McBournie tented a room from floor to ceiling in
striped fabric.

What Fabric to Choose

FABRIC USE	MATERIAL PROPERTIES
Window treatments	• Drapes easily • Lightweight • Dimensionally stable • Sunlight-resistant
Wall treatments and other vertical applications	• Dimensionally stable • Sunlight-resistant • Colorfast
Upholstery	• Dimensionally stable • Strong • Densely woven • Abrasion-resistant
Soft furnishings (cushions, tablecloths, bedspreads, bed skirts)	• Flexible • Drapes easily • Lightweight • Stain-resistant • Abrasion-resistant
Carpets and rugs *For more on soft floor coverings, see page 244.*	• Resilient • Strong • Densely woven • Cleanable • Colorfast

Common Fibers for Residential Textiles

NATURAL AND HYBRID FIBERS	PROS/ATTRIBUTES	CONSIDERATIONS
WOOL	<ul><li>Inherently flame-retardant</li><li>Resistant to wrinkling, abrasion, and soiling</li><li>Very durable</li><li>Has natural crimp or twist</li><li>Top choice for floor covering</li></ul>	<ul><li>Attracts moths</li><li>Feels scratchy/has a rough hand</li><li>Low light reflection creates dull coloration</li></ul>
COTTON	<ul><li>Smooth hand</li><li>Strong</li><li>Inexpensive</li><li>Can be dressed up or down</li><li>Breathable</li><li>Extremely versatile</li><li>Relatively easy to clean</li></ul>	<ul><li>Lacks resiliency</li><li>Absorbent</li><li>Has short fibers, so wears easily</li></ul>
SILK	<ul><li>Translucent and lustrous</li><li>Connotes luxury</li><li>Superstrong</li><li>Drapes nicely</li><li>Offered in myriad hues</li></ul>	<ul><li>Rots when exposed to unfiltered sunlight (draperies need to be lined, but will eventually disintegrate nonetheless)</li><li>Attracts moths</li><li>Flat structure does not hide dirt well</li></ul>
LINEN	<ul><li>Strong</li><li>Pleasing texture</li><li>Does not make lint</li><li>Crisp hand and nubby texture</li></ul>	<ul><li>Wrinkles</li><li>Lacks resiliency</li><li>Absorbent</li></ul>
LEATHER	<ul><li>Supple</li><li>Nice patina</li><li>Evocative scent</li></ul>	<ul><li>Must order overage due to natural imperfections</li></ul>
MOHAIR	<ul><li>More luxurious and lustrous than wool</li><li>Holds a rich dye</li></ul>	<ul><li>More expensive than wool</li><li>Mohair plush (i.e., cut pile) is scratchy</li></ul>
VISCOSE, BAMBOO-RAYON, BAMBOO-VISCOSE	<ul><li>Soft hand</li><li>Flexible</li><li>Drapes nicely</li></ul>	<ul><li>Stains easily</li><li>Not dimensionally stable</li></ul>

SYNTHETIC FIBERS	PROS/ATTRIBUTES	CONSIDERATIONS
ACRYLIC	▪ Soft and lightweight ▪ Mimics spun natural-fiber yarns ▪ Solution-dyed acrylic can be used outdoors ▪ Great for indoor use as a performance fabric	▪ Plasticky hand ▪ Not as resistant to abrasion as fellow synthetics polyester and nylon
NYLON	▪ Strong and resistant to abrasion ▪ Resists mildew and insects ▪ Resilience makes it ideal for floor coverings	▪ Prone to static
POLYESTER	▪ Resists mildew and insects ▪ Resistant to abrasion (great for upholstery) ▪ Strong ▪ Cost-conscious ▪ Excellent resistance to sunlight ▪ Trevira is flame-retardant ▪ Nonyellowing (ideal for window treatments)	▪ Hydrophobic, so difficult to clean ▪ Prone to static ▪ Pills
RAYON	▪ Translucent and lustrous with a flexible, soft hand ▪ Strong	▪ Lacks resiliency ▪ Weaker when wet
VINYL, FAUX LEATHER, MICROSUEDE	▪ Washable with soap and water ▪ Will not crock, pill, or fray ▪ Stainproof ▪ Like fabric, these nonwoven textiles are manufactured in 54-inch bolts and sold by the yard ▪ Much more affordable than natural leather	▪ Doesn't breathe ▪ Coloration is unnaturally uniform

Natural fibers are twisted into a continuous strand to form yarn, but synthetics begin life as a liquid that is extruded through a machine to form a long filament. Sometimes this filament *itself* is the yarn; in other cases, the filament is chopped into small pieces (about the length of natural fibers) and then spun, resulting in a yarn that more closely mimics the feel of a natural product. Acrylic, for instance, was developed to approximate wool. The more twisted (or high-spun) the yarn, the stronger and more consistent it is—but the harder its hand; choosing a textile for durability often means sacrificing softness.

Once twisted into yarn, each type of fiber—from silk to viscose—exhibits a unique combination of the following properties:

ATTRIBUTE	WHAT IT MEANS
LENGTH	The longer the fiber, the less likely the fabric is to pill or shed. Spun silk is an example of a long-fiber fabric. In general, natural fibers are short.
ELASTICITY	A fiber's "give," or ability to stretch without snapping. Nylon is very elastic.
LUSTER	The level of light reflectance, which is based on smoothness. Naturally nubby wool is less lustrous than silk. Fabrics made of short fibers can be "polished" (i.e., smoothed) after weaving.
STRENGTH	The longer the filament or fiber, the greater the strength of the resulting yarn. Synthetic fibers, made by extruding a liquid into a single long strand, are inherently strong.
FLAMMABILITY	Some fibers, such as wool, are naturally fire-resistant; synthetics are usually highly flammable and must be treated.
RESISTANCE TO SUNLIGHT	Synthetics are the most resistant to disintegration and color fading.

Fabrics are made of a single fiber or a blend of two or more varieties: cotton-polyester and wool-silk are common examples. Blended yarns or fabrics strive to maximize the best qualities of different fibers—such as resistance to abrasion and brilliant color—and to minimize the downsides. The label designates fiber content by weight per square yard, a figure that will reveal the percentages of fibers, but not whether they are blended in the yarn or the weave (as in silk for the warp, wool for the weft).

HOW TEXTILES ARE MADE

1. Fiber is spun into yarn or extruded (if synthetic) into a filament.
2. The yarn is then constructed (woven, knitted, felted, etc.) into cloth.
3. The unprocessed cloth (called greige goods) is dyed a color or printed with a pattern (or both).
4. The fabric is often finished, either for decoration, such as polishing or embossing, or for enhanced performance, such as a backing for greater dimensional stability.

PLAINWEAVE

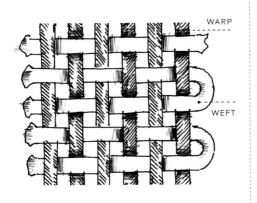

FABRIC CONSTRUCTION

Textiles are made by weaving, knitting, or knotting yarns together, by punching fibers into a backing, or by way of mechanical or chemical bonding (as is the case with Ultrasuede and felt). But most common are woven textiles made on a loom that interlaces the yarns at right angles: warp yarns run vertically, and the weft yarns are inserted horizontally.

The simplest type of weave, the classic plainweave pattern, is also the strongest. More complicated textiles have an extra set of weft yarns woven in for decorative effect.

When specifying fabrics, note the following:

- **The direction of the weft.** The warp yarn is generally stronger, providing the fabric's structure. Fabric has less give when pulled in the warp direction, so installing fabric in the proper direction—along the length of the bolt—will maximize the dimensional stability. Fabrics that are able to be "railroaded" can be used both horizontally and vertically, and are stable in both directions. There are two sides to most fabrics—front and back; very few are reversible. Striped fabrics are almost always intended to be run vertically.
- **Thread count.** Likewise vital to note is the number of yarns per square inch—a tally that includes both warp and weft yarns. The higher the thread count, the more densely woven and thus strong the fabric is.

FINISHING TREATMENTS

Textiles used for interior applications are frequently enhanced with a finish.

BACKINGS

A backing is applied to the fabric's reverse side to stabilize its construction and allow for an unconventional use:

- Bonding the fabric to **paper** enables it to be pasted to the wall as a covering.
- A polyester/cotton **knit** stabilizes the construction for upholstery use and helps prevent sagging when the fabric is installed vertically. A knit backing also prevents delicate fabrics from shredding and their seams from slipping or pulling apart.

FRONT TREATMENTS

These are applied to smooth or texturize a surface, to enhance the design, or to alter the hand (softening it, for instance):

- **Chintz (or glazing).** An applied glaze renders the fabric—usually a cotton or satin-weave fabric—shinier and more resistant to dirt. Durable resin-finish chintz withstands washing and dry cleaning, whereas wax-and-starch glaze washes out over time.
- **Calendering.** Cloth is pressed through hot metal rollers for a soft and glossy result. This is often done to temper the inherent nubbiness of linen or wool.
- **Moiré.** Heat and heavy pressure from rollers applied to a woven rib fabric creates a wavy or rippled effect akin to wood grain; the flattened and unflattened portions of the ribs reflect light differently.
- **Embossing.** Impressing a plate or engraved rollers into the cloth to form a raised pattern.
- **Embroidery.** Needlework applied to cloth by hand or machine, using either wool (crewel) or silk threads.
- **Quilting.** The fabric is bonded to polyester batting (with a knitted top layer) and then topstitched in a pattern.
- **Laminating.** A sheet of matte or glossy vinyl or plastic is bonded to a smooth fabric, to make it usable in high-traffic areas.

CHEMICAL TREATMENTS

These treatments are applied to fabrics to make them stain-repellent, water-resistant, easier to clean (called soil-release), and/or to inhibit the growth of bacteria and mold.

Although some fabrics are sold pretreated, the designer generally initiates the process. Before buying the full amount of fabric, she arranges for the supplier to send a length of it (usually a 2-yard minimum that may have to be purchased) to the finishing house. The finisher inspects the fabric and determines whether it's suitable for the desired backing or treatment. If it is, the sample will be finished and returned for approval. For very expensive fabrics, the designer might send only a memo sample to the finisher in order to gauge his opinion on the likelihood of success before going any further.

WHAT FABRIC TESTS MEAN

All fabric is tested for colorfastness, its ability to withstand wear and tear, and other performance characteristics; the results determine its suitability for various applications.

Abrasion. How much surface wear—caused by rubbing and contact with another fabric—can a textile handle? The more rubs a fabric can take before showing wear, the more durable it will be in a high-traffic area. The test for abrasion is known as the Wyzenbeek double-rub standard.

- 15,000 or more double rubs: a sturdy fabric suitable for heavy use in a residential setting such as a family room
- 9,000 to 15,000 double rubs: a fabric suitable for more formal living or dining rooms
- 3,000 to 9,000 double rubs: a fabric most appropriate for furniture that is used only occasionally
- Under 3,000 double rubs: a fabric best when used for drapery or decorative pillows (not for seating upholstery)

Flammability. How does a fabric perform when exposed to specific sources of ignition and for specific intended uses? Standards must meet a governing code. Testing agencies are the American Society for Testing and Materials (ASTM) and the Association for Contract Textiles (ACT). Standards vary according to category (drapery, carpets, rugs, mattresses); regulations for upholstery are not as stringent.

Breaking strength. How much stress must be exerted to pull apart a fabric under tension? The point at which it breaks indicates whether it's appropriate for upholstery use.

Seam slippage. How well does a seam hold up when stressed? This will dictate whether a fabric is suitable for seating upholstery and if it could benefit from a stabilizing backing.

Pilling. How quickly do fuzzy fiber balls form on the fabric's surface? Quick-to-pill fabrics are not ideal for seating upholstery.

Colorfastness. How well does a fabric retain its color and intensity over time in relation to the dyeing or printing method? Inorganic dyes and pigments hold up best.

Lightfastness. Is the fabric prone to fading with sunlight exposure? This is a key factor when choosing textiles for window treatments.

Sunlight resistance. Does exposure to sun cause a fabric to completely disintegrate? If the answer is yes, it must be heavily lined when used for window treatments.

ORDERING & PURCHASING

Purchasing textiles for interior applications is a very different—and far more technical—process than buying fabrics for clothing or crafts. Be sure to order from a knowledgeable source that understands the many aspects involved, such as a trade showroom or a drapery/upholstery workroom.

Sizing

Upholstery fabrics are commonly 54 inches wide—including the selvage, which is the 1½-inch unfinished edge—although the measurement can range from 48 to 108 inches (the latter is most common for window and drapery fabrics, to obviate seams). Note that fabrics are sold by the *linear* yard—not the square yard—and each wholesaler has a different minimum order, usually 2 yards. A full bolt averages 55 yards, an amount that varies slightly depending on the fabric weight.

Leather

Natural hides are sold by the square foot but can only be purchased as half or full hides. Shaped like the animal they once were, natural hides have a big loss factor; add a minimum of 20 percent to the needed square footage to account for imperfections.

There are three types of leather:

- Full-grain leather is natural.
- Top-grain leather has undergone minor corrections.
- Split leather is only the very center of the hide, without imperfections or markings.

PRICING

Fabric must be paid for in full upon ordering, including shipping and sales tax as applicable. In showrooms retail customers will pay a different price than designers. The universal pricing code is known as "5/10," meaning that 5 is subtracted from the number to the left of the slash, which represents the dollar amount, and 10 is deducted from the number to the right of the slash, which represents cents: for instance, if a fabric is marked as 65/60 then the net (or designer's price) will be $60.50/yard.

Dye Lots and Reserves

Bolts of greige or gray goods are dyed in a large kettle. Each batch is assigned a dye lot number, which will be listed on the fabric bolt. Although the chemical recipe is consistent from batch to batch, there will still be subtle color variegation between dye lots. It is therefore essential to request a cutting (a small 3- to 5-inch-square sample) from the in-stock dye lots and place a reserve for a specific lot. (Reserves are also necessary for imported fabrics and those with long lead times.) A fabric house will hold a reserve for five days; after that it must be renewed to remain in effect. Often, another designer is waiting in the wings to snatch up the desired yardage once a hold expires. Reserving more than is needed is also a smart strategy. Upon placing the order, request another cutting for approval (CFA) before giving the okay to the vendor to ship to the workroom; this ensures that the right lot is sent.

Printed Fabrics

Fabrics were colored with natural pigments derived from plants or animals, such as indigo, saffron, and cochineal, until the mid-nineteenth century. Nowadays manufacturers use more stable chemical colorants. Ground cloth is colored using dyes that react with the textile-fiber molecule to impart integral coloration. In contrast, patterns are printed with pigments, microscopic particles that adhere to the fabric *surface*—but not to the fiber; therefore, prints are often prone to fading, can rub off on adjacent fabrics or clothing (called crocking), and need to be cleaned carefully to prevent loss of color.

TEXTILE GLOSSARY

Bark cloth. A slightly textured, nubby cotton or cotton-blend fabric that imitates ethnic fabric originally made of real tree bark.

Block print (or hand-blocking). Subtle mixes of hue are achieved to create a primitive, informal effect.

Bouclé. An uneven yarn of three plies, one of which forms loops at intervals.

Brocade. A supplementary weft in gold or silver is inserted to create a pattern.

Brocatelle. Initially developed to mimic tooled leather, this stiff fabric has a raised relief created by a satin warp yarn in the pattern.

Burnout. Generally velvet or polyester treated to a chemical process that dissolves some of the fibers, resulting in a semitransparent fabric.

Chenille. A yarn or fabric with a fluffy, protruding pile.

Damask. A satin weave distinguishes both pattern and ground, which reverse on opposite sides of the cloth. Striped imberline is one example.

Dupioni. A strong but irregular silk yarn.

Felt. A dense, strong nonwoven made by matting fibers together.

Dyed. There are a number of ways fabric can be dyed:

Cross-dyed. A fabric composed of two different fibers is piece-dyed to produce a variegated effect: each fiber takes the color a bit differently.

Piece-dyed. The whole bolt of greige goods is dyed in one lot.

Resist-dyed. A decorative motif is blocked out with wax prior to the cloth being dyed, creating a reverse pattern. Batik is one example.

Solution-dyed. Synthetic fibers are dyed when they are in liquid form, before being extruded into filaments, resulting in a very consistent, more integral coloration.

Stock-dyed. Fibers are dyed before being spun into yarn, creating a fabric with a more consistent coloration.

BARK CLOTH

BLOCK PRINT

BOUCLÉ

BROCADE

BROCATELLE

BURNOUT

CHENILLE

DAMASK

DYED

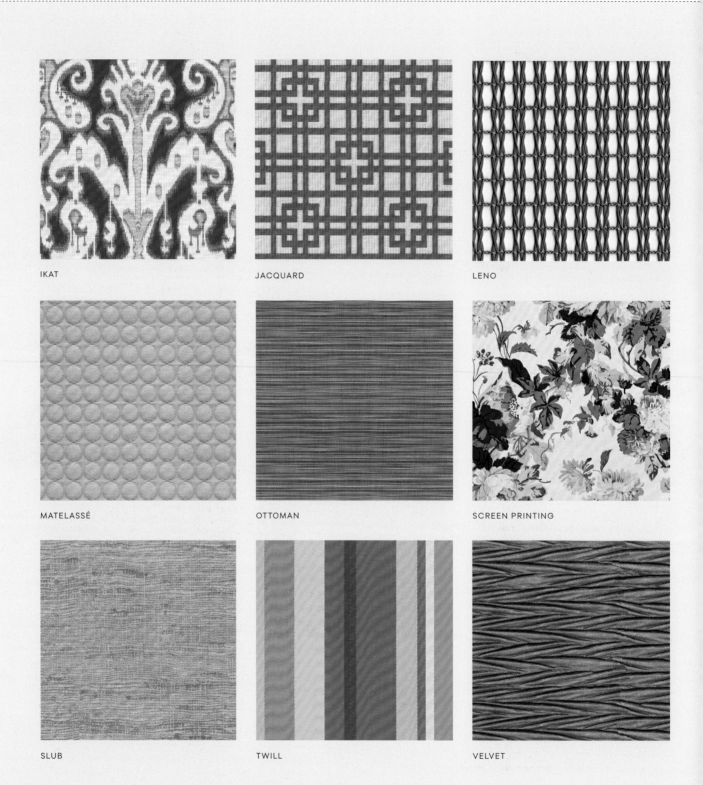

IKAT

JACQUARD

LENO

MATELASSÉ

OTTOMAN

SCREEN PRINTING

SLUB

TWILL

VELVET

Ikat. Yarns are tie-dyed prior to being woven into a distinctive flame-like pattern.

Jacquard. Fabric made on a Jacquard loom capable of producing complex patterns. A tapestry is a type of stiff, heavy Jacquard made with a multicolored "rainbow" warp that adds great visual interest.

Knits. Knitted fabrics include lace and fake fur. They don't have much dimensional stability.

Leno. This open-weave method is used to fabricate drapery fabrics: warp yarns are twisted before each weft is inserted, locking the yarns into an open pattern that doesn't shift. Many patterned casements that are intended to stand alone as the sole window treatment are leno weaves.

Matelassé. A double-cloth fabric woven with a three-dimensional design that creates a puckered or quilted look.

Microsuede. A microfiber is needle-punched onto a felt ground in this nonwoven.

Ottoman (or repp). Using different types of threads for the warp and weft creates this ribbed look.

Plainweave. A fabric made by alternating warp and weft yarns one-to-one.

Roller, cylinder, and machine printing. An efficient way of printing fabric in quantity.

Sateen. A smooth, lustrous fabric, usually made of cotton.

Satin weaves. Weft threads are woven at widely separated intervals, creating a smooth, shiny fabric with a less "woven" look. The spacing between weft yarns creates a more delicate cloth.

Screen printing. Color is applied to a ground in certain areas only using silk screens, layering until the final design is achieved. There may be as many as twenty-five colors used in a single English or French floral print. The two kinds of screen printing are rotary and flatbed.

Slub. Yarn is spun unevenly to create "slubs," or sections of irregular thickness.

Twill. The weft yarns are woven over two (or more) warp yarns; herringbone is one example.

Velvet. A type of satin weave, velvet boasts a thick, soft pile that's created through a second set of warp yarns that are looped up above the face of the fabric. Loops are left as is (called uncut) or sliced to create a fringier feel (called cut). Cut and uncut loops can also be combined to create patterns (looped threads will often outline the pattern). Velvet pile lies in one direction, which is called the nap.

Vinyl or faux leather. Plastic backed with knitted jersey fabric for stability; sometimes called "leatherette."

Worsted. Yarn made from long wool fibers.

FURNITURE & UPHOLSTERY

A room is like a container, and it should be designed in layers: first the architecture; then the walls, floor, and ceiling planes; and finally the objects to be carefully placed within. Furniture selection is not something that should be done in isolation of the space or as an afterthought; rather, it is part of an integrated exercise to create a complete environment.

How does a designer move from the general specs and sizes of pieces on the furniture plan (e.g., an 84-inch sofa and a 36-inch coffee table) to a *particular* sofa (a brown leather Chesterfield) and an accompanying coffee table (a hexagonal midcentury design in walnut)? She refers back to the initial concept, and how line, form, shape, texture, color, and pattern are expressed in the designs of the desired style or period.

An eclectic assemblage of furnishings populate a loft by Carol Egan.

THE OPTIONS

The floor plan will dictate the number and placement of individual furnishings, and the wall elevations will illustrate where the accompanying decorative lighting, mirrors, and art will be sited. But choosing or designing each piece relies on knowing the available options and making a decision about each anatomical part of a particular furnishing.

Furniture falls into three basic categories: tables, case goods, and seating. Every room features something from each one.

Tables

Rooms need to have a variety of surfaces to serve a multitude of purposes: to hold drinks, to make a sketch, to jot down a note, to display an object or table lamp. Below are the main categories, and each type is available in many styles and materials.

- **Coffee table:** Place at the center of a conversation area to hold decorative objects as well as book and magazines, a stack of coasters for drinks, and/or a bowl of candy, nuts, or fruit.
- **Side table:** Use alongside a sofa or chair to support a lamp for reading-height lighting as well as drinks, books, and objets d'art. Side tables can also lend sculptural presence.
- **Console:** Choose a wall-mounted or freestanding one behind a sofa, along a narrow hallway with a mirror or painting above, or to set the tone in a foyer and catch keys and mail. A console's long, narrow proportions make a perfect canvas for a tablescape.

- **Demilune:** A half-round console is often used in pairs flanking a fireplace or other focal point, such as a doorway. The curved edge makes a demilune a bit more space-efficient in tight quarters than a regular console.
- **Dining table:** For meal-taking, of course—and sometimes for doing homework, or paying the bills—it must be lovely yet durable.
- **Library table:** A freestanding, large rectangular table that can "hold" the center of a room with lots of character, it is the ideal place for a large floral display, stacked books, a shawl, or a casually draped rug. Place chairs or ottomans on either side.

Case Goods

Items in this category are a case of some sort: a box that is fitted with open or closed shelves, drawers, doors, or any combination thereof. Case goods can be made of wood, metal, plexiglass, or glass.

- **Desk:** For doing work or, when chairs are placed on either side, nurturing conversation.
- **Bookcase:** Not just for books, shelves can be used to display a collection, small artworks, or mementos.
- **Storage/Cabinet:** A box (i.e., case) with open shelves, drawers, and/or doors.

Seating

For function and visual variety, most rooms need a mix of different types of seating.

- **Dining chair:** Choose host chairs with arms for the table's head and foot, and armless chairs along the sides. Glides on the bottom of each foot will prevent damage to a hard floor.
- **Bench:** A long perch can substitute for several chairs at a dining table or be used to grace a hearth or the end of bed (where it can hold blankets).
- **Sofa:** Intended to hospitably support formal or informal gatherings, sofas can be sized to accommodate two, three, or more people.
- **Loveseat:** A two-seat upholstered sofa is ideal in smaller spaces.
- **Settee:** The defining characteristics of a settee, which can seat up to three, are an exposed, finished frame, minimal upholstery, and delicate scale.
- **Club chair:** An upholstered armchair sized for comfort complements a conversational grouping. Club chairs are often deployed in pairs; a singular one is usually intended for reading in.

- **Occasional chair:** A versatile player in any room is a lightweight chair, generally with an exposed frame, that can easily be moved and spontaneously pulled up to a seating group.
- **Slipper chair:** A lightweight occasional chair, armless club chair, or similar that is generally fully upholstered.
- **Desk chair:** A supportive back, arms, and a comfortable seat are musts in a work chair; casters are optional but practical.
- **Ottoman:** Square, round, or rectangular, this upholstered piece usually functions as informal seating, often as a footrest but sometimes as a coffee table.
- **Footstool:** A small, lightweight ottoman that suits a variety of purposes: footrest, supplementary seat, sculptural element.
- **Pouf:** A large ottoman but with a higher seat, a pouf often has a conical center projection that serves as a backrest.

IN ADDITION TO PROVIDING A PLACE TO REST, SEATING ESTABLISHES THE ATMOSPHERE OF A ROOM, FROM PLUSHLY WELCOMING TO SEVERELY FORMAL.

Five vendors played a role in the fabrication of this simple chair: the frame maker, the frame finisher, the fabric house, the trim supplier, and the upholstery workroom.

UPHOLSTERED SEATING

Designing a custom chair or sofa isn't just about picking fabric patterns and figuring out nice tufting and piping details. Generally, upholstered pieces are the anchors of a seating area and should be scaled appropriately: to the room, to the particular users, and to the surrounding pieces in the grouping. The selection of fabric follows, and then the details such as cushion fill and outside back shape—all of which should be equally well scaled and suited to the concept, use, and location. Custom workrooms will have muslin-covered samples on display to assist in specifying every detail; the subtle differences are easiest to discern when the chairs are dressed in the same plain fabric.

Some options are purely stylistic, while others affect the piece's function or performance. Most functional details also have a strong aesthetic component, of course. Although there are myriad iterations of certain details like arm style and skirt, learning the most common can give a sense of all the possibilities. Once you know all the anatomical parts and details, you can design a chair, ottoman, headboard, etc., since they are all just iterations thereof.

A sofa is just a larger version of a chair, and headboards and ottomans are simpler but will still have a few details.

Frame

The best frames are constructed with dowels and glue and are screwed, corner-blocked, and reinforced to maintain structural integrity over time. Think of the frame as the skeleton of the piece. Decisions to make are:

- **Material:** Kiln-dried maple is the foundation for all fine upholstery, but lesser types are made of various other hardwoods.
- **Shape:** The profile (and size) of a finished piece is largely determined by its frame. The frame shape should complement the details of the finished space: a tuxedo or tailored sofa in a modern room; a curvaceous arm on a piece slated for a boudoir.
- **Exposure:** The frame can be either completely internal (hidden under the fabric) or partially exposed. An exposed frame gives the piece an "outline," emphasizing its shape, and requires a beautiful hardwood that can be stained and finished: oak, mahogany, walnut. Maple is a good base for a lacquered or painted exposed frame.

Arms

When choosing or designing arm details, bear in mind that arms will get the most wear and tear. In addition to specifying arm height and width—a choice that will depend on the scale of the room and the formality of the use—there are many other design aspects to consider:

- **Extension:** How far from the vertical will the arm extend, either through the angle of the arm or its fullness? Note that the flare can add significantly to the width of a piece.
- **Relationship to the front plane of sofa:** Arms may be flush with or set back from the sofa front.
- **Shape:** Straight, rounded, curved, panel-fronted, sloping, or especially low or high are among the options.
- **Style:** The arm shape is one of the most defining decisions made for an upholstered piece. Some popular options:
  » Rolled arm: Curving outward, common on traditional sofas, can be quite dramatic.
  » Lawson arm: A small rolled arm.
  » Sock arm: A simple rolled arm with no panel.
  » Pleated: A sock arm where the fabric is drawn and gathered from the inside of the arm and over the top.
  » English arm: A low-profile arm set back from the front edge of the sofa that does not add to the width.
  » Track or box arm: Straight arms creating a boxy effect.
  » Tuxedo arm: Usually narrow box arms that are the same height as the sofa back and slightly flared.
  » Panel arm: Has a vertical flat panel in front.
- **Welting/piping:** Can be the same as the upholstery fabric (self-welt) or contrasting fabric or special cord or trim.

ARM STYLES

PANEL ARM WITH SQUARE CUSHION

TRACK ARM WITH SQUARE CUSHION

TRACK ARM WITH T-CUSHION

SOCK ARM WITH T-CUSHION

ENGLISH ARM WITH CUSHION TO FRONT

PLEATED SLOPE ARM WITH SQUARE CUSHION

Outside Back

Although usually covered in the same fabric as the body, the outside back is nonetheless an opportunity to instead use a complementary or contrasting fabric. Other details to consider:

- **Shape:** The back can be flared, straight, angled, or curved around continuously to the arms, the latter creating a softer impression.
- **Skirted:** The outside back may be tight-upholstered or the skirt may begin here.

Inside Back and Back Cushions

Back cushions can be square, rectangular, or T-shaped (to extend over the arms of the piece).

- **Tight back:** In this case, the inside back is padded and upholstered, but there are no loose cushions. A tight back may be tufted, button-tufted, or have dramatic vertical channels. A tight back has the firmest feel.

- **Loose cushions:** The back cushions are not attached to the frame; they generally rise 3 to 5 inches higher than the outside back. They have removable covers that can be cleaned.
- **Semi-attached:** Back cushions that give the appearance of being loose but are actually sewn in place (to keep them neat).
- **Pillow back:** A number of large pillows artfully arranged along the back (in lieu of actual back cushions) creates a layered effect. This design offers the softest feel and look.

Upper Edge Shape

The shape of the sofa's top edge should relate to the overall design. Choices include:

- **Straight:** Traditionally falls below the height of the back pillows.
- **Extra height:** This can be 36 inches plus, creating a sense of enclosure and shelter.
- **Camelback:** This curved style is raised in the middle and slopes lower toward the arms.

KEY DIMENSIONS

- Seat depth: The overall seat dimension can be 33 to 54 inches deep, but 24 is the typical "clear" seat depth for sofas and club chairs.
- Seat height: Most common is 16 inches to top of seat cushion crown.

- Back height: 27 to 30 inches. Extra height, to 36 inches plus, creates a sense of enclosure.
- Arm height: Depends on the style of the piece; may be lower than or the same as the back height.

Skirt Style

The choice of skirt is purely stylistic but a key aspect of the overall design. The following styles are the most common:

- **Pleated:** The fabric is folded into regular pleats, which can range in width from small to large. Accent the apex of a pleat with a special flourish such as a button, bow, or passementerie rosette.
  - » Inverted pleat: A pleated skirt with emphasis on the inverted areas. Align the pleat with the break between seat cushions or the seams of a tight seat.
  - » Box pleat: Creates an architectural rhythm on a more traditional piece. Can be finished with tape.
  - » Corner kick pleat: Used with a flat-front skirt that needs a special moment at the corners. May be lined with a contrasting or complementary fabric.
- **Dressmaker:** A version of a kick pleat skirt that falls from directly under the seat cushion, without any intermediate welting or tacking. It's used to create an elegant, modernized take on a traditional look. The skirt can even fall from directly under the arms or from the top edge of the back.
- **Fringe:** Long fringe can be laid over a simple skirt to appear to be the skirt itself.
- **Tight:** A sleek style most often used on contemporary pieces and paired with a recessed base or simple block or tapered legs in wood or fabric.
- **Gathered:** Traditional and feminine. Gather the fabric evenly around the entire base or just at the corners.

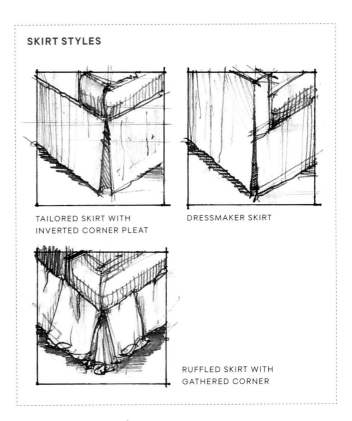

SKIRT STYLES

TAILORED SKIRT WITH INVERTED CORNER PLEAT

DRESSMAKER SKIRT

RUFFLED SKIRT WITH GATHERED CORNER

Seat Support

The seat of an upholstered piece needs support, which can come from a range of systems. The finest is a network of eight-way hand-tied springs. Sinuous spring construction is also frequently used, particularly in a smaller frame as it takes up less space. Web suspension is a third option, but the least desirable.

Like the back cushions, a seat may be either tight (fixed to the frame or decking) or loose. If the seat is loose, then the cushions sit on a "deck" of tight fabric that is part of the upholstered frame. Depending on the piece, there may be one (called a "bench" seat), two, or more seat cushions. They can either be straight in front, designed to stop at the arm (and the seat edge), or they can be T- or L-shaped in cases where the arm is slightly recessed from the seat front. Nicest is when the material used for the decking and the underside of the seat cushions match the overall piece; this is called "self-decking."

Feet/Legs/Base

Seating can be supported by legs, feet, or a base—a choice that depends on the style of the chair or sofa: a settee or dining chair with a higher-than-typical 18-inch seat will require legs; feet or a low base will suffice for a sofa or club chair meant for relaxing and with a 15- or 16-inch seat height.

- **Material:** Legs or feet can be made of any material: exposed wood or metal, or wood fully upholstered in fabric. Wooden legs or feet often have metal "shoes," or casters. Glides are applied to the bottom of feet and legs to lift them slightly off the floor.
- **Style:** Modern or contemporary seats call for simple, straight-lined feet or legs that don't compete with the overall lines of the piece. A recessed base is the least visible and intrusive and may be made of reflective metal or wood, either stained or painted black or to match the fabric. Exposed legs styles include:
  » **Block:** Roughly 4 by 4 inches wide at the top, 64 inches high, and slightly tapered toward the floor.
  » **Tapered:** A straight leg, roughly 2½ inches square at the top and tapered toward the floor.
  » **Upholstered:** Usually a block leg, covered with fabric to match the piece.
  » **Bun foot:** A round, depressed ball shape, approximately 4 inches across, and made of exposed wood or upholstered.
  » **Carved:** Wooden legs, 4 inches high minimum, traditionally carved with natural motifs.

FOOT/LEG/BASE STYLES

TAPERED LEG

QUEEN ANNE LEG

TAPERED LEG WITH SABOT

TRADITIONAL LEG

BLOCK LEG

TRADITIONAL LEG WITH CASTER

TAPERED BLOCK LEG

BUN FOOT

RECESSED BASE

Fill/Stuffing

Seat cushions come in varied fills. The choice depends on the comfort desired and the intended use. Use high-density polyethylene wrapped in polydacron or cotton when you want a firmer sit—for instance a wingback chair in a formal living room (as opposed to a sofa in a media room intended for sprawling).

For a softer and more luxurious experience, choose cushions filled with a mix of down and feathers from waterfowl like ducks and geese. (Down is the fluffier outer part of the feather; goose down is most desirable.) The more down, the softer the cushion. However, all-down cushions are uncomfortably soft, become shapeless, and need lots of maintenance. They aren't specified very often, as they are generally too soft to support most people comfortably. A mix of 80 percent down, 20 percent feathers over a center foam core is the preferred content for both seat and back cushions.

If luxury is desired but better support is needed, a core seat cushion of high-density polyethylene foam wrapped with a channeled blanket of 80 percent down and 20 percent feather fill is a good option. For box or other shaped cushions, the foam core is wrapped with polydacron followed by another batting layer of a down/feather mix. All cushions are wrapped with down-proof mildew-resistant ticking before the final fabric is applied in order to keep any feathers from poking through the finished textile cover.

Finally, seat cushions subject to a lot of use can be made with internal springs for strong support and to keep their shape over time. The springs are wrapped in high-density foam, which itself is wrapped in pads made of Dacron polyester fiber and down.

ANATOMY OF A CHAIR

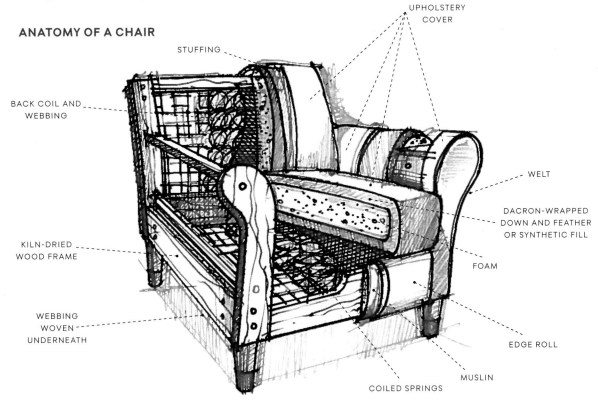

STUFFING

UPHOLSTERY COVER

BACK COIL AND WEBBING

WELT

DACRON-WRAPPED DOWN AND FEATHER OR SYNTHETIC FILL

KILN-DRIED WOOD FRAME

FOAM

WEBBING WOVEN UNDERNEATH

EDGE ROLL

MUSLIN

COILED SPRINGS

Choosing a Fabric

Upholstery fabric has to look good and be a workhorse. The "skin" of a sofa or chair, it must be strong enough to hold the filling in, hug the skeleton and resist abrasion and staining, yet be welcoming to the touch and beautiful to see. Choose tightly woven fabrics backed for dimensional stability and made of fibers with specific characteristics and functionality. The cards and labels attached to fabric samples will often state whether or not they are suitable for use as upholstery. If you're unsure, let the upholstery workroom approve a sample rather than to jump in and purchase 25 yards of something potentially unusable. On some fabrics used for both residential and commercial applications will be a note regarding the Wyzenbeek (ASTM D4157) or Martindale (ASTM D4966) abrasion tests; either is a reliable means of determining the limits of a fabric's ability to withstand abrasion without wear or pilling. (For more on fabric testing, see page 201.) Some of the best fabrics for upholstery are:

- Wool
- Chenille
- Brocade
- Repp
- Plain weave cotton
- Chintz/polished cotton
- Damask
- Blends of natural and synthetics
- Leather or synthetic leather/microsuede

ENGINEERING

Once a fabric is chosen for a piece of furniture, decide how it should be applied: Where will the pattern repeats be presented? Where will the seams fall? This exercise is called engineering, and it should always be done in close collaboration with the upholsterer. A pattern's repeat size and configuration contribute to the amount of waste material that the upholstery process generates—thus adding to the yardage needed. In some cases, a fabric can be railroaded; that is, installed horizontally. It is the upholsterer's responsibility to determine the exact amount of fabric and trim needed based on the chosen fabric type and the pattern repeat.

SEAM SLIPPAGE

Seating can suffer heavy abuse: the repeated action of getting in and out of a chair makes the fabric shift. To accommodate this, fabric must be of a suitable weight and sturdiness for upholstery use, or it should be reinforced with an acrylic backing to render it more durable. Fabric seams on upholstered goods are especially vulnerable to wear. Because some bulky fabrics will pull at these connection points, specialized seams are required to take the pressure off:

- French seams
- Stitching on outside

A good upholsterer will tell the buyer if the fabric needs backing based on the application.

SLIPCOVERS

Stylistically, slipcovers come in and out of vogue, but they serve two important and timeless functions: to protect upholstered furniture, and to give a piece new or extended life. They are also a staple of certain looks; consider the loose and light slipcovers in cotton chintz or gingham that embody the country-house look. Some homeowners, anticipating stains and spills—especially in a household of children and pets—ask for a set of covers just for the seat cushions. A sateen or plain-woven cotton is the best choice. Contrasting piping or a ruched or dressmaker skirt gives a simple cover a bit of energy.

Embellishments: Trim, Buttons, Nails

An upholstered sofa, chair, or ottoman, with or without an exposed frame or legs, is not complete without its "jewelry," or trimmings. Trim come in the form of metal decorative nails, fabric or decorative buttons, and welting, piping, cords, tassels, rosettes, and fringe.

Welting is a special category. Most upholstered pieces have sections where a seam is embellished. The design decisions include:

- Desired thickness
- Contrasting fabric or self-welt?
- Do you want to include decorative cording and, if so, what design?

PASSEMENTERIE

Passementerie was developed in thirteenth-century France to hide seams and tailoring details—a role akin to how moldings are used to cover the joints between building materials. Trimming later came into its own as a purely decorative accent, first on window and bed draperies and later on upholstered furnishings.

Today, trimmings are deployed as special adornments to uphold the creative vision and confer a sense of luxury—which is appropriate, as they can be quite pricey. The most exquisite and ornamental examples are borne of fine craftsmanship, from hand wrapping to special knotting and stitching techniques. Even loomed elements made on small, slow-producing machines require much handiwork. A simple cord might take up to eight manufacturing stages to complete.

Silvina Leone designed a velvet-covered settee with a tassel-accented bolster.

TRIM

Braids, fringe, and other trims are made in running or linear yardage. It is most often used to trace edges of upholstered pieces and draperies, outlining and enhancing their profile.

- **Braid:** Flat, ribbonlike woven tapes used to decorate edges and seams, often on draperies. They can be simple or quite elaborate, and come in widths ranging from 1 to 4 inches.
- **Cording:** Cords are composed of twisted plied yarns. They are available with or without a flange (or lip), a header that allows the cord to be inserted into the seams. The treatment is referred to as decorative welting when ornamenting an upholstered piece.
- **Fringe:** A decorative border of hanging threads or cords. Fringe attaches to a textile by way of its heading, which is either inserted into a seam or sewn, glued, or affixed to the outer surface by brass nails.
  - » Ball and scallop fringe
  - » Onion fringe
  - » Loop fringe
  - » Brush (or moss) fringe
  - » Tassel fringe: tassels can vary in size and length on a single header
  - » Skirt fringe: often used at the base of a sofa
  - » Bullion fringe: frequently used on the skirt of an upholstered sofa or chair
- **Galloon (or gallon):** This tightly woven ribbonlike trim is made of gold, silver, silk, or a combination; the term is from the French for a border or braid.
- **Gimp:** A narrow woven or knitted trim that gets nailed to or glued on upholstery. It is often used to garnish edges and seams.

- **Ruche:** Cord-like twisted yarns are looped and sewn to a flange, and then sometimes cut into a brushy fringe. It serves the same purpose as cording but offers a more decorative look.
- **Tape/border:** A flat banding used to cover and embellish edges and seams. Tape is also used as a header for beaded or tassel fringe.
- **Tassel:** A dangling element made by tying together same-length yarns or cords and fastening them at one end. Tassels are often added to fringe, chair ties, or tiebacks or used to accent a rosette.

ACCESSORIES

Individual decorative items made of passementerie or trim are a nice complement and an extra-special touch.

- **Rosette and button:** An ornament made of finely wrapped yarns arrayed in a circular pattern to resemble a rose; the center medallion is often accented with a tassel. These embellishments are used on the corners of pillows, the front panel arm of a sofa, drapery, and more.
- **Frog:** Ornamental braiding consisting of a rosette/button that passes through three loops, resembling a cloverleaf.
- **Key tassel:** A tassel topped with a cord loop. It is meant to hold a special key but can be used for various decorative accents.
- **Tieback:** Used to gather back a curtain panel at the side of a window. Trim tiebacks are a decorative cord, with or without one or two tassels.
- **Chair tie:** A long stand of twisted cord with tassels at either end. It is used to attach the back of a seat cushion to the chair frame.

Loose Pillows

The standard size is 20 inches square, but throw pillows are often slightly larger or smaller and vary in shape. In spite of their seeming simplicity, a well-designed throw pillow is complex and labor-intensive. Because of that, custom pillows can be surprisingly expensive. Regardless, a beautiful pillow, filled with down and feather (or a soft synthetic substitute) in a muslin insert, can dress up a sofa or club chair, unite the disparate textiles and colors of a room, and add to the general sense of comfort and welcome.

Points of decision are:

- Shape
  » Square
  » Rectangular
  » Cylindrical
  » "Ball" shape

- Same or different colors or designs on the front and back
- Pieced and quilted patterns
- Surface applications
  » Ribbon
  » Lace
  » Braid or tape
  » Faggotting
- Corner treatments
  » Knife edge
  » Gathered
  » Turkish corners
- Edge seam treatments
  » Decorative cording
  » Welting
  » Fringe
  » Flange
  » Ruffles

PILLOW STYLES

KNIFE EDGE

RUFFLE FLANGE

SPECIALTY

GATHERED OR TURKISH CORNER

TURKISH CORNER WITH CORD WELT

TURKISH END BOLSTER

WHAT'S INSIDE A HIGH-END CUSTOM UPHOLSTERED PIECE

Jonas Upholstery itemizes the many layers of support that lie between the kiln-dried maple frame and the exterior upholstery in the finest furnishings:

- **Webbing.** Jute webbing is applied in a basket-weave pattern and tacked down to the frame seat and back.
- **Springs.** Coil springs are placed atop the webbing in a graduated grid pattern, with firmer springs placed for seat and lumbar support and softer springs for the upper back. These springs are hand-tied to one another and then tacked to the frame using twine.
- **Burlap.** A layer of burlap is placed atop and sewn to each spring as well as tacked to the frame.
- **Horsehair.** Curled and sterilized horsehair (sometimes synthetic hair) is loosely placed and hand stitched atop the burlap. This artisanal humane fiber defines the best quality upholstery. It is long-lasting and allows the skilled upholsterer the ability to contour it into refined and elegant shapes. (Often, foam is used instead; it disintegrates over time and has a puffier, less nuanced look.)

- **A second layer of burlap-topped horsehair.** This layer is more "shaped."
- **Cotton batting.** Puffy cotton fills the void and indentations created by the hand sewing.
- **Glazed cotton.** A single layer is tacked down to the frame to cover the hair and burlap to prevent the hair from poking through.
- **Down pad.** A channeled blanket of goose down.
- **Dacron.** A layer of Dacron softens the appearance of the down pad's stitches and provides loft to the exterior fabric.

Many steps are involved in creating custom upholstery at Jonas, from attaching jute webbing to the hardwood frame to topping the horsehair filling with burlap.

DESIGN CONSIDERATIONS

Selecting furnishings requires thinking about the whole setting and the principles and elements of design. Consider proportion and context as the placement for each piece is determined.

Every style has a "vocabulary" of furnishings that expresses the overall feeling. For instance, the choices for a traditional English country house are limited to cabinets and tables in various woods; seating in a mixture of upholstered and exposed frames; a range of fabrics in florals, prints, and solids; shaded decorative lighting; and antique (or reproduction) accessories.

Avoid period rooms, in which every detail and piece comes from one specific era, in favor of a more eclectic mix. Some guidelines:

- **Line.** Mix boxy with straight-lined, organic with curvy, leggy with upholstered-to-the-floor.
- **Scale.** Is the piece oversize or petite? Put like with like.
- **Contrast.** One great piece, such as a Georgian secretary or a Le Corbusier chaise, can be completely different from every other piece.
- **Color.** Create a palette composed of a major color, a secondary color, and an accent color. Collage a room on the floor plan with paint or swatches to determine what color or fabric will be used on each piece—decide *before* shopping. Use a monochromatic scheme and even the same fabric on several furnishings to unify all the upholstered pieces.
- **Unity.** Mix different woods in a single room and never worry about matching the color of a wood floor to the wood of the furniture.

INSTALLATION CONSIDERATIONS

Furniture is often large and strong but it is not indestructible. Consider hiring special art and antiques movers to transport the very best pieces. A workroom or a vendor will often provide its own local delivery person. Fine wood pieces and mirrors are wrapped in blankets; upholstered pieces are covered in brown paper and plastic.

What happens if a large piece doesn't fit into a building's elevator or can't be carried up a stairway and maneuvered through an apartment door? It's vital to require that an upholsterer or a furniture maker visit the site in advance to assess installation challenges. Both hard and upholstered furnishings can be designed or crafted in pieces and assembled (or reassembled) on-site; for instance, the bun feet of a sofa can be screwed in later, or a highboy made in two sections to be put together after placement.

PURCHASING & ORDERING

Ultimately, buyer beware is the rule of all furniture purchases. It is the buyer's—not the workroom's or seller's—responsibility to know the size of rooms, doorways, halls, and stairwells, and to select the right fabric for the application. Custom pieces can never be returned, and with very few exceptions the same goes for antiques.

Many designer showrooms or galleries will work "on approval," sending a special piece to the customer's home in advance of purchase to see how it looks in place.

WINDOW TREATMENTS

Seen from the outside, windows give a building's facade a sense of scale, hierarchy, and rhythm. Inside, they inform a room's purpose and character. Just as windows are important architectural and interior features, so too are their coverings: connecting indoors and out, decor and view. Window treatments can serve many purposes.

As a design feature, they can:

- create a point of emphasis at the window(s)
- add the illusion of height to a low-ceilinged room
- correct poor room proportions
- frame an appealing vista or hide an unpleasant (or mundane) view
- support the decorating scheme via color, texture, pattern, and detail

As a functional element, they:

- offer privacy
- control the glare of daylight and streetlamps
- attenuate sound
- aid thermal control
- boost energy efficiency

Each genre—drapery, shades, blinds, and shutters—performs some or all of the above roles, to varying degrees. Often two or more types of treatments are paired to achieve the needed combination of function and decorative panache: for instance, a Venetian blind with billowing sheers or a fabric-laminated roller shade with straight-hung curtain panels.

THE OPTIONS

Within the four categories of window treatments there are myriad choices of fabric, construction, and trim to be considered. Learning the technical vocabulary of window coverings can help you unlock all the creative possibilities. A strong grasp of the industry vocabulary is essential when commissioning a custom design, in order to communicate with workrooms to ensure the desired results. The best process includes accurate drawings and specifications that are illustrative of the desired appearance and function.

OPPOSITE: Kapito Muller Interiors designed a curtain panel bordered with Greek key-patterned tape that puddles lightly at the floor.

In a room by Caleb Anderson, a metal holdback mounted high on the wall gracefully clasps a drapery panel.

Draperies

These soft window treatments—a genre that includes curtain panels—are typically hung from a wall-mounted rod or a track (also called a traversing mechanism). Draperies offer a unique combination of structure and softness. They can look crisp and folded or loose and billowing. As the strongest vertical gesture in a room, curtain panels can create a sense of architectural rigor and add a dose of color or pattern to the decor. While the final creation may look effortless and elegant, even the most sparely appointed design is anything but simple. Dealing with the various components of draperies requires much planning, not to mention making many decisions.

FABRIC TYPE

A textile's weave structure, pattern, and dimensional stability will dictate what style of drapery it can be used for; what sort of lining may be necessary to add body, volume, and sun protection; and what pleating or heading type is appropriate. Certain fabrics will require that lead weights (string or coins) be sewn into the hem to keep the panel from billowing. A fabric's UV stability is another key factor: some colors and fibers, such as silk, are prone to fading or disintegrating in heavy sunlight.

Window Treatment Functions

TREATMENT	LIGHT CONTROL	THERMAL CONTROL	ENERGY CONTROL	SOUND CONTROL
DRAPERIES	√	√	√	√
SHADES	√	√	√	√
BLINDS	√	√		
SHUTTERS	√		√	

ANATOMY OF DRAPERY

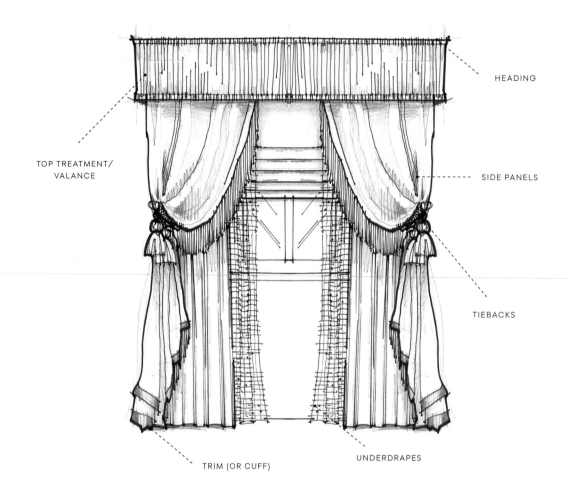

HEADING

TOP TREATMENT/
VALANCE

SIDE PANELS

TIEBACKS

TRIM (OR CUFF)

UNDERDRAPES

PATTERN

Consider scale, repeat, and how the pattern will appear when draped in tight pleats or billowing folds. When choosing a top treatment, such as a valance or a cornice, it's vital to determine how the motif should be positioned: centered or offset. Also think about how the pattern will present at the leading edge of the panels. If the fabric is striped, which color should fall at the edge, and should the full width of the stripe present?

LINING

A lining sewn onto the back of a panel can serve varied functions, including insulation and light blocking. The latter is often desirable for aesthetic purposes: natural light will alter the perception of a textile's pattern and color; some fabrics take on a yellow cast when light shines through. A lining also helps a panel drape nicely and shows off the motif to best effect. There are several types:

- A **decorative** lining can play up the design of the primary fabric by complementing or

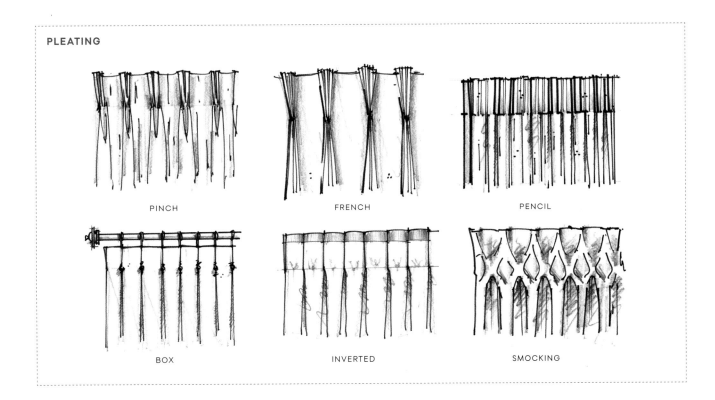

PLEATING

PINCH

FRENCH

PENCIL

BOX

INVERTED

SMOCKING

contrasting with it. Choose a solid hue or a coordinating pattern. Be strategic about color: because the lining faces the window, a bolder hue will give off a tinted glow, which may or may not be desirable.

- An **interlining** is an additional layer sewn between the front fabric and rear lining. It helps the curtain drape and can ensure opacity, so the facing fabric reads better. Interlining adds more weight and thickness to the drapery.

- A **blackout lining** is a must when complete light blocking is desired—in bedrooms and home theaters, for instance.

- For a more casual look or to admit more daylight, leave curtain panels **unlined.** When used as the major drapery treatment, woven casement fabrics or decorative sheers—especially burnout patterns—are rarely lined, since their character derives from how the light passes through them.

UNDERDRAPES

Simple casement curtains are typically made of sheer or semitransparent fabric in a woven pattern. A translucent layer can screen the view out or in to offer privacy (or to soften a subpar vista).

FULLNESS

The fullness of the drapery panel depends on its width in relation to the distance it spans when closed. The general range is two to three times the span; the higher the ratio, the fuller the drape. Fullness is also affected by the style of pleat, if one is chosen:

- Pinch pleats
- French
- Pencil
- Box
- Inverted
- Smocking

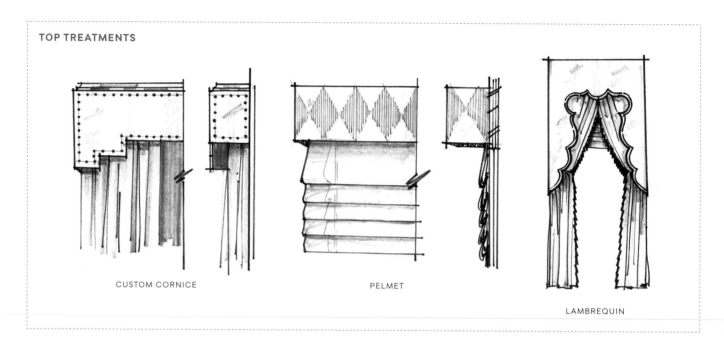

CUSTOM CORNICE

PELMET

LAMBREQUIN

TOP TREATMENTS

A soft valance or stiff cornice offers a complementary gesture to balance the design of the panel. It can finish a drapery by covering up the curtain hardware. (Top treatments are not always appropriate; for instance, avoid them where doors and windows swing inward.) The valance should always coordinate with the panel fabric. In general, run the fabric in the same orientation, even for solid colors; otherwise, the warp/weft threads of the panel and valance will run perpendicular to one another, which can cause the color to read a bit differently. Collaborate with the workroom to decide where seams will fall: the ideal choice is somewhere unobtrusive, not along the centerline. Here are some popular top treatments:

- **Valance.** This is the most common top treatment, and often boasts more elaborate detailing than the curtain panels themselves: ribbons, rosettes, bows, cords, fancy pleating, interesting shapes, and contrasting linings.

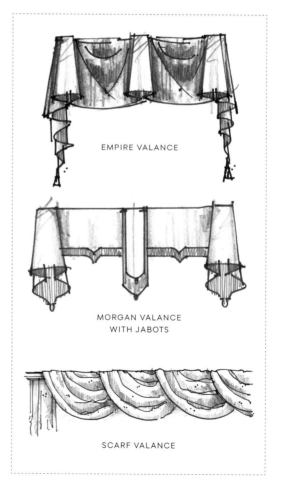

EMPIRE VALANCE

MORGAN VALANCE
WITH JABOTS

SCARF VALANCE

PLEATED SWAG   RUFFLES   SCALLOPING

- **Swag, jabot, and cascade.** These loose treatments extend across the top of the window—sometimes wrapping around the curtain rod—and drape down the sides (about two-thirds of the window height).

- **Cornice.** Sheathed in fabric, this padded plywood or solid-wood form is visually stronger than a soft valance and has a greater architectural presence. Be sure to specify how the fabric pattern should align on the cornice and its exact dimensions, including the depth of the return to the wall. (Each layer of drapery will require 4 inches of depth on the cornice.)

- **Pelmet.** This cross between a valance and a cornice is soft but firm-bodied, padded with jute.

- **Lambrequin.** This stiff, U-shaped treatment brackets the top and sides of the window frame. The fabric should extend about two-thirds of the height of the window, or all the way to the sill.

EDGE TREATMENTS

It's often desirable to embellish the leading edge of a drapery panel (i.e., the side that faces inward, toward the window). Use trims such as welting and braid to add whimsy or lend a bit of geometry. Ruffles or a turned-back cuff can be soft or striking depending on whether executed in the same or a contrasting color. The leading edge itself need not be straight; consider a sinuous silhouette, an arabesque, or a scallop. Bottoms are ripe for decoration too. In fact, leading-edge treatments are often continued along the hem—although not if the panel is supposed to puddle on the floor, which would obscure the decoration. Sometimes *just* the bottom is treated: for example, a 15-inch swath of contrasting fabric at the hem lends elegance.

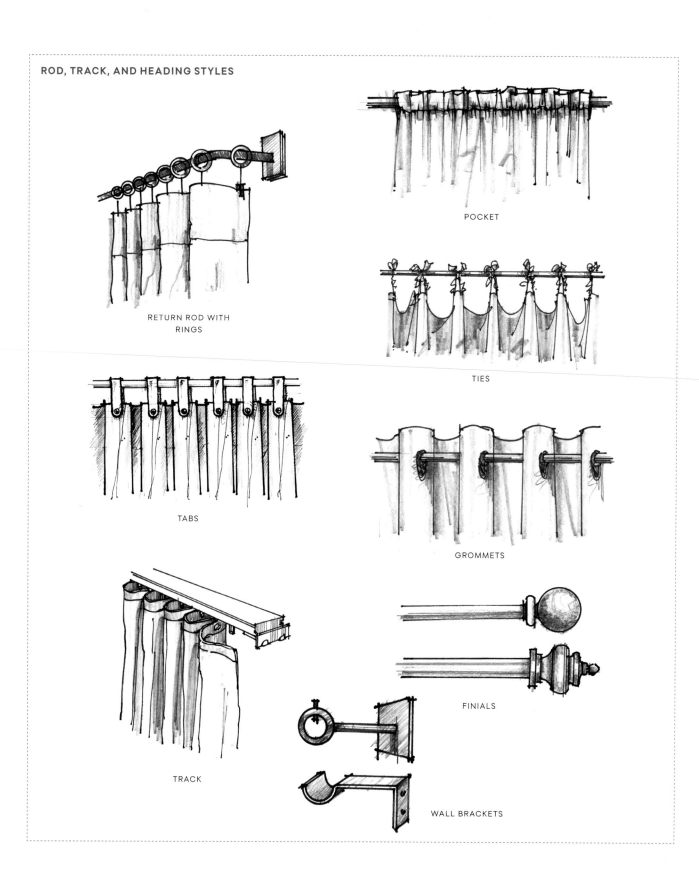

ROD, TRACK, AND HEADING STYLES

RETURN ROD WITH RINGS

POCKET

TIES

TABS

GROMMETS

TRACK

FINIALS

WALL BRACKETS

CINCHED PANELS

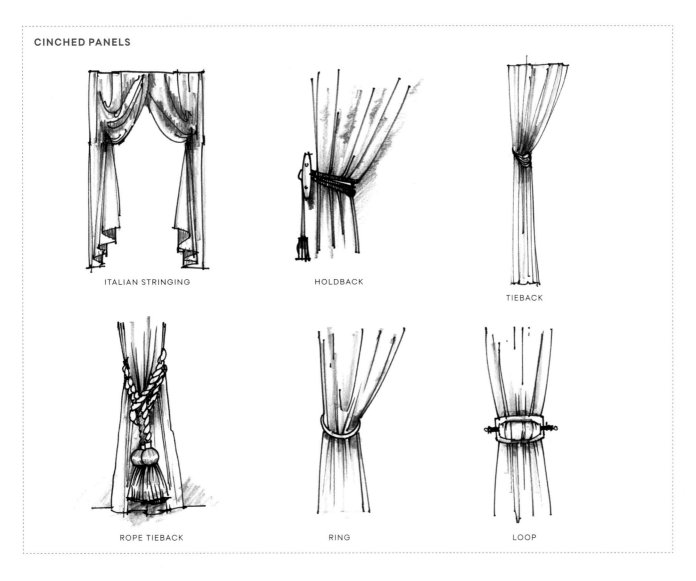

ITALIAN STRINGING

HOLDBACK

TIEBACK

ROPE TIEBACK

RING

LOOP

ROD VERSUS TRACK

Curtains can hang from hidden tracks (or brackets) or from rods. Tracks control the path of the drapery and can be surface-mounted or recessed into the ceiling. Rods are offered in a wide range of styles and materials, from carved wood to burnished metal. Capping the rod's end with an ornamental accent called a finial makes a nice embellishment. The choice of rod is also functional: one that bends around to connect directly to the wall, thus obviating the need for brackets and finials, is great for blocking light, since the drapery panel can "return" (or curve) all the way to the wall. Choose a method for attaching the curtain panel to the rod:

- Hooks and rings
- Pockets
- Tabs
- Ties
- Grommets

OPERATION

Fixed draperies designed to be left open—not pulled shut—are more decorative. These are typically paired with another treatment (a blind, a shade, or a casement/sheer) for light control and privacy. Operable curtains can be drawn closed by using cords, a chain, or motorized controls. When drawn shut, the edges of the panels either butt or overlap.

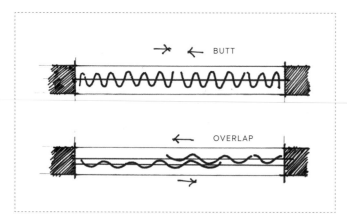

BUTT

OVERLAP

HANGING STYLE

Panels can hang straight or be gathered and held to the side. Panels that hang straight have a crisper look, and this is the preferred style for operable curtains. (Tiebacks wrinkle the fabric, creating an untidy look when curtains are drawn.) Choose one of the following for cinched panels:

- Tableau style (also called theatrical or Italian stringing): drawn up from behind via a cord
- Holdbacks (wall-mounted hardware)
- Tiebacks
- Rings
- Loops

CURTAIN LENGTH

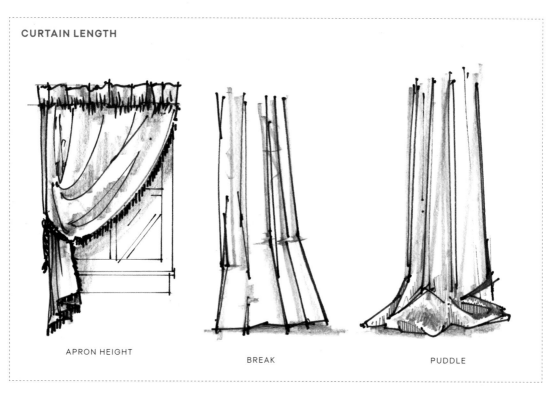

APRON HEIGHT

BREAK

PUDDLE

FULLNESS

Gathered curtains are sized in "fullness," a term that pertains to the actual width of the curtain panel, as opposed to the distance that the panel is intended to span. For example, a 45-inch panel at 2½ fullness will require 112 inches of fabric. A fullness of 2½ to 3X is most common, and creates a luxurious appearance open or closed. Anything less will result in a skimpy panel.

CURTAIN LENGTH

Determining the appropriate length of curtains can be tricky. Short curtains can look unfinished, and overly long curtains can feel dated. Use the window's architecture as a guide:

- **Sill height.** Stopping at the windowsill is preferred when there is an architectural interruption below: a radiator, a window seat, built-in cabinetry, etc.
- **Apron height.** Extending side drapery panels just past the sill can give an awkward window a bit of grace.
- **Above the floor.** Generally not advised, since the draperies will appear truncated or under scale; however, some applications will demand them. The height above the floor should be 3 inches.
- **Break.** Just brushing the floor. Measuring is particularly vital when curtains are to break at the floor—especially if the space is not yet built. Take into account the added height of any wall-to-wall carpeting or large area rugs that will raise the floor height at a later date.
- **Puddle.** More than 2 inches of extra fabric is a bit romantic. Reflective or smooth fabrics are best for this panel length.

Curtains by Lillian August have a pleated header, decorative tape border, and hang from a return rod.

1: A tasseled lambrequin by Silvina Leone. 2: Cuffed drapery with plaid lining, an antler holdback, and Venetian blinds. 3: Alexa Hampton paired Asian-inspired lambrequins with smocked headings and clean-lined curtain panels (held with tiebacks in the same fabric). 4: A Roman shade with lace detailing. 5: Louvered wooden shutters in a den by Villalobos Desio. 6: Simple roller shade in a kitchen by Joan Dineen. 7: In a room by Patrick James Hamilton, a cornice is layered over a sheer shade and louvered shutters, crisply bracketed by pleated panels. 8: Softly draped empire valance by Silvina Leone.

Shades

Shades are used largely for privacy and light control, although they can also provide thermal insulation. Practical as well as decorative, they can serve either as the sole window covering or in tandem with a drapery treatment. Customize them with flat ribbons and tassel pulls, laminate them to blackout linings, or leave them unlined to softly filter sunlight.

- **Plain shades** have a flat surface when lowered. They tend to have a simple and tailored look; when raised, they expose a good amount of window to maximize light and views.
- **Gathered shades** are fuller and more decorative than plain shades. They require more fabric and can often be quite formal. Because they are generally given an "outside" installation—mounted so that they cover both the window and the trim—they obscure more of the window surface. The most decorative variety is the Austrian shade, a ruched and gathered style with a lovely scalloped bottom that is drawn up by a rear cord (sewn into a pocket).

LINING

Shades are simply pieces of lightweight fabric with cords used to gather, raise, and lower them. They have very little structural integrity unless lined. Standard lining options are simple cotton sateen (in white or ecru) or very thin cotton that allows light to filter through. Other common

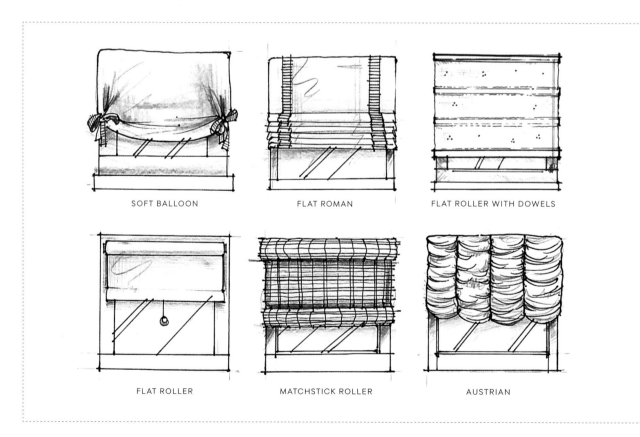

SOFT BALLOON

FLAT ROMAN

FLAT ROLLER WITH DOWELS

FLAT ROLLER

MATCHSTICK ROLLER

AUSTRIAN

choices include flannel and vinyl (the latter is used to render blackout shades completely opaque). Made of delicate fabrics, Austrian shades are always unlined: the trademark heavy gathering provides the needed structure.

EDGE TREATMENTS

Shade edges provide ample design opportunities. Accent the sides and bottom with ribbons, tape, or trims. A flat ribbon set in about 4 inches from all edges of a Roman shade is a pretty accent.

TOP TREATMENTS

Plain shades are often topped by a small 4-inch cornice to confer a finished look and hide the track or mounting device. This element can also be enlarged or adorned with braid or trim.

OPERATION

Like draperies, shades are raised and lowered by using motorized controls or by hand. In the latter case, choose cord (cotton cord or metal chain) or cordless operation, or consider a loop or a wand. Roller shades commonly have a flat piece of wood or plastic inserted into a pocket at the bottom to allow manual pull-down.

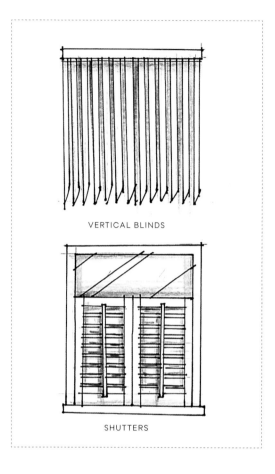

VERTICAL BLINDS

SHUTTERS

Blinds

Blinds are composed of operable slats (called vanes), oriented either horizontally or vertically and made of metal, wood, or plastic. A wand is used to angle the vanes, enabling a great deal of control over light, privacy, and ventilation. While blinds can certainly be colorful or patterned, a neutral look that blends in with the interior scheme is more typical. One exception is wooden or venetian blinds, which traditionally have 2-inch slats and,

courtesy of their dominant horizontal look, confer a strong decorative, even architectural presence. Wood blinds are stained to match standard wood colors, such as cherry, oak, and pine.

Shutters

Usually made of wood, and often louvered, these hinged vertical panels are like doors that cover the window to block light; when swung open, they lie against the adjacent wall surface, bracketing the glass. They are a great option to create continuity in a wood-paneled room. In nineteenth-century row houses and brownstones, shutters were designed to fit flush into pockets abutting the windows so they disappeared when open.

DESIGN CONSIDERATIONS

Every room has certain quirks, and many have windows that are mismatched or asymmetrical. Site conditions—from how windows operate to the placement of their openings on the wall—will affect the design and selection of treatments. Measuring and assessing windows at the start of the project is essential (see page 43). Each has an "inside" dimension: that of the actual opening. Carefully note that measurement and the exact location of the window openings on the wall elevations. Here are some questions to ask during the assessment:

- What is the distance from each window opening to the ceiling, the bottom of the crown molding, and the floor?
- How much wall space is available on either side of the window? This will inform the size afforded the stack back: the width of the curtains when drawn open. (Drapery panels are usually designed to frame the window aperture and therefore need adequate space to "sit" on the walls—beyond the actual window itself, at least 12 inches.)
- How does the window (or door) operate? If they are casement windows or doors, do the panels swing out or in? Be sure to mount valances and shades in a manner that doesn't obstruct an inward-swinging pane.
- Do any handles or cranks protrude?
- Is the window inset into the thickness of the wall, creating a recess, or is the glass pane flush with the interior wall plane?
- Is there a windowsill? Does it project beyond the wall or is it flush?

- Is there a radiator or heat pump under the window? Does it extend into the room? How far?
- Are there baseboard heating units, HVAC floor grilles, window seats, built-in shelving, cabinets, or other architectural interruptions?
- Will the window operation affect how the drapery closes? Gathered drapes are approximately 4 inches deep from front to back. That means that a window treatment with an underdrape, an overdrape, and a full draped valance or cornice may measure a foot deep (or more) altogether. How will the whole assembly look when viewed from the side?

Challenging Configurations

Creative problem solving is required for a number of common window situations.

MULTIPLE WINDOW FORMATS
It is not unusual for a single room to have different kinds (or sizes) of windows on each wall: bay windows, double-hung, French doors. The design challenge is to unify the appearance of all the windows through varied but complementary treatments. This can be done by using the same fabrics, trim, and hardware, as well as consistent overall drapery design and fabrication details.

A PROTRUDING RADIATOR
Select or design curtains that fall just to the sill, or fixed panels mounted wide enough to fall on either side of the protrusion. Layer with a shade or blind that provides light and privacy control. (Consider a cabinet to cover the radiator.)

TWO CLOSELY ADJACENT WINDOWS

Treat the pair as one window, using a single shade (or pair of butt-joined shades) to cover the window surfaces. Frame the whole assemblage with a single valance and just two drapery panels, one on the far left and one on the far right.

A RECESSED BAY WINDOW

This feature is best treated with decorative shades and/or blinds, but full drapery panels can sometimes work. Depending on the architecture, the whole recess can be treated as one window. Return the side of any outside-mount treatment to the wall.

POOR ROOM PROPORTIONS

Windows are arguably the most important architectural feature of a room, and their size, shape, and format give the space its sense of proportion and scale. Manipulate poor proportions by dressing the windows to instill balance; for instance, make windows look taller by mounting drapes high, and enhance the illusion of width with a substantial stack back on either side.

COMPLETE DARKNESS DESIRED

Use blackout shades that extend beyond the window opening and/or operable lined curtain panels mounted on a track.

AN UGLY VIEW

Go for sheer curtains or blinds—solo or paired with more opaque panels. Or choose slatted blinds that can be kept at an angle to screen the view while admitting daylight.

Suzanne Lovell floated a curtain rod in front of a window seat—a typically tricky installation. The panel puddles at the floor for a feeling of luxury.

ARCHED WINDOW

Is the window itself arch shaped, or does a separate arched window sit above it? If the whole window is arched, treat the rounded pane with an inset gathered curtain. Try to eschew coverings if possible for a separate arched top window. Inset a stained- or textured-glass panel to diffuse and refract light, and use standard treatments for the window below.

VERY MODERN ROOMS

Use minimal treatments such as blinds or shades made of fabric or mesh. For draperies, choose solid-color fabric mounted on a simple rod or recessed track via rings or ties.

SLIDING GLASS WALLS

Large expanses of glass walls inset with doors or window openings present a real challenge. Treat these features simply: use only one type of fabric for the drapery panels—versus a more decorative design pairing two colors or prints—and hang them from a recessed or surface-mounted track so that, when drawn closed, the treatment mimics the wall of glass it covers. The curtains should open where there are doors or windows.

FRENCH DOORS

Gathered curtains hung on fixed bars that are attached to the door panel itself work best. Tie a bow in the center of the curtains, which allows for some view. A roller shade or mini blinds can be mounted at the top of the door panel, but this is a more pedestrian solution.

LONG, WIDE WINDOWS

Many designers believe that a shade should be longer than it is wide for aesthetic reasons; however, many *windows* are wider than they are long! In such cases, divide the horizontal span of the window into an odd number of segments (or in segments that align with the window's vertical dividers). Make one shade for each and hang in a row, tightly butted against one another.

INSTALLATION CONSIDERATIONS

Become familiar with the wide variety of window tracks, hooks, pulls, rods, and other mounting hardware. Drapery hardware ranges in appearance from utilitarian to precious, and for some situations the choices are very limited. Work closely with the supplier, workroom, and installer to understand your options and select wisely.

MOUNTING LOCATION

Install treatments either within the window opening or mounted above and outside its frame or casing to allow for additional light and privacy control. The functional and design goals will dictate where the shades and draperies should sit in relation to the window opening. For example, in cases where molding is a prominent feature of the decor, an inside mount is often preferred. Shades that extend over the edge of a window will block more light in most instances.

DRAPERY MOUNTING

Placement and mounting of rods depend entirely on the site conditions; there are no hard-and-fast rules for guidance. Factors to consider include ceiling height and the distance between the window casing and the crown molding. Be sure the pole extends just beyond the curtain stack—which when open should cover about 6 inches of the window (with the bulk of the panel on the surrounding wall).

RECESSING

Recessing the top mounting or track used to support draperies, shades, or blinds into the ceiling, molding, or soffit above will eliminate the need for a valance. Another option is to mount a flat, narrow wooden panel (or fascia) painted like the ceiling over a track to create a mock recess.

COLLABORATING WITH A DRAPERY WORKROOM

Detailed worksheets are used to determine and document every aspect of a custom drapery. These ateliers require drawings to exactly illustrate all the different parts of the drapery; each element of the overall window treatment represents a decision that must be made. For example: What fabric and trim will be used? What's the fullness of the drapery, and what lining and interlining are required? The drawings and specifications should also indicate the method and location of installation.

Curtain panels in a vignette by Linherr Hollingsworth are also a nice touch to bracket a doorway.

SOFT FLOOR COVERINGS

Soft floor coverings, including any kind of rug or carpet, are a fundamental building block for many interiors. Installed from wall to wall, a carpet can unify a room, while an area rug creates an island in a larger space, demarcating zones or seating groupings. A cushy material underfoot warms up an environment and improves acoustics. Soft floor coverings also reinforce the design concept by conveying a certain personality: a rug's color, pattern, scale, ability to reflect light, and even cultural origin or reference can establish or alter the very character of a space.

When selecting a carpet or rug, consider the entire residence. Pay attention to how floor coverings in each room will relate not only to their immediate surroundings but also to the overall design scheme.

THE OPTIONS

Most floor coverings are textiles, either woven or tufted, but hides and furs also fall into the category. Textiles come in two formats: wall-to-wall carpeting, which covers the entire floor (and is sometimes installed directly over the subfloor), and area rugs sized to the configuration of conversation areas or furniture groupings. Within those subgenres are a wide variety of materials—wool, linen, cotton, natural grasses, synthetics—and many methods of fabrication.

CHOOSE CARPETS AND RUGS THAT WORK IN CONCERT WITH THE TEXTURE, COLOR, AND PATTERN OF SURROUNDING FABRICS, WALLCOVERINGS, AND WINDOW TREATMENTS.

OPPOSITE: Carol Egan used area rugs to define discrete furniture groupings in an open-plan space.

"I find wall-to-wall carpets in bedrooms in urban settings to be indispensable. They serve an acoustical purpose in absorbing unwanted noise and have the ability to make a space feel larger than with the use of an area rug. A plush and luxurious rug can set the right tone as your feet hit the ground in the morning. I always try to incorporate silk or viscose in bedroom carpets; that softness and sheen can have a tremendous impact."

—Phillip Thomas, designer

Area Rugs

There are many ways to fabricate a new area rug and numerous materials to choose from. Manufacturers produce them in standard sizes (see box below). Traditional or antique area rugs from around the world will come close to but never exactly match these sizes. Designers frequently commission a custom piece to suit the exact dimensions of a room and its furniture grouping. Area rugs are generally bound at the edges to prevent raveling.

Wall-to-Wall Carpeting

Long rolls of carpeting are laid side by side and stitched or seamed together to cover the entire floor. The most common type of wall-to-wall carpet is broadloom, which is woven in an extra-large format—up to 12 feet wide—so that there are few or no seams in the installations. Products come backed with a synthetic latex coating, sometimes supplemented with a scrim backing that lends dimensional stability, prevents snags and unraveling, and boosts moisture resistance. Broadloom is installed in one of two ways: glued down to the subfloor or tacked over a pad of jute or rubberized synthetic hair.

STANDARD DIMENSIONS OF AREA RUGS

- 3 by 5 feet
- 6 by 8 feet
- 8 by 10 feet
- 9 by 12 feet
- 10 by 12 feet

Carpet Tile

An alternative to broadloom is carpet tile, usually 18 to 20 inches square (or a slightly larger rectangle). The modular format means that tiles can easily be replaced if they get stained or damaged. As such, they are ideal for settings prone to heavy traffic, mess, or water damage: a child's room, mudroom, basement-level play area, or workshop, for instance. Some carpet tiles have an integral pad that enhances their acoustical properties.

1: A hair-on cowhide rug lends texture and interest. 2: Boldly patterned wall-to-wall carpet is like a painting underfoot. 3: Layered carpeting: an antique area rug anchored by wall-to-wall sisal. 4: A zebra-skin rug is layered over sisal. 5: A custom area rug with a sinuous profile has been created to complement the design motif of the room.

DESIGN CONSIDERATIONS

Fundamental choices need to be made about material, construction, size/format, color, and pattern for carpets and rugs.

Materials

Many natural and synthetic fibers are used to make carpets and rugs; the most common are wool and nylon. Each material features unique properties of durability, appearance retention, stain resistance, and ease of maintenance (see page 254).

Construction

The yarns of carpets and rugs are either woven together on a loom or punched (or looped) onto a backing material (a process called tufting).

WOVEN

Woven floor coverings are made on a loom and have a specific weave direction. They boast an artisanal feel, which creates a more casual look but means they may not be perfectly square or lie completely flat. Woven carpets come bound on the ends only.

TUFTED

The majority of carpeting manufactured in the United States today is tufted. In tufting, the fibers are punched onto a canvas backing that stabilizes the textile, prevents stretching, and lies very flat on the floor. Rugs and carpets are tufted either by machine or by hand:

- **Hand-tufting** is an excellent medium for customization; because it is not limited by the constraints of automated mechanisms, it offers much creative flexibility. These floor coverings can be made in any shape and size and tufted in any direction to ensure that the texture correlates with the design motif.
- **Pass-machine tufting.** This mechanized alternative to hand-tufting creates a cost-effective yet luxurious product. (Due to the complex setup, producers usually stipulate a minimum on custom orders.) The canvas backing is passed through a row of needles and then repositioned for the next parallel pass—a process similar to that of a sewing machine. Patterns are limited to stripes, twists, and other linear motifs, although simple designs can be hand-tufted on top. Machine-tufted carpet can be made in any shape and size for an installation with no seams.

The treatment of the pile (the fibers that make up the top of the carpet) affect the performance, appearance, and price of a tufted carpet.

- **Pile type.** How do the fibers adhere to the backing? Are they are cut? How are they cut?
  - » With **loop pile,** both ends of the yarn are adhered to the backing, meaning the side of the yarn creates the surface of the rug. This renders the rug more durable—and the design more visually consistent.
  - » With **cut pile,** one end of the yarn is adhered to the backing and the other creates the surface. The same color appears darker in cut pile since the ends of the yarn absorb more light. It feels more velvety than loop pile, but will show walking patterns and vacuum lines and can pill, pool, or shade.

» **Shearing** is done with a tool that partially cuts the looped surface, exposing tiny end fibers that are darker than the side of the yarn to lend depth and richness. The level of shearing varies from 30 to 80 percent (100 percent shearing equals cut pile).

» A combination of **cut and loop pile** is often used to create textural emphasis or subtle patterns.

- **Density.** Denser tufting holds the pile up firmly, which allows for better wear and more detailed patterning. The denser the carpet, the more durable and dirt-repellent it is—and the more it costs.

- **Pile height.** When the pile is high, the individual yarns have less support and may fall over or be crushed. Footsteps will show on a high-pile sheared or cut carpet. (Longer yarns will read as a "shag" carpet.) Low pile is the more durable option.

- **Special effects.** Various effects can be achieved by treating the yarns in a specific way prior to tufting:

» **Twisting.** Tightly winding together twisted yarns in two or more colors before threading the tufting needle creates a tweed-like or heathered texture. Tone-on-tone hues offer a subtler effect than do contrasting yarn colors.

» **Stria (or striation).** Loosely winding together two or more different-colored yarns before threading the tufting needle creates a watery pattern.

» **Ombré.** A gentle gradation between hues is created by using twists and/or striations of colors.

HAND-KNOTTED

Area rugs are woven in linear rows, so small, curving details may have a slightly pixelated look at lower knot counts (i.e., fewer knots per inch). Color, design, and pile can be customized in this labor-intensive method. Hand-knotted rugs may be slightly irregular in shape and size; corners don't always lie flat.

Which Tuft to Choose

When commissioning a custom rug, pile heights and different qualities may be combined.

APPLICATION	CHOICE
Graphically complex rugs or carpets	Tight, low loops or a dense, short cut pile
Small design details	Small, dense loops or a low cut pile (larger loops—or a less dense or taller cut pile—will distort)
Textural effects	Mix of loop and cut piles, or piles at different heights

NEEDLEPOINT

Needlepoint rugs based on the centuries-old Portuguese Arraiolos stitch are entirely hand-made, and the format does not lend itself to small design details. This expensive and labor-intensive process translates to longer lead times. Needlepoint rugs should not be used in high-traffic areas.

AUBUSSON CARPET

The Aubusson carpet industry was originally established to service the Royal Court of France. These carpets are labor intensive to produce—but the result is strong and durable. The tiny knots characteristic of this method allow for great detail and elaborate design.

Coloration and Dyeing

Carpet showrooms present their color selections on "poms": small balls of yarn that are looped on one end and cut on the other. The loop side of the pom is always lighter in color than the cut end, because the latter reflects less light. When analyzing a pom for color, be sure to inspect the end that corresponds to the final carpet design, whether loop or cut pile. And always squeeze the pom end tightly, since it will better represent the density of the final carpet—and thus the true color.

Yarns are dyed in one of two ways:

- **Vegetable** dyeing uses natural materials; therefore, the result will show natural variegation. Vegetable dye is typically used for hand-knotted and antique rugs.

- In **solution** (i.e., chemical) dyeing, the color is integral to the fiber; therefore, the result is long lasting and resistant to fading, and the coloration is even. Solution dyeing cannot be used for natural fibers and yarns.

Customization

When an interior designer is involved in a project, she will often pursue the custom route, envisioning a rug or a carpet that is the perfect size, color, and pattern for the space. Customization is necessary when traditional or standard options are not available. Custom rugs must be ordered well ahead of installation, to allow for approval of the color rendering and sample (called a strike-off) prior to fabrication. Lead times can be very long (up to twenty-six weeks); specially commissioned needlepoint rugs can take an entire year from order to installation.

Custom rugs are most commonly made of wool, silk, a wool-silk blend, or nylon. Hand-tufted rugs offer the most versatility and options for customization, but even leather and hide can be made into bespoke designs. Irregularly sized spaces and stairways should be professionally measured and templated to ensure a proper fit. Developing a solid relationship with a quality vendor is advisable, given the myriad variables involved in customization.

1: A wool rug with silk accents creates an aqueous vibe in a beachfront home. 2: Varying pile heights create a geometric pattern on a tufted wall-to-wall carpet in a living room. 3: A high-pile carpet with silken threads.

Fiber Options for Floor Coverings

FIBER	PROS	CONS	BEST USE
WOOL	• Wears very well • Extremely resilient • Cleans easily	• Stains easily • Requires pretreatment • The pile can wear away over time	• High-traffic areas • Area rugs
SILK	• Lustrous shine and reflectivity	• Very strong and long-lasting fiber • Very porous and will stain easily • Requires professional cleaning	• Accents or borders on wool rugs • Only low-traffic areas (if a large percentage of silk is used)
LINEN	• Beautiful color	• Stains easily • Difficult to clean	• Low-traffic areas
COTTON	• Natural • Inexpensive	• Stains easily	• Informal residential settings
NYLON	• Excellent durability and texture retention • Highly uniform color • Very resilient, cleanable, and easy to maintain • Can be pretreated for enhanced stain resistance • Resists soil and mildew • Can be recycled	• Not inherently stain-resistant • Feel underfoot is not as soft as a natural fiber	• High-traffic areas such as halls, home offices, and playrooms • Stairs
OLEFIN (POLYPROPYLENE)	• Good resistance to wear • Excellent stain resistance	• Not resilient	• Carpets with high surface density or low-pile loop
POLYESTER	• Wears well • Resists staining • Good texture	• Shows soil • Less cleanable and resilient than other fibers	• Low-traffic areas

FIBER	PROS	CONS	BEST USE
SISAL, JUTE, COIR, AND SEA GRASS	• Sustainable • Offers a natural, organic look • Varies widely in cost • Can be dyed and woven into interesting patterns • Available with simple cotton bindings	• Hard and scratchy to walk on • Highly susceptible to staining from liquids or foot traffic • Cannot be cleaned • Will disintegrate over time	• A neutral anchor for a more decorative area rug or to define a seating grouping
LEATHER AND COWHIDE	• Unique texture • Wide variety of looks and styles	• A natural material that will wear as such (but beautifully)	• Accent pieces and focal points • Low-traffic areas
VISCOSE	• Emulates silk at a lower price • Soft and durable • Natural	• Does not always dye evenly • Cut-pile viscose will crush • Flammable	• Areas with moderate foot traffic • Keep away from fireplaces or hearths
KHAMPA WOOL, NETTLE, ALOE, BANANA SILK, AND BAMBOO SILK	• Natural • Sustainable	• Delicate	• Hand-knotted rugs

CHRONOLOGY OF A CUSTOM ORDER

The process of designing and fabricating a custom hand-tufted rug is quite involved. Here's how one company, Martin Patrick Evan, executes a bespoke design.

1. Conceptualize the design.
2. Draw the final design to scale.
3. Pick the colors. To color-match a fabric or other design element that has already been selected for the space, the maker will use a spectrometer, a gadget that helps identify the exact dye solution needed.
4. The maker prepares art boards of the chosen design, with colors called out and approved yarn colors attached. This artwork—called a rendering for approval—is later translated into a line drawing and silk-screened onto the canvas (or scrim) that becomes the rug's backing (see step 9).
5. After the client and designer have signed off on the rendering, a portion of the rug, called a strike-off, is made for approval.
6. An installation expert carefully measures all aspects of the room or space. He uses sturdy but supple Tyvek paper (or similar) to make templates of stairways and any irregularly shaped areas, odd angles, built-ins, hearths, etc. This process is very tricky when the space is not yet built; in that case, it's best to wait until construction is complete, or create a design that has some room for error.

7. Fibers are processed and spun according to the approved specifications. The yarn is then assembled in bundles (called hanks) in the proper quantities for each color featured. Hanks are dipped into high-pressure dyeing vats and treated to a chemical dye solution. For hand-knotted rugs and others using vegetable dyes, the yarns are instead boiled and churned with natural dyestuff.
8. The dyed yarns are spun onto spools that will be used in the tufting process.
9. The scrim (generated in step 4) is tightly nailed to a vertical rack (or frame) and then tufted from the back. Consistent pressure, speed, and angle are critical to ensure a smooth, even quality.
10. Once tufting is complete, the rug is removed from the rack, placed on the floor, and inspected. Samples and art boards are referenced to ensure exact color matching, scale, and design integrity. Any irregularities or weaving discrepancies are corrected right on the floor.
11. Excess scrim is trimmed, and the carpet is sheared and finished.
12. The rug is ready for delivery. It is important to carefully coordinate the delivery or installation with the rest of the project.

INSTALLATION CONSIDERATIONS

Wall-to-wall carpet will be more complicated to install than an area rug, since it is fixed to the floor. It will also be vital to resolve issues like where seams are to be placed and how the carpet edge interfaces with adjacent hard flooring.

TEMPLATING

Custom wall-to-wall installations—as well as area rugs that are not rectangular—generally require that a template of the exact dimensions be made at the project site. This is especially true if the rug must be shaped exactly to a furniture grouping or to surrounding baseboards, hearths, built-ins, or other margins.

ORDERING

Wall-to-wall carpet is sold by the square yard and comes on a roll, typically 12 feet wide.

SEAMS AND DIRECTIONALITY

The designer or client must collaborate with the installer to create a seaming diagram that stipulates exacly where the seams of wall-to-wall carpet will lie to make them least visible—ideally in areas less prone to foot traffic, as they tend to fray when walked on. Because broadloom is directional, all rolls needs to be laid in the same orientation and come from the same dye lot so that color is consistent across the floor. The location of the seams will determine the amount of carpet to be ordered.

PADDING

In residential installations, broadloom is typically attached to wooden strips nailed around the room's perimeter, which feature sharp, protruding tacks that grab the carpet. (Borders, if specified, are made separately and hand-seamed on-site before the carpet is "kicked" into place.) Installation over a pad increases the life of the carpet and enhances its insulating properties. Padding is typically made of rubber or a combination of synthetic hair and jute. Higher density equals increased durability—of the pad *and* the carpet. Pads differ in the amount of cushioning they provide; a ⅜-inch-thick pad is recommended for most residential wall-to-wall applications. Area rugs should be installed over a 1/16-inch-thick nonskid rubber mat (available when purchasing the rug).

GLUE-DOWN CARPET

A more budget-conscious method is to glue carpet directly to the subfloor using heavy-duty mastic. This is not recommended for high-end carpeting, as any discrepancies in the subfloor will be telegraphed, or show through the carpet. Glue-down carpet is also hard to remove.

WHERE CARPET MEETS A FLOOR

Transitioning from a fully carpeted floor to tile or wood is tricky. Counterintuitively, it is the edge of the *hard* material that is delicate and needs protecting. There are a few transitional choices, including aluminum strips that cover both edges and rubber extrusions that ease the change in height or material. For wood floors, a small saddle or wood strip is best.

CARPETING STAIRWAYS

Stairway installations are complex and generally pricey. There are two methods:

- A **waterfall** installation allows the carpet to fall diagonally from the riser above to the crotch below, where it is tucked in.
- A **Hollywood** installation wraps the carpet around the bullnose of the tread, and hugs the riser down to the crotch; this is more labor intensive, but more tailored.

When applying a carpet with a linear weave direction, run the weave perpendicular to the step. Rows will separate slightly when they bend over the bullnose, showing the canvas; this is referred to as a "smile." (The backing can be dyed a similar color—at an additional cost—so the smile will not show.) The type of stairway determines how the carpet is installed:

- Carpet for a **straight flight** is made in long or individual pieces. Each step is calculated at 24-inch lengths (12 for the riser, 12 for the tread). The sides of straight stairway runs are usually bound and the ends unbound.

- Carpet for **curved** or **shaped** stairways is made individually for each step and installed on-site. Templating is a must for an exact fit. This requires making a blueprint of each tread and engineering the pattern and border specifically for it. Each step is ordered with 3 inches of overage on the ends, and the sides are bound (unless borders are to be seamed on-site, as is the case when ordered before stairs are built or completed).

- **Margins** are measured from the rug to the inside edge of the banister post(s)—not to the outside of the step. The margin depends on how wide the steps are and how much of the flooring material is to be shown on the sides. If the project is under construction at the time the order is placed, actual stair widths can only be determined from a plan. Add overage to the sides of the steps and have borders seamed on-site.

OPPOSITE: A zebra-print runner installed using the waterfall method dresses up a straight-run staircase in a townhouse by Joan Dineen.

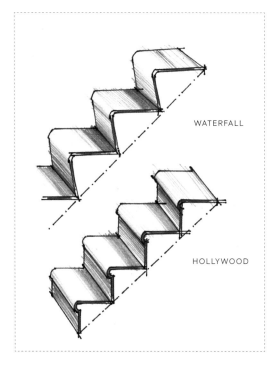

WATERFALL

HOLLYWOOD

LIGHTING

Lighting has a huge influence on a room's ambience, imbuing atmosphere and evoking emotion. The right scheme can create mystery, excitement, richness, or calm. Illumination also has a psychological and physiological dimension, essential as it is to physical and mental health. With increased access to natural light, schoolchildren achieve higher literacy scores and hospital patients recuperate faster; in a residential setting, a well-lit room improves mood and well-being. Full-spectrum artificial light can provide similar benefits to daylight.

Of course, light is not only a design feature in its own right but also the means by which the eye discerns form and detail. Full appreciation of every facet of an interior decor depends on proper illumination: a nuanced and layered scheme.

"PEOPLE ARE VERY PARTICULAR ABOUT LIGHT. SOME LOVE AMPLE ILLUMINATION—THE BRIGHTER, THE BETTER—WHILE OTHERS FEEL COMFORTABLE IN LOW, EVEN LIGHT."
—Addison Kelly

THE LIGHTING CONCEPT

The key to creating a smart lighting plan is to approach the exercise just as you would select a color palette or fabric scheme: with a vision for the entire room in mind. "You can't start by asking, 'Should I choose incandescent or LEDs, a chandelier or ceiling track?'" explains lighting designer Addison Kelly. "Begin with a concept. How do you want the space to feel: dramatic, soft, sharp?"

With a concept in hand, it will ultimately be much easier to determine what the focal point of the lighting scheme should be, whether concealed or exposed fixtures will make sense overhead, and if they should be minimal or decorative. For example, if the concept is "retreat"—often the case for bedrooms—then a quiet and restful scheme may be preferable. This may translate to dimmable fixtures, delicate bedside sconces with pastel silk lampshades, and warm low-wattage bulbs. In a dining room, the idea of a congenial, emanating glow could be upheld by a large pendant with a drum shade, while a master bath could be designed to switch between a range of effects, from soothing to glamorous to makeup-studio bright.

OPPOSITE: Precious sconces flank a large-scale artwork above a fireplace. A Sputnik-esque ceiling pendant and industrial-inspired floor lamp round out the mix in an eclectic living room by James Rixner.

1: A dramatic, layered lighting scheme by Charles Pavarini combines a wall sconce, picture light, and table lamp to artfully illuminate fine finishes, including lapis-hued strié walls and embossed leather drapery. 2: An overscale round pendant light creates a focal glow over a dining table in an apartment by Laura Bohn. 3: In an all-white room by Darryl Carter, an elaborate chandelier with black shades pairs with candelabra sconces in the same hue. 4: Donald Billinkoff illuminated a corridor with recessed architectural lighting. 5 + 6: Subtle recessed architectural light and spotlights inset into the floor keep the focus on the spare, gallery-like room design.

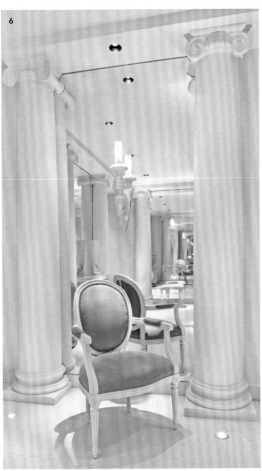

From Concept to Scheme

DESIRED EFFECT	LIGHTING ACTION PLAN
SHARP	Illuminate high-luster surfaces with brilliant light sources that have clear coatings.
COZY	Use fully dimmable soft-edged light from diffused sources with relatively low Kelvin ratings (between 2700K and 3000K).
DRAMATIC	Highlight objects and features with accent lights.
THEATRICAL	Graze surfaces with light to exaggerate texture and color.
SOFT	Illuminate low-luster surfaces with soft light sources that have frosted coatings.
WARM	Illuminate warm color palettes via light sources with relatively low Kelvin ratings (between 2700K and 3500K).

CALLING IN THE PROS

A residential project can be greatly improved with the input of a lighting designer. As with all specialists, enlisting one as early as possible in the design process—ideally at a project's inception—nets the best results. That way, he can both devise a suitable concept (or help discern if the proposed scheme is viable) and advise on structural matters: for instance, will a dropped ceiling or soffit be required to accommodate recessed fixtures? A trained designer knows how to balance the subtleties of color and light with energy and sustainability code requirements and considerations. Depending on the scope of work, a lighting designer will typically charge an hourly consulting rate or a project-based fee.

ABOVE: Special elements accommodate recessed lighting in an apartment with concrete ceilings. Tamara Hubinsky unified the open-plan living/dining area via a shared materials palette and a contrast of light and dark elements. **OPPOSITE:** A feathery pendant reiterates this vignette's textural theme.

THE PLAN

Every space needs a mix of lighting types, from general illumination to lighting for specific activities such as cooking, grooming, and reading. "It is so important to have varied light sources in a room," says interior designer Timothy Corrigan. "Mixing task and atmosphere lighting at staggered heights—overheads, desk lamps, floor lamps—is key. Having only a single overhead makes a room look washed out." Think about a space holistically, taking every surface and activity area into account. "Don't just fixate on task lighting: You must formulate the whole room together," explains Addison Kelly. "Lighting design is about layering." A carefully calibrated mix of sources will also ensure an even, not spotty, glow. Rooms should have a combination of the following:

- **Ambient lighting.** Fixtures providing overall illumination: for instance, a ceiling-hung pendant that combines uplighting and downlighting.
- **Task lighting.** Focused and controlled illumination—such as a desk lamp or under-cabinet kitchen lighting—to support a particular activity. Site the light source in close proximity to the surface to be set aglow, and in a manner that minimizes glare.
- **Accent lighting.** Lighting used to set off certain features of the architecture or decor, such as a fireplace, prominent works of art, or a focal wall. Sconces or library lights, for example.

These categories were derived from the writings of the late architectural lighting designer Richard Kelly, the founding father of the discipline. He described these necessary qualities as focal glow (making it easier to see), ambient luminescence (which makes surroundings safe and reassuring), and a "play of brilliants" to stimulate the spirit.

A properly illuminated space will feature all these elements, but the exact ratio will depend on the uses for the space, the overarching design concept, and the desired effect. In a foyer, ambient illumination may be most important; task lighting less so. In a utilitarian home office area, task lighting is essential but accent lighting not as much of a priority. Regardless, a designer will first identify the activity areas or special moments in a room deserving of focal lighting and use these as starting points, seamlessly layering in the additional lighting needed.

A lighting plan should not be permanent and set in stone. Remember that a space is always in flux, Addison Kelly advises. "Rooms evolve over the course of the day, as sunlight shifts and different activities take place. And life changes too—you have a baby, you take up pottery. Your lighting will also need to change and evolve." It can take time and observation to understand what a space needs, and how daylight comes into the room. "Sometimes the best thing is to live in and understand the space gradually, and then finesse the plan as you go," Kelly adds. With this approach, the fixed lighting should be designed for flexibility and applicability across a range of design schemes.

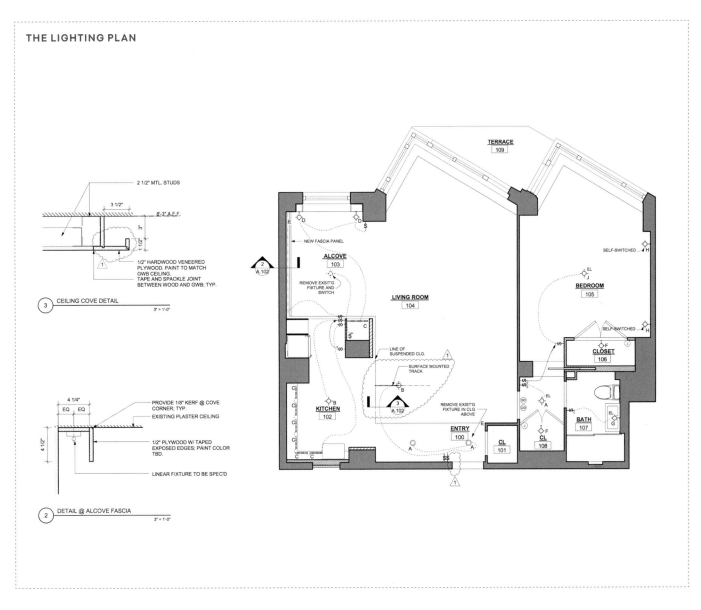

The lighting plan of an apartment by architect Terry Kleinberg.

ABOVE: In an apartment by Cullman & Kravis, a ceiling cove uplit with hidden fixtures creates an ethereal glow that highlights the moldings. **LEFT:** Joan Dineen designed a multipurpose bedroom that's calm and comfortable all day long, thanks partly to a layered lighting scheme—including a vintage chandelier and low bedside lamps.

THE OPTIONS

There are various genres of fixtures to choose from, each capable of adding a different layer to the overall composition. Lighting can also be poetic or utilitarian—or some combination thereof. Chandeliers, pendants, sconces, and table and floor lamps—decorative lighting—are often highly sculptural and works of art themselves. Use them for great effect over a dining table or above a console.

Lighting Types

In determining the right fixtures, plan for a combination of these types of light:

- **Indirect light.** Wall washing, reflected light, and ceiling coves fall into this category. Casting a glow on walls and ceiling—the room's boundaries—makes the space seem bigger that it is.
- **Direct light.** This category includes task and accent light; it confers a greater sense of coziness and intimacy in a room.
- **Focal (or point).** The light itself creates a point of interest.

Light's defining counterpart is, of course, darkness (or shadow). Exploit a contrast between light and dark to focus a pool or a spot, wash light over a beautiful surface, or frame an important image.

Fixtures

Every room should have a mix of the following fixture types:

- **Architectural lighting.** The choice between concealed (i.e., recessed into the ceiling plane) and exposed (as in track lighting) will depend on a few variables. In some cases, the building structure prohibits inclusion of recessed lights; a surface-mounted fixture is therefore the only option. Aesthetics is also an important consideration. To reinforce a loftlike ambience, exposed fixtures are appropriate and desirable. Recessed cans offer a cleaner, sleeker look and are generally preferable in a traditionally minded space. Hidden fixtures are more mysterious too, emanating a glow without drawing attention to the source itself.
- **Ceiling fixtures.** Whether surface-mounted flush with the ceiling or hung like chandeliers and pendants, these fixtures illuminate while creating visual interest in the dead space just below the ceiling plane.
- **Wall sconces.** Usually installed in pairs, these decorative wall-mounted fixtures can be positioned to provide symmetrical emphasis—on either side of a mirror or a fireplace, for example—or at regular intervals to break up and illuminate a long passageway.
- **Floor and table lamps.** The illumination workhorses of most spaces provide ambience as well as task light. Their shades also play a strategic role by adding layers of softness, color, and texture.

Light Source

Besides the function, design, and location of the fixture, the light source itself, or the bulb, is an integral aspect of residential illumination. In the field of lighting, bulbs are referred to as "lamps." Every lamp has specific attributes—focus, color, and distribution—that should be part of the design process. For architectural lighting, lamps are detailed in drawings as part of the specifications.

LAMP	CHARACTERISTICS	LIGHT COLOR
LED	Low energy consumption and low maintenance—but bright white light	Warm-cool (2400K–6500K)
FLUORESCENT/CFL	Poor color rendition	Warm-cool (2800K–4500K)
INCANDESCENT	Offers a decorative appearance and warm color	Warm (2700K–2900K)
HALOGEN	Moderately higher efficiency than incandescent	Neutral (3000K–3500K)

KEY DIMENSIONS

Determining the proper height and location for different types of lighting is a challenge and depends on the design context. For the best results, consult with an expert. Here are a few guidelines:

- Sconces: mounting height in a room should be no less than 60 inches on center above the floor; in a hallway, 72 inches minimum above the floor
- Chandeliers: should descend about 30 inches above the dining table and 84 inches above the floor when floating in the middle of a room
- Pendants: 24 to 30 inches above a kitchen island or other surface
- Reading height: should be within 18 inches of the horizontal reading surface
- Foot path: roughly 12 inches above the floor

ABOVE: Set over a credenza, a sconce bathes the wall in light and serves as a decorative accent in a vignette by Ingrao. **OPPOSITE:** Swing-arm sconces above a sofa.

DESIGN CONSIDERATIONS

Lighting effects are achieved through the selection of fixtures, their arrangement within the interior, and the choice of bulb. Specialists (and seasoned designers) use calculations to determine each of these; however, there are some simple ways to think about the placement and selection of lighting within the home.

Focal Points

To get from concept to scheme, start with a focal point. What about the room does the homeowner want to emphasize—a tapestry, an artwork, a rug, or a fireplace? It needs to be properly lit. Each seating group in a living room will need its own glow, to draw people in. Even a beautiful reading nook can serve as a focal point. Personal preference can hold sway here: for instance, lighting a beloved book collection may call for bookcases washed in light, accented with gleaming, shelf-mounted library lighting. But if the intent is for the bookcases to recede a bit, then no special lighting is required.

Factoring in Finishes

Be sure to consider the connection between lighting and the surrounding materials and finishes. Glossy surfaces will reflect light; textured ones will absorb it. The exact same lighting scheme will read much darker in a red-lacquered room than in a whitewashed one.

Dimmability

Adjustability is an important feature of lighting, to allow for a change of brightness and mood. Install dimmers wherever possible to ensure the greatest flexibility. Dimmability also depends on the type of lightbulb: for instance, some LEDs are completely dimmable, while compact fluorescents are only dimmable to 20 percent. Halogen and incandescent bulbs give the widest range. The technology is currently undergoing rapid change, so do your research.

LIGHTING IS A DESIGN ELEMENT LIKE ANY OTHER: THE PRINCIPLES OF REPETITION, RHYTHM, BALANCE, AXIS, EMPHASIS, SHAPE, AND FORM GOVERN ITS USE.

1: Library lights are mounted over built-in shelving. 2: Bookshelves illuminated from within set off a special collection, creating a focal point at one end of a living room by Addie Havemeyer. 3: Under-cabinet lighting in a kitchen by Laura Bohn is supplemented by the warm, lantern-like glow of internally lit translucent upper cabinets.

Recessed lights are designed to look as though parts of the
wall are peeling away in a stairwell by David Scott.

INSTALLATION CONSIDERATIONS

Decisions about where to place permanent lighting must be made long before fixtures and bulbs are purchased. When preparing for installation, keep the following elements in mind:

- **Channeling.** In cases such as concrete-slab construction, where there is no "pocket," or depth, for installation, recessed ceiling fixtures will require costly channeling or a dropped ceiling over some or all of the space—solutions that will drive many other architectural decisions.
- **Junction boxes.** A designer will note specific locations for sconces and chandeliers in his drawings based on the furniture plan. These placements must be determined before renovations begin, because the electrician will install a junction box early in the process.
- **Electrical cords.** Think about the furniture plan and the proximity to an electrical supply. Are there ample outlets to plug in all the specified lamps, and are they well placed to avoid awkward stretching of cords? For instance, a cord for a Parson-style console in an entrance hall can be hidden more easily if an outlet is placed at tabletop height to avoid seeing it dangle below. Consider flush-mounted floor outlets for groupings that float in the center of a room.

- **Floor outlets.** Advance planning allows for outlets to be mounted flush to the floor surface under a side table or a seating area. A small slit is sometimes made in a rug or wall-to-wall carpet to allow access.
- **Controls and switches.** New construction or renovations require a switching diagram (or plan) that illustrates which fixtures (or sets of fixtures) are controlled by which switches, and their locations. The diagram will include simple switches, dimmers (rheostats), occupancy sensors, timers, and touch pads. Details that deserve attention include locations, groupings of multiple switches, three- or four-way switching of one set of fixtures or outlets, and special situations such as installation into tile or upholstered walls.
- **Cover plates.** A small but critical design element is selecting or customizing cover plates for light switches and outlets. There are long lead times for them.

LAMPSHADES

The right shade can impart grandeur to a decorative lamp and reinvent its character. Attentiveness to details such as edge trims and proper sizing in relation to the base is the key to a professional touch.

In sizing a shade properly, it is vital to use standard measurements; this will help the designer write a PO for a custom order.

ABOVE: David Scott chose a subtly curved lampshade for a sinuous base. **OPPOSITE:** A simple white silk lampshade contrasts with a faceted black base.

HOW TO SCALE A SHADE

Measurements are expressed as *top diameter* by *bottom diameter* by *length of slant.* A fourth dimension sometimes listed is the *drop* created by an Uno harp (or washer).

- **Height.** The height of a lampshade (i.e., its slant) must be proportionate to the height of the lamp base. For a table lamp, the shade should be 65 to 80 percent of the base-to-socket height. For a floor lamp, the shade should be about 47 percent (or slightly less than half) of the base height.
- **Diameter.** Lampshade sizes are typically described in terms of the *bottom* diameter. This measurement should be within (and never exceed) 2 inches of the base height. The appropriate diameter is also a matter of safety: shades on floor lamps should clear the widest part of the bulb by 3½ inches all around—particularly when hot-burning incandescent, halogen, or high-wattage bulbs are used.

Start with these basic guidelines but then scale up or down a bit to fit the dimensions of the room and the surrounding vignette, advises Lisa Simkin of Blanche P. Field, a maker of custom shades. "A half-inch difference is a lot; it's like two inches visually. Scaling a lampshade is like attempting to find the right hat for your head; try different shade sizes and shapes on your base."

ANATOMY OF A LAMP AND SHADE

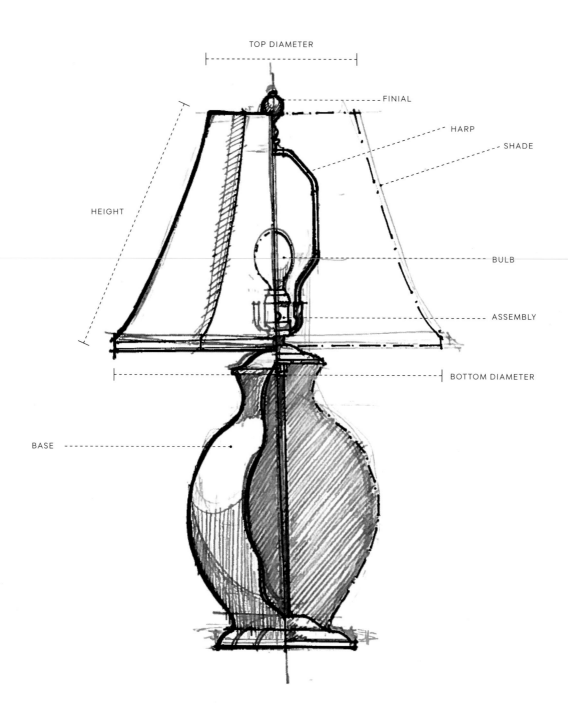

TOP DIAMETER

FINIAL

HARP

SHADE

HEIGHT

BULB

ASSEMBLY

BOTTOM DIAMETER

BASE

SHAPES

PLEAT STYLES

CUSTOM LAMPSHADES

THE OPTIONS

There are many choices to make when designing a bespoke lampshade or buying one off the shelf. From fabric to trims to shape, no detail should be ignored.

SHAPE

The profile of the shade should somehow complement—or deliberately contrast with—the base. For a fully custom lampshade, the metal frame that supports the shade material is handcrafted to order. Therefore, almost any shape is possible so long as it's structurally sound. If a lamp is to be placed close to a wall, an oval, a rectangle, or a flattened shape will create the narrowest footprint. Here are some of the most common profiles:

- **Bell.** This sinuously flared profile lends a girlish flourish.
- **Cone.** The steep, straight slant—like a poodle skirt caught midtwirl—looks best on thin, attenuated forms, such as a lamp with a candlestick base.
- **Drum.** A simple, classic cylinder suits a variety of lamp styles, and is especially apropos for a curvy or gourd-shaped base.
- **Empire.** This slightly tapered design suits myriad lamp-base styles.
- **Hexagon.** With its faceted form, a six-sided shade confers a traditional touch. It demands a lamp base with a similar spirit of rigor and shapeliness.
- **Square.** The bold geometry of a square shade pairs well with a slightly architectural base, such as a rectangular or faceted one. It also looks nice capping a spherical base.

SOFT VERSUS HARDBACK

Shades are either laminated to a backing such as plastic (also referred to as hardback) or hand-sewn. Laminated shades confer a more modern look but will show every nick and dent. Softer hand-sewn versions are often quite traditional and elaborate, as well as more forgiving of wear.

MATERIAL

Many materials are suited to shades: paper, silk, cord, cork, and even string, which can be wrapped around plain paper or a printed fabric for a layered look. "I've even had clients bring in a favorite vintage shirt to sew into a shade—a Pucci or Etro print is especially cool," says Simkin. Soft fabrics are either sewn around an armature or laminated to a backing. When choosing a material, consider both the style of the lamp base and any surrounding decorative elements, such as wallcoverings and upholstery.

- **Paper.** The most commonly used (and affordable) material, paper comes in various colors and opacities and can be detailed with painting, stenciling, cutouts, and other decorations. Paper can even be shellacked to a patinated sheen. Most fabric shades are laminated to a paper backing for support.
- **Cotton.** Versatile cotton is ideal for many applications. It has a nice body that lends itself well to pleating treatments.
- **Silk.** The most formal of fabrics, shimmery silk also has a subtle texture that bestows depth and dimension to a solid-color shade. The material transmits light beautifully. Note that certain silks cannot be laminated.
- **Burlap.** Rough-hewn burlap—as well as jute and raffia—offers a casual flavor, injects texture, and works well with aesthetics ranging

from midcentury modern to French country. The relatively open weave also admits a fair amount of light.

TRANSLUCENCY

Some applications will demand a relatively translucent, light-emitting shade, notably work and reading areas where ample illumination is a must. For accent or mood lighting, a greater degree of opacity is often desirable to impart an atmospheric glow. The choice of shade material (as well as any embellishments applied to it) will affect translucency. The bulb can create a visual hot spot on hand-sewn fabric shades, which can be diffused with the addition of a lining.

DECORATIVE TRIM

Fringe, gimp, tape, ribbon, beads, ruffles, and piping are among the many accents that can enhance a shade's design. Contrasting tape encircling the top and bottom bestow a graphic look that can swing modern or traditional, while pom-pom edging can add a sweet touch to a lamp destined for a young girl's bedroom.

PLEATING

There are many pleating options, from spare to fancy. How much fabric is needed depends on the diameter of the shade: from ¾ yard for a 6-incher to 3-plus yards for a shade spanning 30 inches. Bear in mind that not all fabrics will be suited to all pleating styles.

- Flat pleat
- Open box pleat with space
- Opaque box pleat with space
- Flat pleat with cuff
- Shirring
- Smocking

TYPE OF CONNECTION

A shade typically connects to the light fixture by way of a harp. This wire armature is integrated into either the fixture or the shade itself. The existing connection will dictate the *inner* structure needed for a custom shade. When purchasing a ready-made shade, choose one for the particular connection type you have. A lamp can also be rejiggered to accommodate a different connection style (harp being the most flexible). There are three types of harps:

- **Spider.** A spider harp clicks into grooves near the lamp socket and wraps over the bulb; the shade is set on top and secured with a screw-on finial. New shades may require swapping out the existing harp for a new size. (Fortunately, they are inexpensive, readily available, and easy to change.)
- **Uno (or recessed).** This type of connection is integral to the shade itself. Affixing the shade to the lamp is a matter of simply unscrewing the bulb, slipping the Uno ring over the socket, and screwing the bulb back in. No finial is required; the bulb locks the shade into place.
- **Clip-on.** Rather than connect to the lamp base, this simpler style clasps directly to a round (not spiral CFL) bulb.

FINIAL

Many lamps are capped with a finial, the element that secures the shade to the harp. Although its purpose is overtly functional—it's essentially a screw—the finial also allows for decorative indulgence. Styles range from simple, unobtrusive metal cylinders and small wooden balls to figurative elements (leaves, shells) and precious materials such as crystal and coral.

DESIGN CONSIDERATIONS

Account for the type, style, and shape of the lamp base, the interior of the room within which the lamp is being installed, and the function of the light source. Those factors will narrow the choices and help refine the selection of color, pattern, and material. Here are some questions to ask.

What Is the Purpose of This Lighting?

- **Ambient lighting.** An open or broad shade in a translucent material will be most effective to admit ample illumination.
- **Task lighting.** Shades for task lighting are often integrated into the lamp itself. Opt for a translucent or opaque shade in a style that concentrates a pool of light on the reading or work surface below.
- **Decorative lighting.** Take creative license by experimenting with opaque shades or ones made of unusual materials, such as metal. Incorporate ribbons, fringe, or other decorative trimmings.

Where Will the Lamp Be Placed?

The bulb-and-socket assembly must be completely hidden from view. Most designers like to cover the base cap unless it's decorative. In addition, the bottom of the shade should fall at the user's eye level. For a lamp placed on an end table, the shade can be a bit shorter in proportion, because its bottom edge will likely fall below the line of vision anyway. A return—whereby the bottom of the shade folds under to screen the bulb from view—is also possible. A lamp set on a higher surface, such as a tall cabinet or dresser, demands a shade sized to cover the bulb and socket assembly. A top diffuser, which is a translucent disk that shields the direct view of the bulb, is desirable in certain situations—for example, when a lamp on a console alongside a staircase will be viewed from above. (The design must allow heat rising from the bulb to escape.)

What Is the Design of the Lamp Base or Fixture?

In general, it's best to choose two related styles or play against type: echo the shape of the lamp base or deliberately contrast with it. A 1950s ceramic base with textured glaze might suggest either a similarly tactile burlap Empire shade or a more polished, sophisticated variety that echoes its silhouette.

What Is the Style of the Room?

Where does the aesthetic fall on the continuum of traditional to modern? Choose a style that reinforces the design concept and overall decor.

DESIGNING A CUSTOM SHADE

Envisioning a custom shade requires collaborating with a workshop or an artisan who can help evolve and finesse the design. It is the designer's job to communicate her intent and work out how the shade will fit into the surrounding interior.

Custom lampshade fabrication process at the New York atelier of Blanche P. Field.

ART & ACCESSORIES

Decorative and functional art and accessories—from paintings and family photos to vintage pottery and desk sets—are an essential means of bestowing a space with character, quirk, and a lived-in patina. "Art and accessories are a layer of decorating that's every bit as important as the bigger items—the furniture, the rugs, the window treatments—and make a house look like a home and not a showplace," says designer Allison Caccoma.

While not everyone has important artwork, even the tightest budget has room for framed posters and photographs, or the display of a personal collection of memorabilia. Without paintings, prints, objets d'art, and the like, a room can look unfinished, even a bit generic. Accessories channel and telegraph the history and personality of a home's inhabitants. Although the term "accessory" can imply something incidental or secondary, the smaller goods bring meaning to one's everyday surroundings, especially if items are curated and arranged with personal significance and emotional attachment in mind.

"PUTTING TOGETHER A ROOM OR A HOUSE IS A COMPREHENSIVE PACKAGE, THOUGHT OUT DOWN TO THE TINIEST DETAIL."
—Allison Caccoma

ARTWORK

Even a budding collection of art can express or support the space's design concept. Apply the principles of repetition, rhythm, and symmetry, and group items according to color, shape, or theme.

Where to Put It

Walls are the obvious place to hang artwork. Above the sofa or the dining room credenza are popular focal points. But look beyond those expected areas; an odd corner of a room without much else going on can become a special moment of pause with the addition of an artwork cluster. A hallway or a staircase is ideal for conversion into a gallery. So is a bookcase: intersperse small paintings and sculptures among the books, and hang framed works from the front edges of the shelves.

How to Hang It

The method of hanging the artwork is an important consideration. Most common are standard picture hooks, but rails are a more decorative option that allows for frequent rearrangement. Shelves and brackets can also be serviced to display collections on walls. Propping artwork—on a ledge, atop a console, on the floor—is an informal style that affords the ability to switch arrangements frequently. Artwork and mirrors should always be hung by a professional.

Stairwell walls are a willing canvas for a more-is-more installation of art. Philip Mitchell hung a salon-style array of framed works against patterned but softly toned wallpaper. The free-form arrangement of artworks is unified by shape.

The Arrangement

Framed art is usually hung in a linear arrangement, an asymmetrical cluster, or a salon-style collage; keep the following two display strategies in mind:

- **Alignment.** One secret to displaying framed art is to imagine a line from which pictures can "hang," aligned along their top edge. Alternatively, pictures can all be lined up across their horizontal centerlines, set at about 64 inches from the floor. Art can even be leaned on a shelf, thereby aligning along the bottom edges.
- **Free-form compositions.** "Many people are afraid of venturing beyond a uniform grid, but there are so many other hanging options," says designer Alexis Givens. The primary decision is whether or not the installation should be symmetrical. "Template everything with paper first to test out arrangements; adjustments will inevitably happen once you begin hanging pieces." It pays to enlist an expert installer to help with this task.

Framing

The choice of frame and mat color, size, and style can make a big impact. Gilded or metal-leaf frames impart a rich, classical look, as does carved or shaped wood in a rich tone. Frameless mounting adds a modern gallery-like edge to an arrangement.

To unify seemingly disparate images, frame them all the same way: for instance, in a square profile matte black or steel frame. This will put the emphasis on the artwork.

A good frame shop can guide frame and mat selection, which is often a bewildering task. "You can even create renderings in Photoshop to better envision the final result," advises Givens. "I often do this to help clients visualize what their artwork will look like in the chosen frame style."

LIGHTING

Art requires proper illumination. Spotlight it from specially framed recessed downlights or track fixtures, or from individual decorative picture lights mounted above.

The Backdrop

The wall surface behind hung works must also be considered. Should it be neutral? Patterned? Dark or light in hue? The color of the plane behind a framed work impacts the perception of it. Think about the wall as a key part of an overall composition comprising the artwork, the frame, and the larger setting. Dark or neutral tones can set off monochromatic photography. The hues in an important painting might inspire the color scheme of the wall or surrounding room.

Commissioning Artwork

Team with an art consultant or directly with a fine artist to commission a custom piece: a painting, a photograph, a portrait, a work on paper, a sculpture, or even a functional object. Every artist has a different working process, but most commissions will require that the homeowner (or designer or art consultant working on his behalf) make a few trips to the studio; some degree of back and forth via phone conversations, drawings, samples, maquettes, and models will also be needed to finalize the creative direction. If the work is a site-specific installation or being commissioned for a particular spot—above the sofa, in an entrance gallery—then the artist may need to come and take measurements and observe various aspects of the space, including lighting, wall construction, and moldings.

In terms of payment, many artists request a 50 percent deposit. Always discuss financial terms up front, and find out what amount (if any) might be refundable or transferable to a new artwork if necessary.

TOP: The New York apartment of an art collector by Cullman & Kravis. **ABOVE:** A hand-painted decorative screen is a work of art in its own right.

1: A site-specific installation of porcelain flowers seems to spout from an entryway's molding. 2: Lucite wall brackets form pedestals for vases that flank a drawing spotlighted with a picture light. 3: Crayon and pastel sketches of nudes create a delicate collection in contrast to the heavy piece below. 4: In a dining room by Villalobos Desio, a spotlight easel stands beside a dining room display case—one part china cabinet, one part cabinet of curiosities.

ACCESSORIES

Accessories are often chosen to add a dose of color—bringing a jolt to a more neutral space—yet their scale and shape are just as important. Pint-size possessions confer a sense of intimacy, adding an ornamental layer to the many horizontal surfaces that make up an interior. They also help to round out the scale of larger furnishings. Think about objects that could enhance the function of a room or an area while adding a design component: a sterling pencil cup and stationery pad next to the phone, a crystal carafe set on a nightstand in the guest room, an ornamental box to hide remotes on a table in the family room.

How to Choose Them

Accessorizing a space generally entails a combination of editing existing items and adding new ones of varying scale and size to round out the mix or finish a tableau. Items should not only fit in with the decor but also suit the homeowner's personality and lifestyle.

Even the most acquisitive collectors often neglect to procure the slightly larger objects that form a sort of connective tissue. "People tend to have small objects, but what you really need on a tablescape are items that bridge scales and add height," says Allison Caccoma. "Often the task at hand is to add in some new, bigger accessories: decorative boxes, porcelain bowls, a glass hurricane, a stack of books."

OPPOSITE: Kapito Muller Interiors propped an étagère with artworks and sculptures grouped by hue.

Finding the Gems

"Sometimes my clients say they don't have anything suitable for accessorizing, but then I go through their china cabinets, attics, and closets and discover all sorts of forgotten gems," says Alexis Givens. "Most people can't see through their own stuff." Take a cue from how designers approach the exercise of establishing arrangements: gather all your accessories in one place—a dining room table—and then group items by color, material, form, or another common element. Then test out the arrangements in various locations around the house.

Where to Put Them

Consider not only the obvious canvases for vignettes—coffee tables, glass-fronted china cabinets, sideboards—but also oft-overlooked spots such as bookcases and dining room tables. And don't attend to special-occasion spaces alone; windowsills, kitchen counters, bathroom vanities, and other locations used every day make wonderful surfaces for "scaping" too, whether with vases or functional items like pretty soap dishes. And don't ignore these good spots to accessorize:

- **Accent tables.** From coffee to side tables, this genre of furniture is an ideal anchor for an arrangement. Choose objects of different heights to create a sort of skyline; use books as props or pedestals to anchor smaller objects. "I can't overstate the importance of height on a coffee table, which can be achieved by complementing small objects with taller ones like candlesticks and hurricanes, or even a plant in

LEFT: A niche fitted
with glass shelves forms
a de facto showcase
for sculptural objects.
OPPOSITE: Open shelves
are used as display niches
for objets d'art united by
form and color.

a decorative cachepot," says Caccoma. On a low table, consider a bowl that's ornamented on the inside, so it looks nice even when empty. Use an accent lamp to anchor a tableau. Of course, don't give over the whole surface to an arrangement of ornamental objects; save space to put down a glass or a book.

- **Consoles.** From a styling perspective, the long surface allows ample room to play with color, scale, and texture. Consoles also provide vertical space above (on the wall) and below (the empty space and floor underneath). This extremely versatile piece works in myriad locations, from entryways to bedrooms. Sideboards and credenzas offer the same styling opportunity.
- **Dining room tables.** Even when not in use for mealtime, dining room tables are great canvases. "People neglect their dining rooms—they'll just put a few random bowls or a pair of candlesticks there and call it a day," says Givens. "Not much thought is typically given to the table. But the large surface is perfect for displaying a collection"—a mélange of vintage pottery, stacks of dishes, or a sculptural array of mismatched candlesticks.
- **Nightstands.** Keep the arrangement neat and spare. These surfaces are often used to stash a bedside glass of water, a book, and a watch or eyeglasses. Select functional objects such as trays and bowls that double as catchalls.
- **Desks.** Keep form and function in mind when choosing accessories such as blotters, penholders, and tape dispensers. A desk can always benefit from decorative boxes, trays, and other organizing devices.

- **Fireplaces.** The mantel is an expected home for art and accessories, but don't forget the firebox itself. A well-designed fire screen or set of andirons is always nice. Consider propping the firebox of a nonworking fireplace with decorative objects.
- **Bookcases and shelves.** Bookshelves are ideal for showcasing collections. Use them as framing devices for an artful assemblage.

How to Arrange Them

There are many design elements and compositional strategies to put into play when styling.

- **Symmetry and pairs.** The surest route to balance and calm is to exploit sameness. Place two identical objects on either side of a long console or mantel, or choose ones with similar visual weight.
- **Color balance.** Varied objects all in the same palette or color harmony will look like they belong together. Grouping by color keeps an arrangement from feeling too busy.
- **Rules of three.** A trio of accessories, whether disparate or of a piece, is always a safe bet. Choose items of different shape, color, height, and material to give a grouping some frisson.
- **Elevation changes.** Pair low with high to give a tableau a sense of energy.
- **Positive/negative space.** Important objects need breathing room while less special pieces can benefit from being grouped together so the beauty is in the aggregate.
- **Telescoping.** Stack and arrange objects from large to small.

ONE BOOKCASE, FOUR WAYS

Alexis Givens styles a bookcase in various arrangements.

1. TIE TOGETHER A TABLEAU WITH A THEME: Here, a bird motif takes center stage through images and sculptures; even the leaning books look like wings. Turn colorful spines to face in for a quieter look and neutral palette—although this strategy only works for infrequently referenced books or those not in heavy reading rotation!

2. SHOWCASE COLLECTIONS: Similarly hued books have been grouped together to create stripes that mimic the decorative box on the left, giving the composition some energy and visual weight. Outfitting a shelf with a small mirror and lamp brings light to a typically shadowy space.

3. KIDS' POSSESSIONS: For shelves in kids' rooms, the goal is to display and play. Use bookcases as a rotating space for artwork, block creations, and beloved books so that kids feel pride and a sense of ownership. Add whimsy by trimming a shelf with fabric bunting, ribbon, or washi tape.

4. MOUNT ART: Transform simple shelves by hanging a piece of art in front.

THE ART OF STYLING

Alexis Givens explains the design principles she deployed to create alternative scenarios for a console. She used artwork, accessories, books, and natural ephemera as props. The same thinking could be applied to a tabletop, shelves, or any other surface. It's possible to learn the fine art of arrangement through both trial and error—keep tweaking until a tableau starts to gel.

1: This symmetrical and rectangular setup is very balanced visually, largely because of pairs: two ottomans, two ginger jars (decorative elements that double as bookends). The eye settles nicely on a central point. The large painting becomes the background for everything else and introduces verticality to the composition. Sculptural objects in classic shapes like triangles, squares, circles, and rectangles intermingle to impart geometric balance. Be attentive to the area below a console: a pair of ottomans fills the dead space (generally a great spot for tucked-out-of-the-way supplementary seating).

2: A few of the same items were reused for this scenario. A pair of desk lamps adds symmetry, while their unexpected shape introduces a curve. (They also act as spotlights.) Books function as platforms for small decorative items and add height. The two stacks helped fill the sliver of visible wall space between the table and painting. Below, just one ottoman was used; filling the space is a bowl in a similar metallic finish as the lamps and ginger jars. Light and dark items invite a play of contrast.

3: Wall-hung mini canvases coupled with an array of small items on different-level platforms work in concert to make an intriguing vignette. The triangular tabletop setup comprises a jam-packed assortment of books. A round mirror throws a curve into the otherwise linear arrangement of books and helps to pull light into this corner of the room. The smaller items may look haphazard, but taken as a whole the grouping creates a pretty shape.

4: The two paintings in this arrangement are layered to give the elevation an angling that speaks to the topography of books below—the eye moves in a zigzag to take it in. Here, the negative space below the console was serviced for display: towers of books grouped by hue and casually stacked. Flowers add life and an organic shapeliness. With so much dynamism and color below, the tabletop itself merited a sparser approach.

4

COLLECTING & CONNOISSEURSHIP

Ranging from fine art and antiques to small-scale design objects and vintage furnishings, a collection can give a home a sense of culture, taste, history, and pedigree. "The market for collectible design has exploded in recent years as more movements and makers from design history—especially twentieth-century modernism—have been rediscovered and appreciated," explains decorative-arts specialist Daniella Ohad. "The industrial aesthetic of French midcentury design, the biomorphic sculptural curves of the '80s, the unpretentious forms of mid-century Nordic, the crafted pieces of the Studio Movement, the colorful plastic objects of Italian Postmodernism—all are now highly coveted."

It can be quite challenging for novices to get started. It's best to begin with something you love—a historic period, a color, a place, an artist—and let that be the kernel of a collection. Love 1930s kitchen canister sets? Acquire five sets and line them up in a glass-doored étagère. Inspired by a Caribbean vacation? Start a collection of paintings from the islands. As you go, you will become more aware of which artists are more well-known and which scenes or images you love best, and that will guide you as you grow and refine your collection.

An understanding of value and an educated eye are more necessary than ever in the process of creating a home, and this is an area where the assistance of a professional is often a plus. Whether her work tends to skew more classic or more contemporary, a well-educated designer will be versed in all periods. "A grounding in the history of design is important even when embarking on a modern collection," explains historian and writer Judith Gura. "Knowing the terminology and the common language and signature motifs of each era is key to knowing what pieces go with what, what eras are compatible, and why." In other words, it takes some expertise for a collection to work with—or in contrast to—its setting.

Whether you hope to build a collection, upholster your early-nineteenth-century Gustavian settee in a fabric appropriate to the time, or simply expand your knowledge, here are some ways to educate yourself and become conversant with design history and the collectibles landscape:

- **Visit museums.** "The growing popularity and awareness of design has brought museum curators to expand their collections and to assemble exhibitions that shed light on formerly neglected chapters in design history," says Ohad. A museum is also a great place to look at antiques and gain a sense of what contemporary reproductions are high quality.
- **Peruse galleries.** Galleries have also taken a leading role in promoting vintage gems and in discovering new talents. Many have become producers of contemporary collectibles, working with artisans and designers to release furniture and objects in limited editions.

- **Attend auction previews** and review catalogs (in hard copy or online). "Auction houses have adopted the notion of curated sales, resulting in dozens of elaborate and didactic catalogs every year," says Ohad. Experts are often present at previews and are happy to answer questions about a piece or provide insight on a particular genre or era. Some auction houses host classes and public-education programs.
- **Seek out antiques shows and design fairs.** The dozen upscale fairs that make up the annual circuit have made collectible design available to view and more accessible to acquire, explains Ohad. In most cases, the proprietor is present in the booth and happy to share knowledge about their specialization.
- **Attend lectures.** Design schools and cultural organizations are among the institutes that offer continuing-education programs and lectures targeted to the public.
- **Read books and design magazines.** Books on period design are one of the best ways to educate yourself. So are designers' monographs and other interiors tomes: See how designers use a client's collections to create drama and focus, emphasize color or line, and express the personality of a home.
- **Work with a consultant.** If you are intent on building a valuable collection, retaining an art consultant is a must. Many gallerists or curators often also work independently with individual clients. Or find a designer who seems comfortable with art and antiques of particular periods, and see if he would be willing to assist.

NOTES ON PROCESS

Despite the fun and whimsy accessories impart, the selection process itself can be laborious and time consuming, especially if the project scope entails purchasing all of them (as in the case of a second home or for a major upsizing).

STAGING

Designers sometimes borrow an array of items on approval and stage them in the client's home during the installation process for a test drive before committing. "It's one thing to admire a beautiful objet d'art or figurine in a boutique, and quite another to observe it in context, arrayed just so," says Allison Caccoma.

BUDGETING

Many designers reserve a budget for accessories and art at the project's inception in order to purchase or specify them over a period of time. Some clients choose to wait until the project is close to completion before deciding if they want the project to include the final layer of accessories.

PLAN AHEAD

Thinking about accessories early in the design process helps with selection of finishes. "We start talking about them in the design-concept phase," says designer Pam Shamshiri. "When we present clients the kitchen finishes, for instance, we show the cutlery and the glass and the plates at the same time. You want to think of what will live on the countertop when you pick the material."

UNIVERSAL DESIGN

The built environment should be designed to guarantee ease of mobility and habitability for people of all abilities. That includes young children, the elderly, and those with temporary or permanent physical, psychological, or visual disabilities or challenges. This is the goal of universal design, a philosophy—and set of standards—that expands upon accessibility tenets codified in the Americans with Disabilities Act of 1990.

Although accessibility is obviously paramount in public spaces, it's no less essential in private residences. Even if a homeowner is able-bodied, she may plan to have children one day, welcome guests or visitors with varying needs, or wish to remain in her abode as she ages. Maximizing daylight and minimizing tripping hazards are smart ideas for *every* room. Anyone can benefit from being able to find the light switch in a dark and unfamiliar room, and not having to crawl on hands and knees to unplug a cell phone. A universally designed space is easy to navigate and use no matter what one's limitations or abilities.

Keep the following principles in mind when designing a space:

- Accommodating a wide range of preferences and abilities where possible—for instance, both right- and left-handed access
- Eliminating unnecessary design complexity to ensure simple, intuitive use
- Designing and specifying features that require minimal physical effort to use, such as lightweight doors, lever handles, and soft-close drawers
- Allowing users to maintain a neutral body position (without stretching or bending) and to minimize repetitive actions
- Providing adequate space for wheelchairs and other assistive devices and for approaching, reaching, and using elements from a seated position

A UNIVERSALLY DESIGNED HOME SUPPORTS THE RITUALS OF DAILY LIVING, ENSURING COMFORT, SAFETY, AND SOUND ERGONOMICS.

AGING IN PLACE

Most elderly people need to leave their home (or independent living situations) when they can no longer perform daily tasks unassisted: preparing meals, dressing, bathing. But long before that point, many older adults experience difficulty seeing, hearing, maneuvering, and with memory. They have uncertain gaits and reduced stamina, feel dizzy or unsteady, and can no longer see well enough or distinguish colors and the edges of furnishings and interior elements.

If the residents intend to remain in their home for as long as possible, then specific features should be planned from the inception of the design process:

- Designing a stepless entry
- Locating a bedroom and an accessible bathroom on the ground floor and stacking two closets for a future elevator install
- Specifying lever handles and pulls instead of knobs
- Installing a curbless walk-in (or drive-in) shower
- Siting kitchens cabinets, counters, equipment, and fittings within easy reach from a seated position
- Installing outlets, switches, and receptacles at 42 inches above the floor, or at counter height if possible
- Accommodating wheelchair use via 32- to 36-inch-wide doorways, minimal level changes, and hard flooring
- Incorporating open shelving and low counters

VISITABILITY

The principle of visitability is a pillar of universal design. A home should welcome guests of all abilities by offering a way to gracefully and easily enter, join a gathering, and fully and independently navigate main spaces. Key points include stepless entries, low door saddles, wide doorways, halls and rooms with areas to turn, and circulation paths with few obstacles. Kitchens and baths are high-use areas for residents and for visitors alike; see pages 379 and 427 for incorporating universal features in those spaces.

BEING MOBILITY-IMPAIRED SHOULD NEVER PREVENT SOMEONE FROM FEELING WELCOME. ACCESSIBLE FEATURES ON THE MAIN FLOOR ARE FUNDAMENTAL TO A PHYSICALLY, PSYCHOLOGICALLY, AND SPIRITUALLY BARRIER-FREE HOME.

DESIGN CONSIDERATIONS

Universal design is an all-encompassing world-view that ensures not only physical usability but also visibility (via bright and high-contrast finishes) and audibility (loud-enough doorbells). Another essential detail is preventing scalding from hot water. Many design features customary in health care settings can be reinterpreted for private residences, from nonslip flooring to flat-entry shower stalls.

Think about providing the following:

PATHWAYS AND NAVIGATION

- Clear, obstacle-free walkways: hallways at least 42 to 48 inches wide; exterior pathways of at least 36 inches
- Doorways to all rooms (and closets) that are 32 to 36 inches wide, with a half-inch (or lower) beveled-top threshold
- A 5-foot-diameter clear, open space in every room for turning a wheelchair
- A 36-inch clear space on both sides of the bed (60 inches on the closet side)
- Secure, easy-grip handrails on all ramps, steps, stairs, and porches
- Lever-set easy-to-grasp door handles mounted at 37 inches and, for front and back doors, a dual-function release dead bolt
- Lightweight interior doors requiring no more than 5 pounds of force to open
- An absence of floor elevation changes in rooms (and wherever else possible)
- Windowsills no higher than 30 inches for fire egress

VISIBILITY

- Thermostats and touch pads with easily readable large-print numbers and controls, mounted at 53 inches above the floor (48 inches for wheelchair users)
- Contrasting colors between doorjambs and adjacent walls
- Light or off-white walls and countertops; avoid dark-colored paint and finishes where possible

FLOORING

- Easy-to-maintain commercial-grade nonslip flooring and dense low-pile or -loop carpeting over thin, dense commercial-type padding
- Antislip backing for all large area rugs (avoid using small throw rugs)
- Use dense low-pile or no-pile rugs as much as possible
- Easy-to-maintain water- and slip-resistant floor-surface materials in light colors for the kitchen, laundry, and bathrooms
- Avoid ceramic and porcelain tile unless it has rectified edges that allow it to be installed butt-joined, without grout

FURNISHINGS

- Furniture with rounded corners that is properly scaled for the room and adequately firm (so it's easy to get into and out of)
- Mattress top no higher than 22 inches
- Chairs and sofas with arms to facilitate rising

NATURAL AND ARTIFICIAL ILLUMINATION

- Glare-free illumination
- Use skylights wherever possible to maximize daylight
- High-quality general-illumination and task lighting
- Light fixtures with electronic ballasts and linear or compact fluorescent lamps in 3500K to 4100K color range or LEDs
- Large illuminated rocker-type light switches located within easy reach of room entrances and mounted at 42 inches above the floor
- Automatic on/off night-lights in bathrooms and along the pathway between bed and bath
- Energy-saving motion-sensor controls for bathrooms (also consider for closets and exhaust fans)

HOT WATER

- Whole-house antiscald valve set at 120 degrees max (100 degrees for those with spinal-cord injuries) and located at the outlet-line side of the main hot-water heater; alternatively, install at the hot-water line of all sinks and the bathtub
- Heat-insulate all exposed waste and hot-water lines and site them below the sink or place behind an easily removable recessed panel

MATERIALS

- Products and finishes requiring minimal maintenance and upkeep and that do not produce VOCs

ELECTRICAL

- Ground fault interrupter (GFI) electrical wall outlets mounted at wet locations 42 inches above the floor
- Mount telephone jacks in all rooms at 12 to 16 inches above the floor; install wall-mounted safety phones in bathrooms, the laundry room, and the kitchen
- Choose Energy Star–rated exhaust fans with correct airflow capacity and very quiet operation (1.0 sone or less). Mount control switch at counter front (or where it is easily reachable when seated)

CLOSETS

- Height-adjustable poles and shelving
- Pull-out open shelves
- Fluorescent lighting with switch mounted outside and directly adjacent to the door (or automatic door switch)

LAUNDRY/UTILITY ROOM

- Front-loading washer and dryer with front-mounted, easy-to-use and -read controls; platform-mount both approximately 9 inches above the floor

Note that all measurements are to center and above the finished floor.

ROOM-*by*-ROOM CONSIDERATIONS

Certain design elements are common to every room in the home. These include an appropriate (and suitably diverse) lighting scheme, a good sense of spatial flow, and a functional layout. No matter the space, it should be designed to support the short list of primary activities taking place there, which will differ depending on the homeowner's lifestyle. (Some people read or work in the den, others watch TV there.) So while every dining area shares signature features—namely, an eating surface plus seating—they could be specified in any number of ways depending on the size of the room, the number of diners, and the desired ambience: a quartet of bentwood chairs around a Parsons table, a pair of leather-covered stools at the kitchen countertop, long benches spanning a refectory table. The key dimensions included throughout this section aren't hard-and-fast rules—much depends on a particular space—but are useful guidelines. Indeed, there is no formula or recipe for designing a room, but there are frameworks and specific questions to ask, and considerations to keep in mind for every type of space.

ENTRYWAYS

Entryways create an experience, a sense of physical and psychological pause upon arriving and departing. An entry is a threshold, a word that has a concrete definition as well as symbolic content. "Crossing a threshold" can mean simply entering from the outdoors in, or passing from room to room, but it's often used narratively to describe transitioning into a new phase of life, making a serious commitment, or entering an inner sanctum. All entrances tap into this deeper meaning, conjuring a sense of anticipation and heightened awareness and, conversely, creating a moment of release and exhalation.

AN ENTRYWAY IS ALSO A PLACE
TO EXPRESS THE PERSONALITY
OF THE HOME AND ITS RESIDENTS
THROUGH CAREFUL SELECTION OF
COLOR AND PATTERN, LIGHTING
AND FURNISHINGS.

RIGHT: David Scott balanced a sense of airiness and enclosure in the foyer of a Southampton home, cladding the expansive space in rich wood slats. The bare floor and wide span of glass instill a gallery-like feel, reinforced by the sculptural console. **PREVIOUS SPREAD:** A millwork element that accommodates overhead lighting folds down to create a fireplace surround in an apartment by Tamara Hubinsky.

THE BIG QUESTIONS

- Is this the front or back entryway to the residence? The main or auxiliary one? Location and status will influence the level of formality as well as practical considerations regarding storage for items such as shoes, coats, packages, and mail.

- Who will be using the entry and how often? Is this portal primarily for guests or for daily use by the inhabitants?

- How do the homeowners want to present themselves to visitors?

- Where does the homeowner's lifestyle fall on the spectrum of casual to formal?

- Does one enter this space from the outdoors (a walkway, a front porch, etc.) or from another interior, such as the hallway of a large apartment building or a garage? Exposure to the elements—and whether those entering will have wiped their feet already—may inform how hard-wearing the finishes need to be.

- Is the space enclosed by walls or a door, or does it open directly onto (or offer sight lines into) a number of other rooms? (In the latter case, it is important to choose cohesive wall and floor finishes and give attention to the visual flow between the spaces.)

- What is the atmosphere and color palette of adjacent spaces?

- Is the main staircase located here?

- Does the entry need to serve other purposes, doubling as a library or an art gallery, for instance? In space-challenged urban apartments, entries are often used as a dining area or an auxiliary sitting spot, or for storage.

KEY DIMENSIONS

- Door clearance: 36 inches
- Console or counter height: 34 to 38 inches
- Mirror height: the center point should be roughly 5 feet above the floor
- Electrical outlet height: just above the counter or console surface
- Runner: surround with 3 to 15 inches of floor space on either side
- Coat closet: 2 feet deep inside and 5 to 6 feet wide; allow 4 to 6 inches of pole width for each coat, and about 18 inches of depth

An oversize artwork and tableau of special pieces transform a small entryway by Villalobos Desio into a special moment. The pieces offer a preview of what's to come—announcing the home of a collector—while the space addresses functional needs like seating and storage.

SIGNATURE ELEMENTS

Whether the entry is a grand foyer or a more serviceable arrival zone, these areas provide welcome, shelter, and a practical place to store coats, keys, packages, handbags, and the like. The following elements should be included as part of an entryway:

1 LIGHTING

Appropriate lighting—a table lamp, decorative chandelier, or wall sconces—to supplement recessed overhead fixtures. This combination creates a sense of atmosphere and helps people find shoes and keys more easily. Ceiling fixtures should be as bright as possible—ideally fluorescent bulbs or track lighting. Be sure to locate light switches within arm's reach of the door.

2 COAT CLOSET

A closet large enough to accommodate approximately twenty coats, short and long. To maximize usability, avoid sliding doors in favor of hinged ones, for a wider opening. Ideally, a closet also needs an upper shelf for items such as hats and bags. Many homes without a closet use an informal coat tree or wall-mounted pegs and hooks to hang everyday jackets and hats. A common feature of country or eclectic interiors is a multipurpose hall bench that combines seating, coat pegs, hat shelf, and basket storage (for gloves, mittens, shoes, and scarves).

3 SEATING

A place to sit—such as a chair, an ottoman, or a bench—for one or two people to put on or remove shoes (and, in some cases, change into slippers). It's common to flank a console with two chairs or to tuck an ottoman below. Even a small stool will suffice in a snug space.

4 MIRROR

Aside from its primary purpose—to check a reflection upon entering or before leaving—a mirror also visually expands a space, which can be a desirable feature in small quarters.

5 SURFACE

A console table, a small chest, or a wall-hung shelf can serve as a surface to corral keys, packages, mail, and other items. Or, if square footage permits, use a central table, ideally round (for better circulation).

Cullman & Kravis envisioned an elegant foyer that reflects its owner, an art collector. Next to the door is a sideboard with mirror above; on either side of the portal to the living room are low benches upholstered in a tiger print. Grandly scaled moldings and a ceiling sheathed in glazed aluminum leaf amplify the sophistication.

DESIGN & DECORATING CONSIDERATIONS

The design scheme of the entry area should introduce the homeowner's lifestyle and aesthetic preferences, and relate to or complement the palette of the adjacent rooms.

Neutral or Bold?

If the entry is fairly open to contiguous spaces—with wide doorways and abundant sight lines, for instance—more neutral colors and finishes are generally favorable, so as not to clash with what's to come. Even if the foyer is relatively self-contained, it should still feel of a piece with the surrounding rooms and consistent with the overall scheme and vibe. At the same time, because transitional spaces are for passing through, not lingering, they provide an opportunity for making a dramatic statement that would be overbold in a living area: rich or bright paint colors, overscale wallpapers, precious surfacing treatments such as silver leaf, fanciful lighting, and artwork—or all of the above.

Creating Architectural Presence

Often devoid of architectural interest, entries, hallways, and stairwells are rarely destinations in their own right. However, they can often serve perfectly as galleries for showcasing art, photographs, and collections. Such a display can transform a boring pass-through into a spatial experience. Treating a foyer or a hallway as a "gallery" (and even referring to it as such) implies that people will pause there to look more closely.

"ENTRIES ARE A MOMENT OF PAUSE— A DECOMPRESSION CHAMBER. SOMETIMES THEY'RE QUITE CALIBRATED, SOMETIMES *POW!* BUT EVEN WHEN YOU DO A BOLD GESTURE, IT'S IMPORTANT TO RESTRAIN YOURSELF SOMEWHAT: YOU DON'T WANT TO GIVE IT ALL AWAY THE SECOND THAT PEOPLE WALK IN THE DOOR."
—Amy Lau, designer

OPPOSITE: Kati Curtis accented an entry's existing tin ceiling with a vintage light fixture.

What to Do When Walls Are Few

Although front entries are commonly a dedicated and enclosed room or hall, wall space is often limited due to the presence of multiple doorways, or when the space houses a staircase. In this case, cohesion and decorative interest can come from a special floor or ceiling treatment or a hanging light fixture, such as a pendant or a chandelier. Establish a focal point with a bold door color, or create a sense of place by using a strongly patterned or whimsical wallcovering.

Carving Out an Entry Zone

In smaller and less formal homes—and in many urban apartments—the front door often opens directly into a living area (or the kitchen). In this case, strategic use of furnishings and floor, wall, or ceiling treatments—a bench or slipper chair for removing shoes, coat hooks on the wall—can help establish an entry zone that's suitably special. Conjure the illusion of a discrete hall through a well-conceived furniture plan: facing the sofa away from the door and placing a console behind it, for instance, or selecting a custom rug with a bold border to evoke the feel of a room within a room.

UNIVERSAL DESIGN

- Full-length sidelights (or in-door window) or double peepholes: one at 54 inches in height, one at 42 inches
- Front doorbell able to be heard throughout house
- A minimum of 18 inches on the "pull" side of every door; 12 inches on the "push" side

ABOVE: Palm-frond wallcovering makes a welcoming statement—and graphic impact—in a room by Pamela Banker Associates. OPPOSITE: A super-functional entry nook by Gideon Mendelson features a built-in bench with storage drawers below and a row of wall hooks for stashing coats and bags.

BACK ENTRIES & MUDROOMS

Located at a back door or at the transition from garage to home, mudrooms are primarily for use by the homeowners and are more overtly functional and hardworking than their front entry counterparts. Sometimes mudrooms even house washers, dryers, and ironing boards, or are used to store groceries and bulk paper goods, thereby functioning as a laundry, pantry, or housekeeping closet. All of the signature elements of a front entry should be present plus the following:

- Somewhere to store dirty boots, sneakers, sports equipment, and jackets
- As much storage and shelving space as possible
- Durable, stain-resistant, and easy-to-clean flooring, such as porcelain tile, slate, or washable indoor/outdoor rugs

LIVING AREAS

A living room is a place to tell a story, appealing to different moods, purposes, and personalities. More than any other room in a home, the living area takes on many guises—from a laid-back family room, frequented morning till night, to a formal space used primarily when entertaining. A living area can be a large den furnished with multiple seating groups or an intimate conversation area for four in one corner of a studio apartment, with a bed set up to double as a sofa.

Regardless of its demeanor, a living area must be designed to support the specific activities taking place there, whether solo time or social gatherings, quiet reading or group TV watching. The other imperative is to determine exactly how formal or casual the room should be; will users perch or sprawl on the sofa, for instance? The answer will guide everything from the choice of fabrics to the furniture layout and plushness of the seating. Experienced through the senses, it should be designed with deep attention to surfaces to be touched and to visual delights—how views are framed or an artwork showcased—inviting the eye and mind to linger.

"DON'T LISTEN TO THAT OLD SAW ABOUT HOW THREE PEOPLE NEVER SIT ON A SOFA. BEAUTY OR POWER (OR A COMBINATION OF THE TWO) WILL LOAD A SOFA WITH ARDENT OCCUPANTS IN A MINUTE."

—Mark Hampton,
Mark Hampton on Decorating

Strong but quiet patterning and abundant texture distinguish a window-wrapped living room by Stefan Steil.

THE BIG QUESTIONS

- Who are the primary users? Consider everyone in the family: adults, children, pets.

- How many should the room seat?

- What activities or pastimes will take place here: reading, knitting, listening to music, game playing? When and how often? Each activity will likely need its own furnishings and lighting, and a sense of separation.

- Are there electrical outlets near the activity areas? What type? How many are needed?

- What kind of illumination do the activities need? Balance lighting for close work such as crafts or reading with a general ambient glow from table lamps, floor lamps, and ceiling downlights.

- Does the homeowner entertain, and in what manner? Does she host small seated gatherings, large family affairs for seventy-five, or cocktail parties at which some guests sit and others stand?

- Is the inhabitants' lifestyle casual or formal?

- Where are the doorways and main circulation routes? Their placement will often suggest where to position the main and secondary seating areas.

- Is there an architectural focal point, such as a fireplace or a picture window?

- Will important artwork or a collection be displayed?

- Do people watch TV here? Should the monitor be the central focus of the primary seating arrangement? Should it be exposed or hidden?

- What is the flooring material, and can (or should) it be changed?

- Will there be area rugs? If so, it's important to size them appropriately, relative to the furniture groupings and circulation paths.

OPPOSITE: To make a snug living room appear grander in scale, Villalobos Desio specified a wall-to-wall striped carpet and streamlined window treatments that extend all the way to the ceiling.
ABOVE: Kristin Fine faced a challenge in designing a furniture plan for this living room. Although large in size, it features an overabundance of doorways: two leading to the adjacent sunroom, and two into the entry hall. She followed the logical flow of foot traffic, using natural circulation routes to define boundaries between seating groups: a pair of benches facing off on either side of the fireplace, and a conversation area with a bay window as backdrop. Bold fabrics are relegated to a small canvas—the pair of Louis side chairs—and specified textured neutrals for the larger pieces.

SIGNATURE ELEMENTS

Given the myriad activities that take place in a living area, it must include a mix of seats and tables, layered illumination, and carefully integrated AV and electronic equipment. Storage is another critical feature, whether built-in or freestanding (a hutch, a cabinet, or an armoire).

1 LIGHTING

A living space needs both general ambient and task lighting. Place fixtures to support the diversity of activities and gatherings expected to take place. Where will someone read a book? Knit? Sketch? Watch TV? Let function—and natural illumination—guide the scheme. A multipurpose space that houses activities throughout the day needs a wide spectrum of light sources:

- Table lamps
- Floor lamps
- Wall sconces
- Art lighting
- A chandelier
- Overhead ambient lighting, recessed or track
- Cove or concealed lighting to impart a glow

2 FOCAL POINT

Every living area needs a focal point of some sort to anchor the primary seating group. It could be a prized artwork that commands attention, or an architectural feature, such as a fireplace or a window wall. In many living areas, it is the TV.

3 SEATING

Every living space revolves around a comfortable seating area, to bring people together and to serve as a restful setting for individual pursuits. To nurture conversation, seating vignettes should be sized for two or more people to talk. If the room is spacious enough, a secondary furniture group is preferred to one large, hotel lobby–like assemblage. Here are some common types of seating:

- **Sofa.** The standard-bearer in a living room offers ample surface area for sitting.
- **Sectional.** Both L- and U-shaped varieties are best for casual hangouts and family snuggling; they're less appropriate for formal interiors.
- **Chairs.** Commingling a diversity of chair styles can lend personality to a room. Chairs also visually balance the larger scale of a sofa.
- **Ottomans and benches.** Ranging from petite footstools to bed-size platforms, they bring another element of scale to the space and can be moved to service different groupings.

4 FLOOR COVERING

A strategically placed area rug anchors and outlines a furniture grouping, enhancing the feeling of enclosure, togetherness, and coziness. Use one large area rug to tie together two seating groups or a pair of smaller, matching rugs—one for each vignette—to create the illusion of rooms within a room.

5 SURFACES

Every seat needs a horizontal surface within reach to support drinks, books, remotes, and the like. Coffee tables can range from a cluster of small pieces to a huge piece holding its own with a grand sectional. Side tables, consoles, nesting tables, and footed stacking trays are other good choices, as is a mobile bar cart.

Every seat in a living room by Cullman & Kravis has a table surface within arm's reach. In addition to making for a highly functional decor, the tables add visual variety in a room typically dominated by seating.

ABOVE: A pair of sofas face off in a sparely appointed living room by Donald Billinkoff, in which modern classics lend sculptural presence. OPPOSITE: A mix of light sources—including a swing-arm sconce—and an offbeat art arrangement distinguish an inviting living area by Neal Beckstedt. The sconce can be repositioned as desired to wash different parts of the room with light or switch up the mood. To give the large canvas hanging over the sofa even more emphasis, he hung two smaller works near a top corner.

SPATIAL PLANNING

Human beings yearn to feel physically and mentally secure when at rest, an idea rooted in evolutionary theory. Since living spaces are for relaxing—for literally letting down one's guard—the furniture arrangement must provide psychologically "safe" places to sit. Essentially, people prefer to sit where their personal space is protected, even a bit sheltered. Accordingly, most conversation areas array seating in an L- or U-shaped configuration. Ideally, seating faces the entry to the space, which abets circulation through the room. In most living areas, spatial constraints and the location of doorways dictate that seats and tables be pushed up against a wall in order to fit. But where square footage permits the grouping to be positioned in the middle of a room, the furnishings and area rug together can create and define a protected outer boundary.

A seating group needs four elements:

- A way to get into it
- A focal point
- Circulation around it
- Comfort

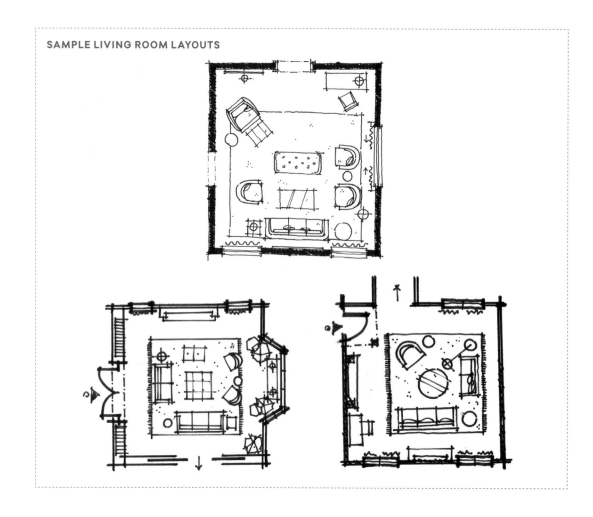

SAMPLE LIVING ROOM LAYOUTS

CONVERSATION AREAS

A room is always based on a module. Although a handful of basic arrangements predominate, variations within the theme are many. Most conversation areas will fall into the framework of a square doughnut: roughly square in proportion, delimited on two or more sides by seating, with an open area in the middle for a coffee table and circulation. One side will typically be devoted to the sofa plus one or two end tables. The secondary seats should be arranged across from the sofa and/or perpendicular to it (which is more conducive to conversation). In either case, the secondary "arm" of seating plus an attendant side table should be arranged to correspond to the length of the sofa arm.

For example: A typical sofa is roughly 8 feet long and 36 inches deep. Bracketed by a pair of end tables, the span equals about 14 feet. Perpendicular to it could go a pair of club chairs and, across, a chaise.

SQUARE DOUGHNUT EXAMPLES

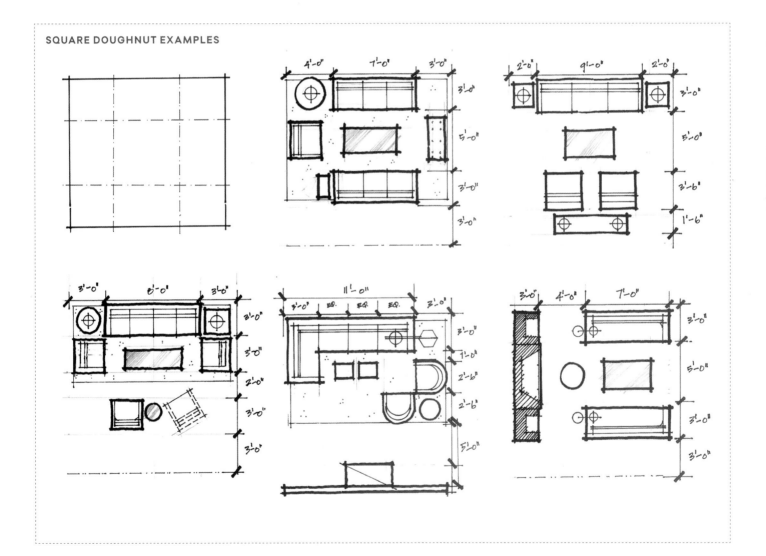

DESIGN & DECORATING CONSIDERATIONS

Living areas are complex, all-day spaces, so a deft layering of scales, colors, textures, and patterns is essential to enlivening a room.

Designing for Interaction

When designing any living area, consider how many people it should seat and what type of interaction it will support: one-on-one conversation, group chitchat, big parties? To create a welcoming, comfortable living area, take a cue from anthropologist Edward T. Hall, who outlined four zones of physical interaction:

- Intimate: 0 to 18 inches for solo time
- Personal: 18 inches to 4 feet for tête-à-têtes
- Social: 4 to 12 feet for groups of three to six
- Public: 12 to 25 feet for large gatherings

Use these zones to determine how many guests a space can comfortably sit. While it may be possible to fit twelve people into a small 10-by-10-foot room, they will likely feel uncomfortable in such tight quarters.

One Seating Area, or Two?

Even in a small room, it is essential to include both a primary seating group—at minimum, a sofa plus two chairs and a coffee table—and a secondary one nearby. "Having more than one furniture group in a room always works better," says designer Bunny Williams. "The scale of furnishings in a living room is so important: you need intimacy, for people to be close to one another. A ten-foot-long sofa with a twin-bed-size coffee table doesn't work—even in a big space where you entertain large groups." The secondary group can be simply an armchair and an ottoman, two chairs flanking a table, or a small settee or loveseat. Table or floor lamps will create a pool of light to emphasize each grouping.

Mix Mobile with Weighty

It's a good idea to balance solid, permanent furniture with pieces that are lightweight and mobile, such as occasional chairs and ottomans on casters. The heavier furnishings anchor the grouping, while the movable ones allow for flexibility in the arrangement depending on the activity or users. "Keep the layout simple, because you can't lock all the furniture into place," says designer Matthew Patrick Smyth. "Once you have guests over or your cleaning person vacuums, things will move around a bit."

How to Size an Area Rug

Think of the area rug as a sort of place mat for a seating arrangement: always size the rug so its edges outline the entire furniture grouping. This means that *all* furnishings should fit *entirely* on the rug—no errant feet stepping beyond its borders. There are two exceptions to this rule. A large rug can sometimes take up much of an entire room, defining and unifying all the furniture atop it, leaving exposed just a few feet of gleaming wood floor. Consoles, bookcases, additional pull-up chairs, or other occasional pieces can occupy the bare-floored perimeter. The other instance is when layering two rugs; for

example, placing a small, precious antique rug atop a larger, neutral stretch of sisal (a great trick to boost visual impact). The sisal should outline the grouping, while the decorative piece should float within its *inside* edges. In no case should furniture sit on a bare floor, grouped around a small rug—an arrangement that does justice to neither rug nor room.

UNIVERSAL DESIGN

Plan conversation areas to allow gracious access for wheelchair users by including a 36-inch-wide circulation path and a 5-by-5-foot clear area for turning around. Rugs should be very flat and dense and well anchored to the floor, providing a good surface for traction. Make everyone feel welcome by removing all obstacles.

ABOVE: Gray tones and metallic accents bring the view—of cityscape and sky—into a living room by Stefan Steil. RIGHT: Carol Egan put a funky twist on a traditional seating group, using a low bench in lieu of a sofa, with a pair of colorful shell chairs across. A small stool serves as the coffee table. The lightweight pieces can be moved around during casual gatherings or to enlarge other conversation areas.

Matthew Patrick Smyth adhered to a traditional furniture plan for a formal living room replete with modern art. Near the fireplace, a secondary seating group combining an eclectic mix of pieces is oriented around a library table.

Specifying a Sofa and a Coffee Table for Comfort

Sizing guidelines for sofa-seat height vis-à-vis the coffee table—its height and distance—are somewhat flexible and interdependent. What's essential is that people can easily reach the table-top from a relaxed sitting position. Accordingly, consider the softness and fill of the sofa cushion; leaning forward from a sink-into-it seat to reach the coffee table can be difficult. In this case, keep the table a bit closer or taller. Or specify a slightly higher sofa when plush cushioning is desired.

Carving Out Space for Kids

Children yearn to exercise their independence, but can do so only in settings in which they feel secure. They naturally gravitate to areas where they have privacy and can play freely. At the same time, they want reassurance that an adult is near. When designing a living space (one not so formal as to be off-limits to children), incorporate alcoves, nooks, and similar features where young ones can play on their own yet within sight or earshot of an adult. A small, comfy chair or a beanbag can beckon them to join the family in reading or other activities.

ABOVE: Overstuffed seating brings a lived-in touch to a living room by Ellen Fisher. Because the upholstery is so plush, she chose a slightly higher-than-usual coffee table for ease of use. **RIGHT:** Suzanne Lovell recessed a flatscreen TV into a stone hearth, ensuring that, when it's turned off, attention stays on the verdant views through the windows.

Incorporating the TV

"In a living area, a television can be quite limiting designwise," says designer Elizabeth Pyne. Think about hiding a flatscreen behind an artwork or a mirror that lifts up or slides aside, or in a custom cabinet with retracting doors. Does the TV even need to be there? "I believe a living room should be a drawing room, a space for entertaining, whereas television watching is an intimate experience, best in a smaller den," Pyne adds. "Unless it's part of how you socialize—or this is the home's only living space—consider relegating the TV elsewhere."

Designing Media Centers

There are a few things to keep in mind if the room is to be used as a media center—mostly for TV watching, video-game playing, and listening to music. Ensure good acoustics by deploying as many soft textures as possible: a rug, window treatments, upholstered furniture or walls, cork wallcovering, and the like. Speaker systems are all-important for enjoyment; an AV specialist can assist with the technical side. To eliminate glare, opt for blackout shades.

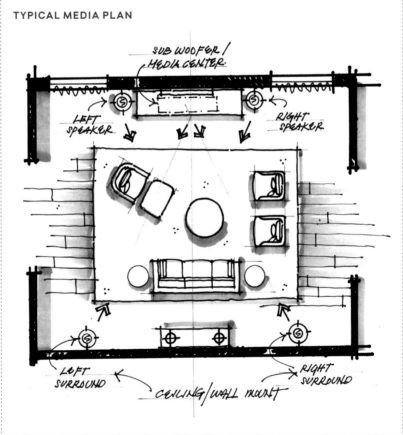

TYPICAL MEDIA PLAN

SUB WOOFER / MEDIA CENTER

LEFT SPEAKER

RIGHT SPEAKER

LEFT SURROUND

RIGHT SURROUND

CEILING/WALL MOUNT

WORK AREAS

Work can take many forms—reading, writing, number crunching—and so can a work area. Residential spaces conceived for these activities range from a large, wood-paneled library to a sliver of kitchen countertop just big enough to house a computer and a notebook or calendar, making it "command central" for a busy family. Thanks to laptops and Wi-Fi, work can be accomplished from any corner of the home, yet most people still prefer a dedicated station for stashing files and accomplishing focused tasks. A home office will ideally offer a work surface and some measure of quiet and visual privacy, plus organized storage.

A WELL-DESIGNED WORKSPACE—
HIGHLY FUNCTIONAL BUT ALSO
INSPIRING—CAN BOOST CREATIVITY
AND PRODUCTIVITY.

A lively but smartly designed office area by Thom Filicia supports serious work while also giving the eye—and mind—plenty to linger on: fine artwork, well-placed accessories, and graphic patterns.

THE BIG QUESTIONS

- Who will be working here?
- What type of work does she do: real-estate sales, household management, legal work, PTA coordination, tutoring, philanthropic efforts?
- What activities does the work entail: talking on the phone, interviewing people face-to-face, spreading out visuals, crafting?
- Is the workplace situated in a public space at the heart of family activities or somewhere buffered from the busy traffic of home life?
- Will visitors need to access the office?
- Will the space be used daily or only occasionally?
- What time of day will it be used most often?
- Are privacy and freedom from distractions a concern—either to aid concentration or because the work requires confidentiality?
- Is a meeting area or a sitting area needed to supplement the work surface?
- What type of equipment will the space house: a computer, a printer, a scanner/copier? Large machines can eat up sizable real estate and need electrical outlets and sometimes surge protection.
- How much and what type of storage is required? Common items to be accommodated include reference books, files, folders, desk accessories, random papers, office supplies, and bulk items such as copy paper, ink, and toner.

For a busy mother of three, Kristin Fine designed a secluded home office that serves as an adult retreat. Dead space below the eave was utilized for low built-ins, while the angular desk stands close to the center of the room. The table lamp has a clear base so as not to block the view.

SIGNATURE ELEMENTS

Regardless of their style or square footage, all home office areas require a work surface, proper lighting, and accessible storage. These same features could fulfill the needs of an informal kitchen "command center," a traditionally appointed library, or a lounge-like study.

1 WORK SURFACE

These can vary in size and format, from a freestanding desk to a shelf or built-in countertop sited in an odd nook. The surface should be ample enough to allow for a laptop or a computer monitor, a pad of paper, and basic necessities such as tape, a stapler, and pencils. File cabinets and a pencil drawer below are added bonuses.

2 TACK SURFACE

An immediately adjacent tack surface or corkboard offers a place for creative types to curate a mood board, for a parent to display school notices and shopping lists, or for an author to pin important papers. Also helpful is a magnetic whiteboard, a blackboard, or another temporary writing surface. (Whiteboard or chalkboard paint is a great alternative to wall-hung boards.)

3 SHELVING

Most work areas require some kind of shelving nearby for books and memorabilia, such as family photographs, diplomas, or trophies. Home offices are also nice venues for displaying artwork and collections of objects.

4 POWER SOURCE

Work areas require appropriately placed electrical outlets and receptacles for Internet connections, routers, base units, phone chargers, and landlines. Outlets wired for surge protection are crucial to accommodate computers and hard drives. Multifunction scanner/copier machines and similar equipment need dedicated circuits and special receptacles.

5 LIGHTING

More than almost any other area of the home, a study or a desk needs to be carefully lit in order to be fully functional. These spaces require general ambient light as well as task lighting to illuminate the work surface. Under-cabinet strip lighting (either LED or fluorescent) can serve this purpose in a kitchen or another room with upper cabinetry. The task lamp should cast a glow that can be focused on the desktop without throwing glare into the eyes of the person working. A lamp is also a design statement that can support the overall look and feel of the room.

OPPOSITE

1: Vintage furnishings—a shelving unit and a leather-topped desk—bring a collected feel to an office by David Scott. A combination of open shelving and closed cabinetry accommodates collectibles and office supplies alike. 2: A wall-mounted shelving system establishes a work zone in an apartment by Stefan Steil. White-painted walls and pale-wood floors uphold the sleek and restful tone established by judiciously styled open shelves. 3: Lacquered walls dignify an alcove office area by Amanda Poole Parisi, Hong Molitor-Xu, and Jamie Drake of Drake/Anderson. Wraparound shelving maximizes available space and helps keep the work surface free of clutter.

KEY DIMENSIONS

- Desk height: 29 to 30 inches
- Counter work surface height :
  36 inches
- Work surface depth: 18 inches or
  more—24 inches is typical; 30 inches
  is best. Freestanding desks should be
  at minimum 30 inches deep.
- Work surface width: 30 to 66 inches
- Outlet height: no less than 12 inches
  above the finished floor; ideally 6
  inches above counter height
- Lateral files: generally 30, 36, or 42
  inches wide and 18 to 20 inches deep
- Vertical files: 24 to 28 inches deep
  and 18 inches wide
- File cabinet drawer: 12 inches high
- File cabinet base: 4 inches
- Pencil drawer: 3 inches high
- Deeper "box" drawer for medium-size
  items: 6 inches high

DESIGN & DECORATING CONSIDERATIONS

The location of the work area within the home will guide numerous design factors: the degree of privacy and protection from distraction needed, the size of the surfaces or storage that can reasonably fit, and how to accommodate visitors. If the office space is being integrated into a living area, it will be important to ensure it looks appropriately residential and not too workaday.

OPPOSITE: Alan Tanksley used a large-scale painting to anchor an airy work area. A stool placed at one end of the desk serves as an auxiliary perch or a place to stash books and objects, keeping the work surface neat. Ample daylight is supplemented by a table lamp that illuminates the primary reading/writing spot. **BELOW:** Matthew Patrick Smyth floated a desk near a bay window to carve out a work zone in a living room. An ottoman placed in front of the vignette keeps it from looking too utilitarian.

Creating a Private Zone

Privacy requirements will vary depending on the nature of the work being done, the documents being used, and the personal preferences of the inhabitants. Scholars and professionals who work at home often require a separate room, with a lockable door, to provide acoustic privacy and prevent interruption. A home office for an accountant or a therapist requires confidentiality for the clients and, by virtue of space planning, a barrier between home and work. A kitchen work area will be effectively open to whoever passes by. When doors and walls are not an option, good storage (including closed shelving and lockable drawers) can safeguard important papers.

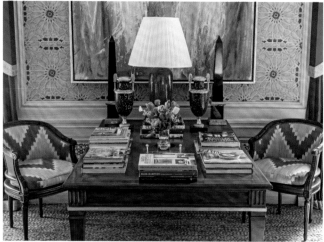

ABOVE: In a grand salon by Alexa Hampton, a large library table flanked by armchairs offers a spot to peruse books—or type on a laptop.

A tonal color palette and dynamic art installation give a home office by CetraRuddy quiet glamour. Since this is not a heavy-duty work area, finishes and materials can be more precious: a sheepskin-upholstered chair, a glass-topped table with Lucite base, and an angular settee.

Avoiding Cord Disorder

Plan in advance where equipment such as printers, scanners, fax machines, routers, and even phone chargers will go, and place their corresponding outlets accordingly. This will help prevent the tangle of cords and wires that inevitably plagues work areas. Under-counter channels and cord ties also help create a professional atmosphere. If a freestanding desk is not anchored to a wall, locate electrical receptacles in the floor, right nearby, so cords don't need to be stretched across the room—which is both a safety hazard and visually undesirable.

How to Store Items

Office supplies and paperwork demand tailored storage: file drawers, shelving, cabinets with doors, and different sizes of drawers specific to their contents. A home office can really benefit from a custom millwork solution.

- **Cupboards and cabinets.** It's preferable to have flexible space to keep stationery, copy paper, ink, toner, and paper towels close at hand. The best kind of storage for miscellaneous objects is a cabinet with shelves, either a cupboard or a closet. Drawers of varying sizes are a great help. Depending on the design of the work area, mount cabinets or shelves directly above the desk.

Cullman & Kravis designed an intimate work spot for a guest bedroom. To one side of the antique desk, built-in shelving showcases personal mementos.

A zebra-print rug grounds an artful study by David Scott. Strong profiles and rich textures, including flannel and mohair, telegraph a masculine vibe.

- **File cabinets.** Both types—vertical and flat files—can be specified with two, three, four, or five drawers. Two-drawer file cabinets for letter- or legal-size paper are sized to fit under a typical 30-inch-high desktop or work surface. Custom desks and cabinets follow the same dimensions.

A Soft (and Softening) Touch

Given the hard surfaces that predominate in home workspaces, these areas can benefit from softer elements to dampen noise and improve acoustics: area rugs or wall-to-wall carpeting, upholstered seating, curtains, fabric-upholstered walls, and even a corkboard or a leather desktop.

Containing Clutter Artfully

Offices can present a challenge for people who like to keep current projects out on their work surface, or who file papers by piling them in stacks on a desk—even when there is enough room for closed storage. The trick to instilling order is to create frameworks to contain clutter: box shelves, trays, and other elements that define a border around—or boundary for—clutter. When office accessories are carefully selected and part of a coordinated set, they create visual order and express the overall aesthetic.

DINING AREAS

Dining areas aren't just where meals are taken. They are a source of nourishment on an emotional level. As places for people to come together and bond with others or to sit down for calming solo time, they play an important role in a home and have deep-rooted cultural significance. Mealtime is a primal moment; the ritual of eating connects people to each other—and to wherever they are.

Contemporary lifestyles have altered the stature and shape of the dining room. Today, many people adopt this underused and formal space for daily activities: to gather with friends, do homework, read a book, play a game, pay bills, write the shopping list. Accordingly, dining spaces are often designed to double as a library, home office, or study. And as modern residential interiors have become more open and fluid, so too has the dividing line between dining and living areas. Meals occur in many more locations in the home (at the kitchen island, at a table in the family room) and often more casually. While a dedicated dining room implies a certain formality, a place for eating within another room connotes relaxed welcome and individuality— and efficient use of space.

Cushioned window seating supplements vintage cane-back chairs in a dining area by Gideon Mendelson.

THE BIG QUESTIONS

- Who will use the dining room?
- Will one person usually eat here alone or share meals with others? How many?
- Is the inhabitants' way of living casual, formal, or somewhere in between?
- How does the family wish to present themselves to guests?
- Will all meals be taken here, or will it only be used at certain times of day (breakfast, dinner) or year (primarily during holidays or weekend dinner parties)?
- What other activities—working, reading, listening to music—occur in the space or on the dining surface?
- How often does the family entertain, and in what manner (cocktails, seated dinners, potlucks, pizza parties)? Will they sometimes use the dining room for buffet service?
- What relationship should this space have with the kitchen? Should the two be separated or more unified?

The dining room of designer Joan Dineen's turn-of-the-century townhouse features elegant wood paneling that is original to the space. Deco-influenced furnishings reiterate the period vibe, while more modern elements such as contemporary art and a vintage 1970s chandelier bring an element of contrast.

SIGNATURE ELEMENTS

Whether in the form of a tucked-away nook or a window-wrapped breakfast room, all dining areas share two elements: seating plus eating surface. Eating spaces present a prime opportunity for indulging in special decorative treatments: scenic wallpaper, a sculptural lighting fixture, an art installation, and mementos. Diners are a captive audience, after all.

1 EATING SURFACE

When people come together to share food and conversation, the focus is on the center of the table or eating surface. The size and shape are usually determined by the number of diners it will accommodate, the proportion and layout of the room, the placement of doors, and the circulation paths.

2 SEATING

The choices are endless: simple, ornate, with or without arms, counter- or standard-height stools, upholstered or bare wood, banquette or bench. Maintain one style or mix two variations, placing the more monumental or formal seating at the heads of the dining table.

3 SERVING SURFACE

A serving surface should be within easy reach of the table. A credenza or a sideboard for storing fancy wedding china and extra linens does double duty as a buffet for serving platters. If space permits, deploy two serving surfaces: a hutch, a movable cart, or even a bookcase will suffice as the auxiliary piece.

4 LIGHTING

Choose illumination that sets the right mood and flatters guests and food alike. Be sure to include the following iterations—all on dimmers, if possible:

- General ambient light
- A large decorative fixture to create a focal point over the center of the table
- Sconces for character and to wash the walls with light as a focal point

5 PASSAGE SPACE

Sufficient passage space around the furniture is needed for ease of circulation and graceful service.

6 ART AND ACCESSORIES

These decorative items should round out the mix and bring a sense of scale to the room, not to mention personality.

7 FLOORING

A rug is optional and depends on personal preference and functional considerations such as cleanliness and acoustics. The flatter, heavier, and larger the rug the better, both to allow ease of movement and to ensure that all chair legs will fit on top even when pulled out.

OPPOSITE: Donald Billinkoff positioned a vintage credenza at the head of a dining table. The attenuated form of the lighting pendant helps wash the entire eating surface with illumination during mealtime. Armless side chairs are easier to shimmy into when the table is full.

A bordered rug gives the dining area of an open-plan loft
by Coffinier Ku a sense of enclosure.

SPATIAL PLANNING

The arrangement of furniture in a dining area will depend on the inhabitants' lifestyle and how meals are taken. For example, large extended families who dine together can benefit from a long table with relaxed seating nearby. If the homeowner hosts formal holiday celebrations, consider several small tables set up near—but not adjacent to—one another. Expansive rooms for frequent entertainers allow for one large or several small tables for sit-down meals; those who lean toward semiannual cocktail parties need open space for a crowd. Certain cultures may also have preferred furniture arrangements.

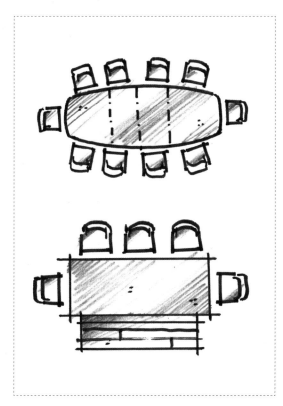

KEY DIMENSIONS

- Dining table height: 30 inches
- Table width: no less than 39 inches (to accommodate dishware) and no wider than 54 inches (to nurture conversation). The width should be proportionate to the length. Square tables should be a minimum of 42 inches across (for reference, standard card tables are 36 inches square).
- Table length: 48 to 120 inches
- Chair seat height: 18 inches
- Chair seat size: a minimum of 18 inches square—usually 18 inches wide by 21 inches deep (arms can add substantial dimension)
- Chair back height: at least 3 inches taller than the tabletop
- Clearance between edge of table and wall or other object: at least 36 inches for circulation
- Distance between midpoints of adjacent chairs around a table: 24 inches
- Distance between table and serving credenza: 36 inches minimum
- Distance between bottom of overhead hanging light and dining surface: about 30 inches (or 60 to 66 inches above the floor)
- Carpet: should extend 36 inches beyond the table (wide enough so all chairs rest on it, even when they're pulled out)

DESIGN & DECORATING CONSIDERATIONS

Dining spaces can range from formal, dedicated rooms to California kitchens, which are a combination of great room and cookery made de rigueur by interior designer Mariette Himes Gomez in the 1980s. Loft living requires designing the dining area as a space within a space, and studio apartments call for double-duty furnishings and activity zones. The selection of table material and base, the lighting scheme, and the chair style—how each looks from the front *and* the back—are critical decision points that will add up to a particular ambience.

Deformalizing the Dining Room

"A formal dining room can be such a waste of space unless you have a big, traditional house," says Neal Beckstedt. "Make it more functional by adding shelving so it can be used as a library, or specify a table that's comfortable for working on a laptop." To create a more versatile space, consider using two small tables (in lieu of one big one) that can be pushed together as needed.

Avoiding an Empty Look

Think about what the room will look like even when not in use. Dining rooms—especially those not frequently in service—can appear woefully uninhabited (and a bit like conference rooms) with abundant empty chairs around a bare table. "I'm not a fan of what I call the 'cluster': a massive table surrounded by tons of chairs," says Beckstedt. "I prefer a smaller table with just one or two chairs, so the dining room looks like a study, and then sprinkling the rest of the chairs around the home or apartment—you can just round them up when dinner guests come. The look is more casual." Or consider designing the space so that extra chairs can be pushed up against the wall, perhaps flanking a credenza or side table.

Accessorizing a Tabletop

"People often neglect their dining room tables—especially in larger homes where daily eating occurs elsewhere," says designer Alexis Givens. "Dining rooms are often just furnished with a table and chairs so they don't have much going on decorwise; a single bowl or pair of candlesticks won't cut it in this case. Use a large, underutilized dining surface to create an installation or showcase a cool collection of larger items: vases, stacks of dishware, an array of different candlesticks."

Dramatic Lighting for Mealtime

Overhead fixtures, such as chandeliers and pendants, are the jewelry of the room and can make for a dramatic statement, but they often don't give off enough light. A dining room is a stage, and it can benefit from a theatrical approach to illumination. Supplement a chandelier with sconces or lamps to vary the heights of light sources around the room; add discreet recessed downlights to provide an ambient glow, to focus on the china collection or food display, and to spotlight the table surface. Cove lighting in the ceiling adds an elegant touch.

Rug or No?

The casual dining space of a family with young children is not a good spot for a hard-to-clean rug; an unadorned floor will probably be best. In a less used or more formal dining space, however, a carpet will add a decorative layer, soften sound, and warm up the room. Choose a pattern busy enough to hide stains, and avoid hard-to-clean fibers such as wool. Some decorators avoid carpets no matter what. "I think rugs look awkward below the dining room table," says Amy Lau. "They also trap crumbs. If the flooring in the room is tile, I'll sometimes design an inset faux rug using another tile pattern or variety, but usually I just leave the floors bare and put the design emphasis elsewhere." Put pads on chairs' feet to protect a wood floor.

Pick the Right Tabletop Material

Natural finishes, such as wood and stone, are most common for tabletops. Wood offers the most traditional mien and greatest stylistic variety, from a rough-hewn weather-beaten farmhouse table to a more formal French-polished gem. But functional needs must guide the selection too. Factor maintenance into the decision, and be realistic about the degree of use and abuse the table will receive. Hot plates can mar certain finishes, silverware can scratch, and wet drinks can leave behind rings. More modern man-made options—glass, laminate, quartz composite, and solid surfaces such as Corian—are nice alternatives, especially for countertop dining. Regardless, no material is impervious, and all need care during and after use.

Choose Integrated Leaves

The most versatile table style is one with built-in leaves that slide out from the ends or rise from the center when needed. (Keep in mind that it is unusual to find a glass table with the ability to expand.) A caveat: drop-leaf or insert materials such as wood may fade, age, or patinate differently from the tabletop proper if the leaves are not exposed to light—if they are stored in a closet, for example, or even within the table itself. Leaves can also warp over time.

1: A sunlit family room by Suzanne Lovell accommodates both living and dining areas. The latter is furnished in a mix of leather director's chairs and slipcovered armchairs that tie into the decor of the sitting area. For ease of maintenance, the stone floor below is left bare. 2: A restful palette of blues unifies varied elements in an open-plan living/dining space by Amanda Poole Parisi, Hong Molitor-Xu, and Jamie Drake of Drake/Anderson. 3: Paul Siskin chose a walnut dining table for the eating area of his open-plan (and open-to-the-elements) residence. The timber top nicely coordinates with wood slats cladding the nearby fireplace wall. A collection of candlesticks dresses up the tabletop.

OPPOSITE: Villalobos Desio lent a pass-through dining area presence with prominent artwork and a modern pendant light. Bucking conventional wisdom, a pair of backless stools anchor either end of the table where armchairs typically preside. **ABOVE:** A slim, spare console accompanies a dining vignette by Stefan Steil—and serves as a pedestal for a cluster of objets. The chair legs and table base have a simpatico sensibility, creating a dynamic composition of angled lines.

ANATOMY OF A DINING TABLE

The minimum table length to comfortably accommodate six standard-size dining chairs is 72 inches. A rounded top, such as an oval, will seat even more than a rectangular format. Also consider the base design: a central pedestal is more user-friendly than perimeter legs.

TOPS

The layout of the room and how people will congregate affect the choice of shape.

- **Square or rectangular.** Although it's the most popular shape, a rectilinear top may be less adaptable to accommodate large groups of diners, because the corners limit where chairs can be positioned. Stylistically this category is quite varied, from a modernist Parsons table to a farmhouse-style refectory table with a trestle base.
- **Round.** Great for square rooms and/or fewer diners. An Eero Saarinen Tulip table is a popular choice that works with a variety of room aesthetics. A round table is especially nice for rectangular spaces that need versatility; positioned at one end of a room, it will leave enough floor space on the opposite end for a secretary-style desk or a full-height bookcase. Hexagonal and octagonal tables are similarly versatile, although the sides will dictate the number of chairs that can pull up.

A pedestal-base dining table works best in tight quarters, like this dining area by Kati Curtis.

- **Oval.** The most versatile surface, an oval is particularly useful in tight quarters given the curved profile. Many diners can congregate around this elongated top, yet still join in on a single conversation. A racetrack top is a variation that has rounded ends but straight sides.

DINING TABLES

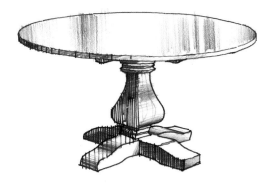

PEDESTAL

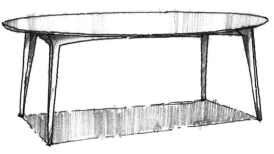

CORNER LEGS

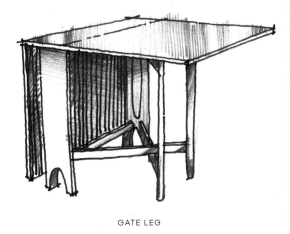

GATE LEG

BASES

The style will affect how chairs can be pulled up under the table.

- **Pedestal.** A pedestal offers the most legroom and is the most flexible design. This style is particularly suited to small rooms or a large number of diners.
- **Corner legs.** The most classic style. The location of table legs will limit both the number of chairs at the table and their placement.
- **Gate leg.** A swiveling leg allows this convertible style to expand as needed to accommodate more diners. It is great for rooms that host sizable but infrequent gatherings.
- **Trestle.** These tables have two or four trestles (or legs) connected by a board at the base. They have a nice, sculptural presence but offer less legroom than others.

APRON

Always check the clearance between the underside of a tabletop or apron edge (the small vertical support beam that is recessed under a tabletop) when calculating the height of dining chair arms.

KITCHENS

In a residential setting, the kitchen represents sustenance and nurturing. The place where food is stored and prepared is indeed the heart of the home—a central hub in which myriad activities and interactions take place. Of all the rooms in a home, the kitchen is the perfect design challenge, marrying purpose with appearance and meaning.

The design inevitably starts with pragmatic concerns: a kitchen's foremost function is to support the specific choreography of cooking and preparing meals. The room's constituent elements—cabinets, counters, appliances, wine coolers, etc.—are fixed in place, can be expensive, and take up sizable square footage. The logistics and minutiae of renovation often eliminate many options and possibilities—which can actually help narrow the sometimes overwhelming options and decisions a kitchen design presents. The most inviting kitchens not only expedite the labor of prepwork and cooking but are also a destination in themselves, welcoming guests and family to relax and hang out.

In designing a kitchen that's open to both a living area and the outdoors, Paul Siskin eschewed overhead cabinets. The result is a more furnished cookery that recedes from view, blending in with the scenery and the surrounding decor.

A wall of full-height cabinetry offers abundant storage in an island kitchen by Donald Billinkoff. The adjacent wall is free of upper cabinets for a streamlined look.

THE BIG QUESTIONS

- Who will be using the space? Consider not only the primary chef(s) but also children who may prepare snacks for themselves. Are there any household helpers—a housekeeper or a nanny—who should weigh in on decisions or be asked to provide additional insight into functional needs?

- Will two people be cooking together at times?

- How does the homeowner live? Does she spend lots of time in the kitchen? In that case, the goal may be to make the room feel convivial, allowing space for others to join. Someone who rarely cooks may only need a small, serviceable galley.

- Do religious or cultural practices, such as keeping kosher, have an impact on the quantity, design, or placement of storage or appliances?

- Does the kitchen need to be handicapped-adaptable or -accessible? A universal, flexible design can give a kitchen longevity and allow for aging in place.

- Which meals (if any) will be taken here?

- What other activities will occur in the space? Homework? Household administration? A dedicated work area, planning station, or surface on which to spread out papers or use a laptop may prove essential.

- Does the homeowner have pets? If so, the kitchen may need to house a dog bowl and crate, a kitty litter tray, or a fish tank.

- What degree of maintenance is the home-owner prepared to handle? The answer will help identify the most appropriate materials and finishes, especially for countertops, flooring, and faucets.

- Do windows need to be treated with curtains or shades? It's important to design cabinetry and moldings to accommodate any tracks or headers.

- Does the homeowner entertain? Does she often hire a caterer? Many people invite guests to congregate in the kitchen, and prefer that it be open to adjacent living spaces. Those who entertain in a more formal manner often desire separation, or at least a door to close off the kitchen from the dining room.

- Does the kitchen require a separate pantry to store serving pieces and place settings, linens, or bulk items?

- Does the client cook in a particular style, requiring specific appliances or extra ventilation?

- Does the homeowner adhere to organic or special diet requirements, such as vegetarian-ism, which may require specialized storage (for instance, a refrigerator with an extra-large produce compartment)?

- Is specialty storage needed for juicers, bread machines, blenders, slow cookers, coffee-makers, and other small appliances?

- How ardently does the homeowner recycle? Does she compost? Can there be a food disposal in the sink? Planning recycling bins and compost containers in advance can save time and costs later.

SIGNATURE ELEMENTS

Technological advances have boosted the efficiency of the kitchen and altered its appearance—yet the basics have remained unchanged for millennia: a source of water for cleaning and cooking, a surface for preparing food, a heat source for cooking, and storage. Additional luxuries include specialty appliances plus space for activities such as lounging, playing, and working.

1 REFRIGERATION

A kitchen needs a refrigerator/freezer, in the form of a standing unit or under-counter drawers. The choice will depend on the overall kitchen design as well as the homeowner's cooking and eating habits. Someone who cooks infrequently and eats out often may not require abundant storage of dry goods and fresh produce, but might benefit from extra space to store leftovers and take-out containers.

2 SINK

Many cooks like to have two sinks—one for cleaning pots and pans, a smaller one for prep work—while others want just one large sink. At least one extra-deep basin is required, serviced by a high spout (with flexible spray for filling big pots) and, ideally, a built-in soap dispenser.

3 HEAT SOURCES

Options for these include a standard or convection oven, a stovetop, a microwave, and broilers. A warming drawer may also be desirable; many newer ovens have a warming option. Make sure there are surfaces nearby to set down hot pans or heavy dishes.

4 VENTILATION

To work most efficiently, the vent hood (or other mechanism) requires adequate power and placement near an exterior wall or window—or at least on a wall or ceiling where hot air can be vented to the exterior. The shorter the distance between the unit and the outdoor vent, the better. If the room does not vent to the outside (as in some apartment buildings), a recirculating model is needed.

5 SURFACES

These are necessary to cut and prepare food, and for use as a holding area for items to be served. Vary counter height to accommodate chefs of different statures, to support specialized tasks such as rolling dough, or to create visual interest by breaking up a monotonous run of surface material. (Height changes are also helpful in solving the problem of where to place counter seams.) Pay special attention to the design of the counter edge; its profile (flat, ogee, bullnose) should reinforce the overall aesthetic. Consider a dedicated spot for a cookbook (digital or print) to be placed when prepping food.

6 TRASH

Kitchens produce garbage of varying types—from food scraps to packaging—and thus require assorted disposal containers: a trash can, recycling bins, and composting centers.

OPPOSITE: Bar stools service the waterfall-edge counter of a peninsula kitchen by Phillip Thomas.

7 LIGHTING

Illumination should be located over the sink, prep surface, and island or peninsula. A mix of decorative pendants, under-cabinet task lighting, and ambient sconces can augment overhead fixtures. LED technology makes bulb changing practically a thing of the past.

8 DURABLE FLOORING

Wood brings warmth to a kitchen but is not the sturdiest choice underfoot, where it will be subject to moisture and wear. Easier-to-maintain ceramic tile, however, is harder on the joints during long periods of standing. An alternative such as cork is more forgiving on knees and dropped glassware and helps dampen sound; nonslip area rugs and mats over hard floors can serve the same purpose. Mixing materials or designing a border or inset can help visually "break up" the wide expanses of flooring that are common in kitchens.

9 SEATING

People often think of the kitchen as a standing space, but seating is just as important: for eating, meal prep, lounging, reading, and working. Supplement stools for counter-height seating with dining chairs or a banquette when there's room for a dedicated eating area. Remember that even the cook needs a perch during a long day!

EXPERT ADVICE

The kitchen is a highly complex and technical space. The location of extant plumbing supply and waste lines can lock a new design into an existing configuration. Many appliances have voltage requirements that may monopolize available electrical capacity. A project can benefit from the expertise of an interior designer and allied practitioners, such as a knowledgeable general contractor, a certified kitchen designer, an architect, and an AV specialist (particularly if flatscreens or sound systems are to be integrated). Such team members are invaluable in helping navigate the complexities and potential complications that can bedevil a build-out, and layer in design advice based on their experience and the site conditions.

OPPOSITE: Decorative painting graces an island in a kitchen by Amanda Poole Parisi, Hong Molitor-Xu, and Jamie Drake of Drake/Anderson.

SPATIAL PLANNING

Kitchens come in many shapes and sizes, but most conform to a handful of standard layouts: single run, galley, U-shaped, L-shaped, island, and peninsula. (Sometimes there's a separate spillover space such as a walk-in closet, a butler's pantry, or a larder.) No matter the configuration, for most people a kitchen ideally features the **work triangle:** the cook should be able to move easily between the refrigerator, oven, and sink in a minimum of steps—no more than four or five. The most important relationship is between the sink and the stovetop or range; locating these on the same stretch of counter is a huge plus. The triangle is a remarkably good guideline but isn't a rule, and a designer-cook who knows how she works can choose a different layout more suited to her style.

OPPOSITE: Wood and marble counters top white-painted cabinetry in an island kitchen by Cullman & Kravis.

WORK TRIANGLE CONFIGURATIONS

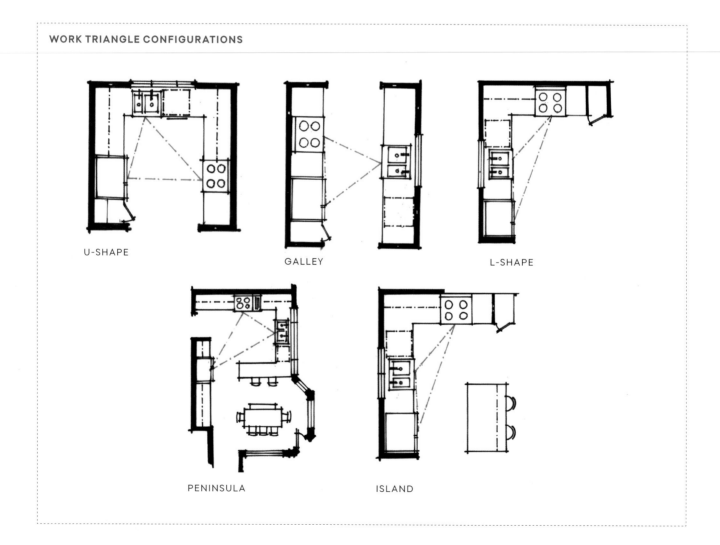

U-SHAPE

GALLEY

L-SHAPE

PENINSULA

ISLAND

KEY DIMENSIONS

- Standard counter height: 36 inches
- Counter height for baking: 30 inches
- Standard counter depth: 24 to 25 inches. When countertop appliances are abundant, consider 30 inches.
- Standard backsplash height: 4 to 6 inches. A full-height backsplash spanning from counter to underside of upper cabinets is most desirable.

- Height of a high counter: 42 to 48 inches. Size the stool to allow 12 inches between the seat and the underside of the counter.
- Depth of a high counter overhang (to accommodate stools): 12 inches
- Maximum distance between the oven, refrigerator, and sink: no more than four or five steps between each appliance

DESIGN & DECORATING CONSIDERATIONS

A kitchen should harmonize with and extend the interior design concept of the surrounding architecture, especially in an open-plan residence. "Don't look at the kitchen in a vacuum," says Robert Schwartz, principal of the kitchen-design company St. Charles of New York. "Its design should reflect elements in neighboring spaces, whether through palette, millwork, or flooring." Approach the kitchen holistically, as a complete *room* rather than an assemblage of discrete elements, he advises. Every plane of the room is related. Cabinetry must integrate with the broad strokes of the ceiling, floor, and tile; the counter material should speak to the wall or backsplash. A well-designed kitchen is a calm backdrop for the food and activity, not an overwhelming collage of materials and colors.

Thinking in Elevation

Be attentive to how the kitchen will appear in elevation—that is, how each wall looks, on its own, when viewed from across a room. Uninterrupted runs of countertop and cabinetry, all at the same height, can read as either clean and streamlined or monotonous depending on the intent and execution. Break up a monolithic expanse by alternating upper cabinets with open shelving and solid panels with glass doors. Regardless of material, align the upper and lower cabinets vertically, creating a sort of column. For instance, use a 30-inch upper cabinet over a 30-inch base cabinet.

KITCHEN ELEVATION

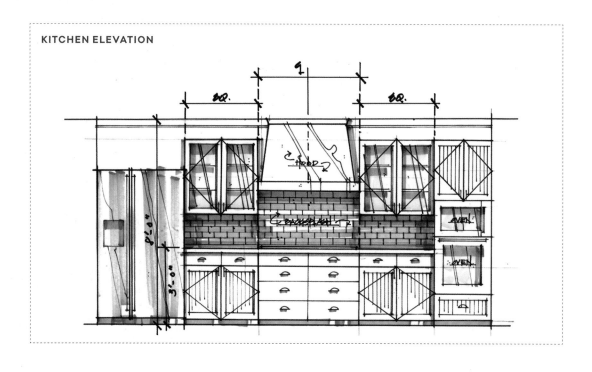

Hide Appliances in Plain Sight

Kitchens are appliance-laden spaces. Double-wide refrigerators, six-burner stovetops, and steam ovens are seductive, but all take up valuable real estate (and can make a space look like a showroom). Determine the wish list and then assess what can physically—and reasonably—fit in the room and prioritize accordingly. If there are many large appliances, consider integrating them into the overall decor with front panels that match the adjacent cabinets. Design cabinetry with pullout shelves, lazy Susans, and drawers specifically made to hold mixers, blenders, and juicers. Create an appliance garage on the countertop: designate one area for the toaster, coffeemaker, and other kitchen gadgets, and hide it with a tambour panel that rolls down from an upper cabinet.

Countertop Choice

Keep in mind how counters will be used. Many people love the look of natural materials, but stones such as marble are porous and thus react to oil, wine, and acids like lemon—even granite is susceptible. A nice alternative is a quartz-composite facsimile, which is impervious and easy to clean. Another authentic touch is solid wood, such as butcher block—and it's not always pricey (but will require some upkeep).

Don't Forget About Dishcloths

Think about where dishcloths, pot holders, and other functional items will be stored. Cabinetry featuring touch latches or recessed pulls creates a sleek-looking kitchen, but there will be no knobs or handles for hanging dish towels. Select hardware with this in mind, or place hooks and rods near the stove and sink.

Soften Hard Surfaces with Textiles

From window treatments to bar stool upholstery, place mats to pot holders, textiles can soften the hardness of surrounding finishes and add decorative panache. Because kitchen fittings and fixtures are a major investment, it is wise to embrace a more neutral aesthetic for these big elements and instead rely on textiles to inject color and pattern. Bear in mind that fabrics can pick up cooking smells, so choose something washable—cotton, for instance.

Custom cabinets faced in zebrano veneer—oriented horizontally to make the room seem more spacious—distinguish a kitchen by Joan Dineen. For a streamlined look, the architect used the same Carrara marble for the countertops and backsplash.

Choosing a Countertop

MAINTENANCE	MATERIALS
LOW	• Quartz composite
	• Solid surfaces (e.g., Corian or Silestone)
	• Speckled granite
	• Solid granite
	• Plastic laminate
	• Stainless steel
	• Butcher block
	• Soapstone
	• Concrete
	• Patterned marble
HIGH (NEED TO BE SEALED REGULARLY)	• White marble

SPLURGE OR SAVE

If a homeowner has set his heart on a handcrafted La Cornue stove, that splurge may require making compromises on other features: an $1,800 stone-composite slab versus an $18,000 marble one, for instance. Sourcing stainless steel counters, carts, and accessories from wholesale kitchen supply companies is a good tactic, especially if funds are tight. Budgets and lead times play a major role in eliminating some possibilities: the cost of fixtures, fittings, and appliances adds up quickly.

Enliven with Accessories

Accessories bring color, style, and functionality to a kitchen. Use sculptural bowls, trays, and containers for storage and service and to break up long swaths of countertop. Change them seasonally or according to mood. Even framed artwork has a place in the kitchen if the medium is chosen wisely (and the piece is mounted at a suitable distance from the cooktop).

"If the homeowner wishes to integrate art and accessories into a kitchen scheme, it's best to plan for them from the get-go," says kitchen stylist Lindsey Katalan of Curated. "Then they can reserve a budget for these final touches, and design cabinets, shelving, lighting, and counters to flaunt them."

USE ITEMS TYPICALLY RELEGATED TO FORMAL DINING ROOMS FOR THE KITCHEN—AND ENJOY THEM EVERY DAY.

Wood accents and woven baskets form a rustic, textured foil for gray soapstone countertops and sleek stainless steel backsplash and appliances in a kitchen by Suzanne Lovell.

Integrating Display Areas

"Showcase collections of Limoges, china, or crystal in a display vitrine or glass-fronted upper cabinet with LED accent lighting and clear-glass shelves," Katalan advises. In high-ceilinged spaces, a second tier of cabinets with glass fronts, illuminated from within, is great for displaying nonfunctional (or infrequently used) items and to draw the eye up, thus enhancing the room's loftlike proportions.

The Backsplash

A backsplash protects the walls from splattering oil and food and is thus integral to a kitchen. Materials range from stone and ceramic tile to glass tiles or even wallpaper behind a glass panel (the choice should be easy to wipe clean). Use the backsplash as a decorative accent: a full-height backsplash in the same materials as the counter is a clean look. Mount GFI receptacles and electrical switches directly in the backsplash at a consistent height all around, and choose coverplates in a compatible color.

Donald Billinkoff designed shelving that wraps around one corner of a kitchen to display a collection of vintage teacups. The colorful china pops against an all-white backdrop that includes a solid-surface countertop.

Suzanne Lovell chose a teak countertop for a wet bar. The rich wood—which would be less practical in a high-traffic, heavy-use area—contrasts nicely with the white cabinetry and concrete surround.

PLANNING & DESIGNING CABINETRY

Cabinetry is perhaps the most defining visual feature of a kitchen—the "furniture" of the room. It spans the stylistic gamut, ranging from streamlined to a more "furnished" aesthetic mimicking freestanding elements such as a sideboard or a hutch. As the most prominent gesture in a kitchen, cabinetry should reiterate the surrounding architecture and overall design concept through detail, ornamentation, and materials. For instance, repeat a molding detail from the living room in the crown molding or panel design. And while an assertively contemporary kitchen with all stainless steel appliances serves as an arresting counterpoint in a more traditional house, it should nonetheless correlate to its surroundings—for example, choose wood-veneer cabinet faces in a similar tone to the millwork in an adjacent room.

Specifying Quality Cabinets

When choosing cabinets, it's crucial to look at the thickness of the door and case materials, the joinery, and how the cabinets are constructed. Best are those made of ¾-inch-thick wood assembled with dovetail joints. Like the cabinet boxes and shelves, the drawers should be made of solid wood, including the bottoms. (Inexpensive poplar can be used for the unseen areas, with a more expensive veneered variety in front.) Cabinetmakers construct doors and drawer fronts with solid-wood frames and edges, using veneers over strong plywood for the main panel: big, flat panels can warp if made of solid wood.

Cabinet Doors: Glass or Opaque?

Opaque cabinet doors hide messy interiors and imbue a space with visual quiet, but glass-fronted cabinets are great for showing off pretty dishware or collections and revealing where items are stored—helpful for guests and homeowners alike. If made of wood, the cabinet doors should have solid frames and edges for sturdiness.

What's Inside Matters

Cabinet interiors—from the shelves to the drawers—are just as important as the exteriors; give thought to their design from the start. Choose or design trays, inserts, and compartments to accommodate your possessions: silverware, linens, china, even a treasured oversize platter. Assess and itemize belongings to determine how much and what type of storage to allot to every genre. Account for pot lids, baking trays, roasting pans, and place mats too. Also handy is a "junk" drawer for odds and ends, or a locked cabinet to safeguard valuables, such as fine silverware or prized wine.

OPPOSITE: In a traditionally appointed kitchen by Hamlin Goldreyer, wood countertops are a warm complement to white-painted cabinets. The long run of cabinetry is broken up with carefully articulated details: changes in counter depth are punctuated by fluted columns. In one corner, a swath of cabinetry was designed to mimic a hutch, incorporating storage to display dishware.

Filling Odd Spaces Between Cabinet and Wall

When a kitchen wall isn't exactly the same length as the cabinets, the cabinetmaker or installer will close the narrow gap at the end of the run with a filler strip that matches the face material of the cabinet. Filler strips are not used in the finest custom kitchens; instead, the end cabinet has an extended stile or a vertical flange, a special customized trim piece that creates a seamless look.

Designing Around Existing Cabinetry

If the scope of the kitchen redesign does not include new cabinetry, transform existing units by refinishing, repainting, or lacquering; or just keep the frame structure and replace only the doors. Achieve an entirely different look with new hardware alone.

Kristin Fine upgraded a kitchen by treating existing wood cabinetry to layers of black lacquer; Carrara marble countertops lighten the look. The result is both more dramatic and sophisticated than exposed wood as well as more visually quiet, receding from view when seen from the contiguous family room.

An accessible kitchen at the Universal Design Living
Laboratory features side-by-side refrigerators, varied
counter heights, and open areas for wheelchair access.

UNIVERSAL DESIGN

Integrating universal design into the planning of kitchens and food-prep areas is becoming de rigueur. The minimum size for such a kitchen—including the smallest possible appliances—is 6 by 11 feet. Install some (or all) of the following accessible features:

- Lower work surfaces, including one or two 30-inch-high counters
- Front-panel controls for stoves and ovens
- Pullout storage and prep surfaces
- High toe kicks and a high baseboard set back 4 to 6 inches
- An L- or U-shaped counter—34 to 36 inches high—featuring bullnose or beveled edges and a contrasting border-edge color and incorporating sink, cooktop, and oven
- At least 18 to 24 inches of clear countertop surface at both sides of cooktop and sink, and at least 24 inches at one side of refrigerator and built-in oven
- Heat-resistant countertop adjacent to oven and cooktop
- A fully finished clear open space below sink and cooktop that's approximately 30 inches wide, 27 inches high, and 19 inches deep—to accommodate seated use
- Lower cabinets with full extension drawers (instead of doors and fixed shelves)
- Easy-to-use pulls, touch latches, or lever handles for cabinet doors

- Use 170-degree hinges on cooktop- and sink-cabinet doors
- Upper cabinets mounted no higher than 15 inches above the countertop (instead of the standard 18 inches)
- Glass-door upper cabinets for content visibility; open shelving where possible
- Removable or retractable doors on sink cabinets to accommodate a wheelchair
- Wall-mounted oven installed so that center of control panel is about 48 inches above floor, and center shelf is about level with adjacent countertop
- Cooktop with easy-to-reach, -see, and -grasp front-located controls
- A freestanding microwave set upon a countertop or in a lower cabinet so it is within arm's reach from a seated position
- Dishwasher elevated at least 6 to 9 inches above the floor
- 18-gauge (minimum) stainless steel sink with 6-inch-deep basins and drains offset to rear
- Lever-handle controls for faucets
- Single-lever or ergonomic dual-handle high-arc faucet with pullout spray head
- Light switches and outlets either placed at 37 inches above the finished floor or mounted on the front of cabinets
- Easily reached light switches for overhead or under-cabinet lighting
- Grease-fire extinguisher mounted in an easy-to-reach location

BEDROOMS & SLEEPING AREAS

For a space whose primary purpose is repose, bedrooms are rather active: in the evening, as a place to prepare for slumber and intimacy, and in the morning, to get ready for the day. Many sleeping areas are also conceived to accommodate reading, television watching, working, exercising, and grooming. As such, the design should be comfortable and relaxing yet efficient. The places where people settle down to sleep are generally regarded as the most private areas of a home. So no matter how busy or multitasking a bedroom is, it should still be a sanctuary for refuge, respite, and centering oneself—for both adults and children.

"I LIKE TO PLACE BEDS SO YOU LOOK AT THE HEADBOARD WHEN YOU WALK INTO THE ROOM—THAT IS, SO YOU WALK TOWARD THE FOOT OF THE BED."
—Neal Beckstedt, designer

Muted shades of silvery gray distinguish a bedroom by Phillip Thomas. At the foot of the bed, a pair of benches in place of a single large one is a nice option.

THE BIG QUESTIONS

- Who will be using the space, and how old are they?

- How many people will be sleeping there? If more than one, will they be sharing a bed, or will each person require his or her own?

- Will the bedroom be used mostly at night, or during the day too?

- What other activities will the room be used for: reading (newspapers, printed or digital books), working (laptop, paper/pencil), playing (board games, free play, interactive gaming and fitness technology, computer games), television watching (flatscreen, laptop, tablet), exercising, lounging?

- Does the bedroom also serve as the main dressing area? If not, is the dressing area adjacent to the bedroom?

- Is the preferred ambience restful, energetic, or somewhere in between?

- Do any inhabitants have sensitivities to light or noise? Is the residence (or room) near a noisy area? Does it receive strong morning sun?

Golden tones prevail in a bedroom by Stefan Steil, carrying through from the mod wallpaper to the headboard fabric and the finish of the bedside table.

SIGNATURE ELEMENTS

It goes without saying that a sleeping place—whether a dedicated room or located within another space—must offer, at minimum, shelter and security (and, of course, a mattress to sleep on). But surfaces and storage areas are no less important, along with a comfortable place in which to dress or disrobe.

1 BED

Naturally, the bed is typically the focal point of a sleeping area and its most important feature. Frame styles range from a streamlined platform to a cocooning fabric-draped four-poster that creates a room within a room.

2 MATTRESS

Vital to consider is the mattress—with respect not only to firmness and comfort but also to its dimensions. Account for the height of the mattress when choosing or designing the bed frame, sheet sets, or nightstands. A custom mattress can be made to suit the desired resilience, softness, and material (including sustainable or organic fabrics, fillers, coils, twines, and cured-wood box-spring frames).

3 NIGHTSTAND

Ensure that the surface is even with—or within a few inches of—the top of the mattress. Ideally it should incorporate a drawer or a cabinet too, or perhaps a pullout shelf with a moisture-proof surface to hold a water glass or a coffee cup.

4 DIMMABLE LIGHTS

Bedrooms require general ambient glow, lighting for the individual sleeping space, and task lighting for reading and dressing. Dressing rooms or areas need illumination strong enough for the user to distinguish black suits from navy and charcoal ones. Careful planning of these features is critical to the flexibility of a room over the course of a day. Switches for *all* lighting should be within reach of the bed. In some cases, a night-light is helpful for guiding users to the hallway or bathroom.

5 DRESSING AREA

This place should include storage for clothing—a closet, a built-in, a freestanding wardrobe, a bureau, or a combination thereof that encompasses space for folded and hanging items, from lingerie to neckties, plus storage cubbies for shoes and purses. Regardless of square footage, a seating perch is a must.

6 SHADES, SHUTTERS, AND/OR CURTAINS

Layer bedroom windows with two or three types of treatments: A roller shade against the window to block the light; a sheer curtain (called a casement) to uphold privacy during the day; curtain panels to maximize opacity, muffle sound, and lend a decorative touch; and to completely block light, use a special blackout lining for the shade and curtains. Mount the curtains so they extend past the window frame and curve back toward the wall in order to thwart all light penetration.

Custom sheets and pillows personalize a bedroom by Suzanne Lovell. The white-on-white palette is crisp yet restful, while layered textures (a cowhide rug and a woven basket) add élan. Dark wood floors ground the space and temper the bright sunlight, which is screened using floor-to-ceiling curtain panels.

To encourage bedside reading, David Scott gave his clients two lighting options: snakelike wall-mounted spotlights that focus a pinpoint of light, plus swing-arm sconces above the nightstand. He sized the custom bed's headboard to fit within the exact dimensions of the wall paneling.

LEFT: In a tranquil bedroom by Laura Bohn, a succinct color scheme and absence of pattern maintain serenity. Soft textures such as a channel-tufted upholstered headboard and wall-to-wall carpeting help dampen noise. Mirrored wall panels and sheer window treatments coax in sunshine during the day. BELOW: Campion Platt chose a canopy-style bed frame to create an enveloping room within a room in a loftlike space. Fine art and an unusual antique wardrobe offer bold focal points. The nightstand design cleverly incorporates a light fixture to free surface area below.

SPATIAL PLANNING

In laying out a bedroom or a sleeping area, start with the bed itself—not only the most important element in the room but also the largest. The bed's placement will dictate the location of all other elements; indeed, in many rooms there is only one logical place to put the bed to ensure circulation around it. Position the bed so that both sleepers can hop out and move easily into the room without having to circumnavigate obstacles. Also requiring dedicated space in a bedroom are major pieces such as a large double or single dresser—often with a mirror or a television above—and a small seating area with a chaise, a settee, or a bergère and an ottoman. These groupings create interesting destinations and visually balance the weight of the bed.

When flexible arrangements for the sleeping area are either necessary or desired, such as in a loft or a one-room apartment, consider taking cues from other cultures and historical periods and adopt a more adaptable approach. In traditional Asian residences, for instance, tatami mats are stowed during the day, which allows a space to be used for other activities.

KEY DIMENSIONS

Add at least 4 inches to the mattress figures to determine the approximate footprint of the mattress plus frame.

- Crib mattress: 28 by 53 inches
- Twin mattress: 39 by 75 inches
- Twin XL mattress: 39 by 80 inches
- Full mattress: 54 by 80 inches
- Queen mattress: 60 by 80 inches
- King mattress: 76 by 80 inches
- California king mattress: 72 by 84 inches

- Spacing between the bed frame and night tables: 2 to 8 inches (to accommodate bedding fabric)
- Nightstand height: plus or minus 3 inches from the top of the mattress
- Circulation area around the bed: 36 inches minimum, all around; for wheelchair access, leave a 5-foot turning circle near one part of the bed

NIGHTSTANDS,
FOUR WAYS

DESIGN & DECORATING CONSIDERATIONS

A master bedroom can be designed as either an understated minimalist retreat, with a monochromatic color palette and varied textures, or a glamorous setting that echoes the exciting and dramatic colors of the living spaces.

BELOW: An upholstered wall backdrops a channel-tufted headboard in a bedroom by Suzanne Lovell. **OPPOSITE:** Soothing peach tones and layered window treatments distinguish a bedroom by Cullman & Kravis.

"I PREFER TO USE WALL SCONCES OR DROP PENDANTS ABOVE NIGHTSTANDS, VERSUS TABLE LAMPS, SO THERE'S MORE SURFACE AREA FOR BOOKS AND OTHER POSSESSIONS."

—Amy Lau, designer

The Materials Palette

The choice of materials for a sleeping area is very important. The selection directly affects the desired atmosphere: sanctum or flexible bedroom/leisure area? Determine how and when a bedroom will be used for purposes other than sleeping: in the daytime for a nap or fitness break, or in the evening for quiet reading time? Rooms that look great at night might look drab in the morning. For a bedroom meant to be a place of retreat or relaxation, include quiet or neutral colors, soft fabrics, a cut-pile rug in wool or silk, and window sheers or shades as part of the materials palette. To create a setting for romance and intimacy, use a rich color scheme with deep hues, textured walls, a dark burnished floor, and warm highlights. A room that needs to be cheerful and welcoming all day long requires contrast, lively patterns, and visual order. The more activities a space is used for, the more layered its decor should be.

Layering Textures

By their very nature, bedrooms are usually fabric-laden spaces. This provides a nice opportunity to create a subtle but complex array of patterns or textures—a comfy nest. "Bedrooms are all about layering subtle textures: a waffle bedcovering, a knotted blanket, a zebra-skin rug," says Neal Beckstedt. "It gives a space a sense of depth yet very little movement, which establishes a nice balance of interest and restfulness."

Nightstands—To Match or Not?

In master bedrooms, it is customary to include a pair of coordinating night tables, one on either side of the bed, which establishes a sense of symmetry that's restful and pleasing to the eye. But why not try a mismatched pair instead, to lend visual interest? "Bedrooms can get a bit boring when they are *too* symmetrical, with the same nightstand and the same light on either side of the bed," says Beckstedt. "When you have a chance to mix it up, take it. Mismatched nightstands give a little personality to each side of the bed, and work especially well for couples, since users often have different needs. The wife may desire tons of storage while the husband just needs a place to rest his watch."

Comfort Factors

Regulating environmental factors—light (both natural and artificial), noise, temperature, interruption of privacy—is a critical design prerequisite in bedrooms and sleeping areas. Many people are sensitive to light, drafts, and noise. Sleep is the utmost in surrender, and such control therefore leads to a greater feeling of security. Design drapery in layers to add levels of control. If city or country sounds disturb, then invest in sound-blocking windows, carpet, and an upholstered headboard or wall. Avoid placing a bed under windows, where there is often a radiator or a heat pump, to reduce exposure to temperature changes or air movement.

Too Small to Be a Bedroom?

Urban apartments will often have a small or windowless room that's billed as a study or home office. Resist the temptation to use this as a bedroom: it's a safety hazard, not to mention illegal. Although building codes vary according to municipality, a bedroom needs to be a discrete room with a window that is a minimum of 24 inches high or 20 inches wide (with a clear opening of at least 5.7 square feet) for fresh air but primarily for escape/access in case of fire. Of course, sleeping areas such as lofts or pull-down Murphy beds are perfectly legal as long as there are no doors or obstacles isolating them from the path of egress.

GUEST ROOMS

Because guest accommodations are used for only a limited time, they need less storage than standard bedrooms, but of a more specific type. Guest rooms can also benefit from hotel-style amenities. Include the following signature elements to ensure a comfortable stay:

- **Bed.** A full or queen bed is most flexible, unless the guest room is small and can only accommodate a twin. A daybed with trundle below is a space-saving alternative that allows the room to double as a den.
- **Nightstand.** A single surface is usually sufficient (as opposed to a pair of night tables flanking the bed).
- **Clothing storage.** A closet, hooks, a clothes rack, or armoire invite hanging a few days' worth of garments.
- **Surface.** Provide a luggage rack, a chest, or a foot-of-the-bed bench for storing suitcases and bags.
- **Seating.** A perch for lounging is also helpful, as is a table or another surface on which to place books or write notes.
- **Proper lighting.** Locate at the bedside or a desk; there should also be ambient lighting from overhead fixtures or sconces.

An upholstered wall, a multifunctional bench, a small chest of drawers, and good bedside lighting are welcoming touches in a bedroom by Campion Platt.

ANATOMY OF A CANOPY BED

A canopy bed creates the feeling of a secret world, enclosed and safe, like a floating island or an oasis—a room within a room. The design provides an opportunity to use fabric to great effect and create an arresting focal point in a sleeping area. The structure of the bed is like a building, with a floor (the mattress), columns (corner posts), and a ceiling (the canopy itself). It can stand alone as a complete environment in an otherwise simple space. Whether luxuriously traditional or monastically minimalistic, a canopy bed is special, an environment for both intimacy and coziness.

1 CANOPY
The canopy rests on a frame, which can attach to the corner posts or be suspended from the ceiling.

- **Exterior valance.** Adorn with shirring, tailored corner details, and cording or trim. Choose lining in either matching or contrasting fabric.
- **Canopy interior.** Detail with contrasting fabric, lighting, and cording or trim.

2 HEADBOARD
Upholster or leave undressed. Extend a drapery panel behind the headboard for an even more cocooning effect.

3 SIDE PANELS/DRAPERY
Panels must be properly designed to enable easy access from the bed to adjacent night tables, lighting elements, and switches/controls—all of which should likewise be carefully located. Elements to design include:

- Lining
- Cording or trim
- Tiebacks

4 MATTRESS AND FRAME
A mattress typically rests on a box spring, and both are set onto a metal frame (often called a Harvard frame). Attached to the metal frame is a headboard, a footboard, or bedposts (or any combination). Some beds and frames are made entirely of wood.

5 BED SKIRT
Bed skirts are surprisingly complex. In addition to specifying the fabric and trims being used and the "drop" (or measurement from top to floor), choose a format that works with the bed frame and accommodates any slats. The most common styles are individual panels, which attach via pins directly to the box spring, and a one-piece design sewn onto a flat sheet that rests between the box spring and mattress. In the case of a four-poster bed, the latter will require split corners to accommodate the bedposts. If the mattress is supported by slats, the skirt will need to drape outside the bed frame rather than to tuck between the sides of the box spring and the frame.

OPPOSITE: A custom canopy bed by David Phoenix offers enveloping charm.

KIDS' ROOMS & PLAY SPACES

Whether a bedroom or a family room, spaces for kids are lively places in which children sleep, work, dress, dream, learn, grow, and so much more. A complexity of uses means that the best-designed rooms have great flexibility and adaptability yet an underlying structure—all of which speak to a child's inner sense of order and freedom.

Children's rooms are places of extremes. They need open areas for play and nooks for hiding; tactile materials that tickle the senses and smooth surfaces that are easy to clean. They need abundant closed storage for containing clutter and open shelves to encourage independence, with ample display areas for flaunting drawings and sports trophies. And children's rooms must be age-appropriate yet forward thinking, capable of evolving with their youthful inhabitants (to last them into early adulthood). A well-designed environment anticipates how not just the child but also the family itself will change: kids' rooms are often designed when a brood is just starting to grow.

Crimson fabrics covering tables, a vibrant duvet, and a zebra-print rug are elements Suzanne Lovell used to create a girlish haven. Yet the room's bones are fairly neutral: pale pinky-beige wallpaper and dark-wood furnishings. Simply switching fabrics and accents would create a much more subdued look.

THE BIG QUESTIONS

- What age child is this room being designed for? If it's a long-track project—for instance, the early stages of constructing a new home—how old will he be when the family moves in?
- How long will the child use the room? If she will be going to college in a few years, it's worth considering whether the room might eventually have a second life as a guest room or a home office.
- Is this area part of another room, such as a play area in a kitchen or a family room, or is it a dedicated kid-centric zone?
- Is this a shared or solo space? If it's a bedroom, how many kids will sleep there?
- Will the room need to accommodate future children as well?

- Will there be overnight guests?
- What specific activities will occur here? Is this the main sleeping area or primarily devoted to play? Will the child study here too?
- Is the child quiet or boisterous? Mellow or high-energy? Social or prone to solo play? Does he love to leave his block towers standing for weeks on end? Does he prefer sitting or standing when painting?
- Does the child have sensory or developmental challenges?
- What is the level of disorder that the parents can tolerate?
- Is there a nanny or an au pair who will share the room or suite?

SPACES FOR KIDS OF ALL AGES SHOULD SPARK THE IMAGINATION, SET THE STAGE FOR CREATIVITY AND EXPLORATION, AND SUPPORT UNINHIBITED, JOYOUS PLAY.

OPPOSITE: A bed frame and club chair upholstered in the same gray plaid lend cohesion and sophistication to a boy's room by Suzanne Lovell.

SIGNATURE ELEMENTS

Important features of children's spaces include play areas, opportunities for personalization, a balance of privacy and openness, user-friendly storage, sensorial stimulation, and a sense of security. Access to light and views of the outdoors is another must.

1 OPEN PLAY AREA

Children need room to sprawl, to construct a fort, to build with blocks, or to make a puzzle that can stay in place for a while. Even in a shared or small bedroom, some floor space should be kept clear for free play. Given the amount of time kids spend playing on the ground, flooring and floor coverings that are comfortable as well as durable and cleanable are vital, especially if finger painting and snack time are to take place. Wood flooring, vinyl, and carpet tile are ideal, as are resilient surfaces like cork, linoleum, rubber tiles, and machine-washable rugs.

2 WORK AREA

Children of every age sometimes need to sit at a table or a desk to do homework, draw, play with clay, and so on. For built-in desks, a standard 29- or 30-inch height is best so the child will grow into it; supplement it with a lower freestanding surface for pint-size statures. The desk can be concealed within a bed unit. Two chairs are ideal, both to support a child's need to socialize and to help him learn to collaborate with peers.

3 SEATING

Beanbags, floor pillows, lightweight stools, and exercise balls provide comfy places for quiet reading. Parents need a place for when they visit or supervise: a chaise, a sofa, a club chair, a floor pillow, or another cushiony lounging spot.

4 STORAGE

Children of every age have the same possessions, in different forms and sizes: clothing, toys, books, and mementos. All require organization and appropriate storage. The best kind allows a child to be independent in dressing and play, and is easy for her to access, manage, and maintain: toy boxes, cupboards, shelves, and drawers. It should also meet the parents' needs for neatness.

5 THE BED

If the space is a bedroom, it will obviously need a bed: a bassinet, a crib, a toddler bed, or a twin (or larger). Even if the space is just a playroom, it might host overnight guests.

- If more than one child will be sleeping in the room, bunks are a space saver (and, depending on their design, a de facto playhouse).
- A trundle bed serves as an unobtrusive alternative for a guest; afterward, it can slide under the main sleeping surface or a daybed.
- A mattress on the floor provides a safe transition from crib to "big-girl bed" and is a soft surface for playing.

Phillip Thomas built bookcases and a desk into the headroom wall of a kid's bedroom. A red, white, and blue palette creates an energizing decor.

6 LIGHTING

Reading in bed requires a small sconce or bedside table lamp. But play areas need ample illumination too—ideally a combination of natural, overhead, and ambient light. And task lighting is essential for homework and crafting at a workspace. Children thrive in daylit environments, so maximizing natural illumination is a must. That being said, modulation of daylight is also essential in a child's sleeping space. Consider a blackout shade or curtain panels with a light-blocking backing or lining. (Curtains also provide a nice canvas for playful fabrics and patterns.)

7 OPPORTUNITIES FOR PERSONALIZATION

Kids develop a sense of ownership when given the chance to individualize their space. Having a bulletin board, open wall space, or even a magnetic whiteboard to display drawings and special items creates an awareness of past accomplishments and milestones while pointing to the future. Even in a shared space, having one bookcase or display area assigned to each child helps reinforce self-esteem and identity.

KEY DIMENSIONS

- Kid-height chair: 12 inches (seat height)
- Kid-height table: 17 to 18 inches
- Full-height countertop: 28 to 30 inches
- Crib: range of mattress sizes is 27⅝ to 28⅝ inches wide and 51¾ to 53 inches long; the frame adds about 5 inches all around
- Twin bed: 39 by 75 inches (sometimes 36 or 42 inches wide)
- Full-size bed: 54 by 75 inches
- Height/clearance between bunk beds: 30 inches minimum between top of lower mattress and underside of upper bed

OPPOSITE: A loft bed/hideaway and drum area are playful touches in a kid's bedroom by Donald Billinkoff.

ABOVE: Electric purple accents inject a lighthearted note into the bedroom of a young girl. Carol Egan specified a space-conscious trundle bed that suits overnight guests and lounging in equal measure. Colorful louvered shades are both unexpected and superfunctional during lights-out time. OPPOSITE: A wall covered in custom graphics personalizes a preteen girl's room by Weitzman Halpern. A deep daybed is an asset, letting the bedroom double as a sort of living space/studio. Textured and furry throw pillows bring just the right dose of glam.

DESIGN & DECORATING CONSIDERATIONS

Spaces for kids should be designed to encourage self-expression—and self-control.

Color Palettes That Delight—and Endure

Big items to be kept for the long haul (bed frames, bureaus) should be neutral and somewhat sophisticated, or at least timeless; save the intense color for wall paint, accent pieces, and textiles that can be easily altered. "A muted background has staying power," says Alexis Givens. "To switch up color, change the fabric and accessories." Kids are particular about their palette, so let them weigh in; for instance, have them choose between two or three vetted colors or fabrics. A little girl's request for "a pink room" need not translate to cloying bubble-gum hues. For the walls, choose an elegant pale gray that's chic, not childish, with white trim, and pretty pink bedding as the accent.

Pair Smooth with Tactile

Tactility holds strong appeal for kids. Their senses are developing, and they love varied textures: soft and cocooning materials such as cotton knit and faux fur, as well as rough and scruffy surfaces. Kids are also busybodies who really *use* their spaces: to drive trains, host tea parties, and fight video-game battles with friends. Choose supersmooth surfaces able to withstand the boisterous rigors of play, sticky hands, and diapered bottoms for finishes; easy-to-clean furnishings; and wipeable wallpaper or paint in a glossy finish. Pair these slick finishes with touchable but still practical materials such as cork flooring, indoor/outdoor rugs, and sturdy upholstery fabrics and slipcovers in heavyweight cotton or Ultrasuede—all with texture and pattern to hide spills and dirt.

Rooms on the Move

Flexibility is a key consideration in young kids' rooms. Set up a multipurpose workstation with a small table and accompanying scaled-down chairs that are lightweight enough to move around. Mobile elements such as small poufs and cushions also allow kids to reconfigure their rooms at whim to suit different activities and enable independent creative play.

Gender-Specific or Gender-Neutral?

Should the decor account for the occupant's gender? Some designers say yes, with respect not only to the palette of colors and materials but also to behavior and even sleeping habits. "As an example, I find that boys prefer sleeping in different beds during a sleepover, whereas girls are more likely to share a bed," says designer Sara Story. "For that reason, I often use two twins in a boy's room and a full or queen for a girl's room." Others think that a child's room should be gender-neutral, neither pink nor blue, and it should change to reflect the child's developing personality—or that the child should design his own space as his interests and identity evolve.

Embrace Whimsy in the Right Places

A kid's bedroom is a perfect spot for a vivid paint color or an exuberantly patterned fabric that might be too bold elsewhere, or a novelty such as a hanging chair or one shaped like a baseball glove.

Areas beyond the grasp of curious hands are perfect for these more precious touches: wallpaper on the ceiling, cool sconces, artwork, or a nice fabric laminated onto a roller shade. A chandelier or a ceiling pendant also presents an opportunity to splurge on something delicate and fanciful or bold and dramatic. Attention to scale can create whimsy too, says Story: "Kids' rooms are perfect places to play with scale: mixing large and small, high and low creates a design statement and is also practical from an end-user point of view."

Encourage Ownership

Children are typically highly opinionated about their environments—and remarkably unfiltered about expressing their likes and dislikes. Encouraging them to voice their passions can make them feel at home in their new space and instill a sense of pride. "Kids need to feel like they contributed to the design and that their viewpoint was considered," says Givens. There are plenty of ways to incorporate what they love in a manner that's not overly thematic, including choosing the wall color, special printed sheets, framed artwork, or an installation of favorite superheroes in recessed shelving.

Stick to Low-Maintenance Finishes

A clear finish applied to an unstained wood such as natural oak is more durable than a painted surface. Opt for sturdy and wipeable plastic laminate, back-painted glass, or a solid surface such as Corian or quartz for worktables and nightstands.

Kids' Room Storage

Kids' spaces must accommodate abundant possessions and are inherently prone to disorder. Enlist a combination of open and closed, freestanding and built-in storage.

- **Built-ins.** Where space is at a premium, custom built-ins are an ideal solution, whether a full span of low storage topped with seating cushions, or cabinetry that extends the full height of the room. Full-size drawers integrated below the bed or a window seat are smart.
- **Open shelving.** Educational theories such as the Montessori Method advocate open shelving to display children's heavy-rotation toys or current projects, which are placed on a tray or in a decorative container. By giving young children a clear indication of where items should be returned, this method allows them to be independent and orderly.

- **Display area.** Children (and their caregivers) love to showcase their creations, collections, and accolades—from drawings to trophies to posters. Corkboards, magnetic wallpaper, and picture ledges both serve the purpose and allow for flexibility. Wall-mounted display vitrines and clear acrylic shadow boxes are another great way to frame objects and memorabilia more permanently.

- **Clothing.** A measure of independence is dressing oneself. Locate a younger child's clothing within easy reach: bottom drawers or shelves, low hooks or closet rods. Put a laundry hamper or basket near where the child undresses, to beckon dirty clothes before they land on the floor.

OPPOSITE: Kati Curtis specified environmentally friendly furniture and finishes in a nursery. Bold patterns are youth-appropriate but rendered in an all-ages palette.

DESIGN FOR EVERY AGE

As children age, their needs change, and their spaces should evolve to meet these new challenges. Consider the following:

- A nursery should provide discrete areas where an infant's basic needs can be met: feeding, rocking, sleeping, diaper changing and disposal, and tummy time.
- Storage for puzzles, books, stuffed animals, and crafts is paramount in a toddler's room. This is an age when kids begin to accumulate abundant possessions, and it's wise to think about ways to contain the piles.
- Put a scaled-down table and chairs in a preschooler's room for drawing, practicing letters, and the like.
- Dedicate space for studying and spreading out homework in the room of a school-age child; include a spot for a computer and other electronic gadgets. Because this is also the age of the sleepover, have an area ready for extra pillows and sleeping bags.
- Preteens have a greater need for privacy than do little ones. Give them a sanctum to call their own—even off-limits to adults—in which they can express their personality, hang posters, and expect their possessions to remain untouched. (Despite being digital natives, kids still accumulate reams of books, trophies, pictures of friends, and souvenirs by the time they reach high school.)
- Teenagers can be orderly or expressionistic or anything in between; they have their own internal sense of order—it's just not always apparent to anyone else. Their bedrooms are where they express their identities through their collections and possessions and learn to make their own order; they need only to look around to see their growth from tot to teenager.

BATHROOMS

No matter how sybaritic or spa-like its design, a bathroom is at heart a function-driven space—one where cleanliness, privacy, ergonomics, and safety are top priorities. The room's main components are permanent fixtures, their placement dictated by the location of plumbing lines. (Indeed, much of the design thinking that goes into a bathroom is hidden behind walls.) Further complicating matters, baths are generally the smallest rooms in a house. Carving out space to accommodate the full complement of desired elements and activities often presents a challenge. In a tiny powder room, it can be quite a task to fit in a toilet, sink, *and* storage—not to mention decorative accents.

The first task, then, involves a bit of puzzling to create a workable layout that incorporates the wish list of features. Next is to counter the technical, inherently functional nature of the bathroom with tactile details that speak to the user's need for cosseting and centering. The problem solving required to reconcile these two imperatives can generate highly inspired solutions; the many challenges bathrooms pose—from spatial constraints to material limitations—often spur out-of-the-box creativity. Whether a private sanctum or a more public powder room, bathrooms are extremely personal spaces ripe for bold gestures, clever ideas, and a nuanced approach to decor.

A curvaceous freestanding tub anchors the raised wet zone of a bathroom by Harry Heissmann, softening the harder edges of walls clad in gradient-patterned mosaic tiles.

THE BIG QUESTIONS

- Who is the user? Adults have very different needs from preteens. Elderly or handicapped users may require accessible elements, such as a threshold-free shower and grab bars. Young children will appreciate features that support their small statures, such as a sink vanity with an integrated step stool.

- Is this a solo or shared space? A married couple may want two sinks, while siblings can benefit from a subdivided space that gives simultaneous users a bit of privacy and as much elbow room as possible.

- Does the sink area need to serve as a vanity?

- Will the sink or vanity area need to support a blow-dryer, an electric shaver, or other items that require an electrical outlet?

- Does the user take baths, showers, or both? Is there enough square footage for both a walk-in shower and a separate bathtub? Will the shower need a seat?

- How many does the shower or tub need to fit?

- Does the homeowner prefer a built-in or free-standing tub, a standard design, or a novelty such as a Jacuzzi or a Japanese soaking tub? (Note that it can be difficult to clean the base area or floor below a stand-alone footed tub.)

- Should the toilet be placed out in the open, or tucked away in an alcove or a water closet?

- Does the wish list include a specialty toilet or a bidet?

- What sort of showerhead is desired: handheld, rainshower, body sprays, or a combination? Is a water-saving model (required in certain localities) desired?

- Can any feature or function (sink vanity, linen closet, soaking tub) be integrated into an adjacent bedroom?

- Will the homeowner use the bathroom for dressing? Is the dressing area or main closet adjacent to it?

- How many and what type of items will need to be stored, and where (e.g., in drawers and medicine cabinets)?

- Does the homeowner desire a clothes hamper or sorter here?

- Do windows need to be dressed for privacy?

- What other activities will take place: exercise, reading, listening to music, watching the morning news? Might a chaise or a chair be a nice touch?

OPPOSITE: To visually enlarge—and maximize daylight in—a modestly proportioned master bath, Donald Billinkoff installed floor-to-ceiling windows. Opaque roller shades pull down when privacy is needed. His-and-hers sinks allow dual occupants to have some measure of personal space and elbow room.

SIGNATURE ELEMENTS

At its most elemental, a bathroom can be reduced to three features: a place to wash, a place to bathe, and a toilet. Any additional amenity—heated towel bar, whirlpool, steam machine—pushes the design forward on the spectrum from minimal to extravagant.

1 WASHING AREA

This should include a faucet/water supply and a sink basin, plus a dish or dispenser for soap and a bar or rack for a washcloth and a towel.

2 GROOMING AREA

This area will require a mirror, space for supplies, and proper lighting. Most often, the grooming area is integrated into the vanity in the form of a mirrored medicine cabinet (a tri-fold style allows the best visual access). But where space permits, supplement it with a separate counter or a vanity that's just for primping. A lighted, extendable magnifying mirror can be useful in either location.

3 BATHING AREA

Opt for a shower stall, a bathtub, or both. But within those two categories are myriad options—and points of decision: shower door material, tub-surround size, type of storage for shampoo bottles. Many modern spaces include both a shower and a tub in a spa-like "wet zone" separated from the bathroom proper by a glass wall. Arrange for extra wood blocking or support to be installed behind the finished wall during construction to securely support grab bars. Other nice features include a ledge for sitting and a 10-inch-high footrest for shaving one's legs.

4 FITTINGS

Specialty faucets, spouts, showerheads, and controls are hardworking tools. Coordinate metal finishes and styles with cabinet and architectural hardware and lighting.

5 TOWEL STORAGE

An array of towels adds easily changeable color and style to a neutral space. Store or hang towels adjacent to the shower on a peg, a hook, or a towel bar. (For children, a low set of hooks fosters independence.) These same hardware options can be placed proximate to the sink—on a nearby wall or a bar integrated into the vanity—so that hand towels are easily reached and neatened. Take a lesson from hotel bathrooms and place beautifully folded or rolled towels on a wall-mounted rack near the tub/shower.

6 TOILET

Every bathroom needs a toilet, of course. Options range from standard to water-saving, from bidets to self-cleansing models with heated seats. Although most toilets anchor into both the wall and the floor, wall-mounted varieties bestow a more streamlined look and allow for easier cleaning and wheelchair access (if mounted at 18-inch seat height). When renovating, be sure to plan the location of the cleaning brush and the toilet paper holders—preferably in recessed or semirecessed niches, which need to be framed before the studs are set.

Joan Dineen deployed full-height sliding panels to separate a wet zone (complete with shower and freestanding tub) from the bathroom proper. The choice of translucent frosted glass helps screen views while still allowing ample influx of daylight. (The same treatment also partitions the toilet, not shown.)

7 STORAGE

Allocate adequate cabinets, shelving, and drawers for the basics:

- Hair implements: brushes and combs, blow dryers, hot rollers, straighteners, curling irons, and the like
- Toothbrushes (electric or manual)
- Toothpaste and dental floss
- Razor or electric shaver
- Medicines and cosmetics
- Contact-lens solution bottles and cases

8 ELECTRICAL OUTLETS AND SWITCHES

These should be situated in a safe and convenient spot—in a medicine cabinet or on the wall above the vanity—where no one who has wet hands or is standing in a puddle can touch them and be injured. To prevent shorts and shocks, all outlets, ground-fault interrupter (GFI) switches, and controls must meet code requirements for wet locations. Steam units must be set on timers, with the controls located away from water.

9 ILLUMINATION

Bathrooms need ambient and task-specific lighting, along with some decorative sparkle. The tasks of a bathroom are usually sited at the sink or vanity or in the bathing area. The general law of bathroom fixtures is that if it looks good, the light is too weak; if the light is strong, then the fixture is ordinary or even offensive. (Witness the infamous Hollywood strip of round bulbs typically found alongside a mirror: it is excellent at fully lighting the face sans shadows yet is aesthetically passé.) Alternatives to utilitarian-but-effective fixtures are recessed downlights in the ceiling. Include them over the toilet (for reading in situ) and in damp locations inside the tub or shower area. At the vanity or sink, the best lighting illuminates the face evenly: use a lighted magnifying makeup or shaving mirror mounted on an adjustable arm that can swing close to the face, and place decorative sconces on either side of the mirror to set a pretty scene.

10 VENTILATION

All bathrooms need adequate ventilation for odors and steam. An operable window will suffice if necessary, but a fan that exhausts to the outdoors is better; a combination vent/heater is ideal. These are best controlled separately, and independently of any light fixture. Steam systems need extra ventilation.

11 DRESSING AREA

If space allows, include a hamper for worn clothes. A shower-convenient spot for hanging a robe is a plus.

OPPOSITE: A master bathroom gets decorative panache courtesy of a sophisticated, artful scheme by Peter J. Sinnott IV. He designed a double vanity with inset fabric doors and an integrated primping area—set slightly lower—with accompanying stool (which boasts additional storage). Framed prints and delicate sconces with fabric lampshades create a furnished look.

Other Bathroom Amenities

Multipurpose bathrooms will require additional features.

ACTIVITY	ELEMENTS
READING	Bookstand, shelves, or an e-reader stand; a shelf for reading in the tub
LOUNGING	An upholstered chaise and small side table
EXERCISING OR YOGA	A nonskid mat; open floor space; video player, tablet/iPad stand, or monitor
WATCHING TV	Wall bracket or niche; wiring
LAPTOP OR TABLET USE	Wireless connection; wall bracket or ledge
LISTENING TO MUSIC	Speakers and controls
LAUNDRY	Washer and dryer; hamper; storage for detergent; surface for folding
STEAM ROOM OR SAUNA	Special controls and equipment; bench; tight enclosure

SPATIAL PLANNING

"The bathroom is a very technical room: every element is attached to a wall and/or a floor, and serviced by plumbing," explains Barbara Sallick, cofounder of Waterworks. "And the smaller the room, the more complicated, from both a design and construction standpoint." Indeed, it can take serious finessing to fit the necessities into roughly 50 square feet—the average bathroom size—since fixtures and fittings eat up significant floor space. Two elements will dictate the layout:

- **The tub.** A freestanding version especially will command a lot of floor space. Determine the tub's position first, since there may only be a few places where it will fit. An especially heavy or large tub will also require additional structural reinforcement due to weight when filled.
- **The location of waste lines.** A new-build project will allow more flexibility than an existing space, where piping is already laid. "Waste lines are exceedingly difficult to move; the simplest solution is to leave the toilet where it currently resides and design around it," Sallick advises.

Next, decide whether the space should be open plan or partitioned into zones or enclosures (such as a water closet with a door or a separate vanity area, perhaps mediating between the bath proper and an adjacent bedroom). When the basic tasks of a bathroom are given their own zone, a new realm of design possibilities opens up.

KEY DIMENSIONS

- Vanity with sink: 24 to 48+ inches wide by 18 to 24 inches deep
- Sink: 17 to 22 inches wide and 14 to 17 inches from front to back
- Pedestal sink: 20 to 42 inches wide and 14 to 20 inches from front to back
- Typical toilet: 18 inches wide, 29 inches deep, and 30 inches high
- Bidet: 14 inches wide, 21 inches deep, and 16 inches high
- Tub for one: 30 to 36 inches wide, 60 to 72 inches long, and 14 to 16 inches deep
- Spa tub: 36 to 42 inches wide, 66 to 72 inches long, and 22 to 24 inches deep
- Shower for one: 31 to 44 inches wide, 31 to 60 inches deep, and 86 inches high
- Walk-in shower: 33 inches wide and 48 to 60 inches deep

Striated Linac marble clads the shower area, walls, and countertop of a bathroom by David Scott. Repeated use of the same material creates a sense of continuity; so does the choice of transparent glass to separate wet area from dry.

Siting of the tub—adjacent to the window, to enjoy the view—dictated the location of other elements in a master bath by Suzanne Lovell.

DESIGN & DECORATING CONSIDERATIONS

As much decorating thought goes into designing a bathroom as a living room. Perhaps because bathrooms are usually smallish, they seem manageable. But in reality, a bathroom design project will involve dozens of decisions, some of them literally set in stone. Avoid irrevocable errors by working with a professional (if you are not one yourself) who will meticulously measure, locate, and plan every fixed element—from faucets to towel bars—and note which will be recessed and which will need wall blocking for firm anchoring.

Picking the Right Materials

Choose materials with performance—and ongoing maintenance—in mind. Bathroom finishes are subject to moisture and standing water and may require annual sealing, as in the case of a marble vanity top. Walls, floors, countertops, shower enclosures, and even faucets should pass the practicality test. Let user preferences guide selection: some homeowners like materials that boast a "living" finish, developing a patina with use, such as bronze faucets; others have no tolerance for variegation. A polished-brass finish is often plated over a less expensive silver metal, and the latter will eventually wear through.

A Well-Groomed Vanity

Vanities can be fitted with special drawers to hold and sort cosmetics, and cabinets can hold pullout shelves and drawers for small appliances such as hot rollers, straighteners, and blow-dryers. Provide adequate electrical outlets for all, and anticipate how to manage the cords. Outlets can live inside cabinets or covered with drop-down panels—and can be wired with automatic off switches to prevent fires.

EXPERT ADVICE

When planning a bathroom, working with a designer and a general contractor is a must. The project can also benefit greatly from collaboration with an architect and an experienced project coordinator in a bath-fitting showroom who not only facilitates the ordering and sequencing of deliveries but also advises on technical matters like waste and plumbing lines and whether pressure or thermostatic valves are needed.

VANITIES, FOUR WAYS

1: David Scott integrated open shelving below a chunky marble trough sink, forming a convenient slot to stash towels within easy reach. **2:** A wall-hung vanity with integral sink distinguishes a glass-tiled bathroom by Terry Kleinberg. Aqueous hues impart a spa-like mood, while the reflective surfaces create the illusion of spaciousness. **3:** Vertical fluorescent light fixtures conjure a faintly deco touch in a modern bathroom by Hamlin Goldreyer. The floating countertop supports a sculptural vessel sink. **4:** David Scott custom-designed a colorful vanity for the bathroom of a waterfront home: a sculptural trough sink of translucent acrylic, complemented by a base cabinet in a similar hue.

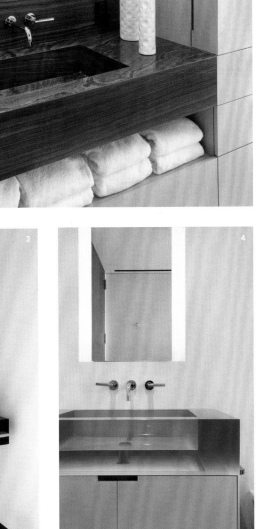

Bringing Warmth to the Bath

Slick surfaces such as granite countertops, porcelain flooring, and glass-mosaic showers prove durable and easy to clean in a bathroom. But when only smooth finishes are specified, a bathroom can feel a little cold. Opportunities to inject warmth and texture abound: window treatments, shower curtains, towels, area rugs (with a nonslip backing, of course). Even a gathered skirt on a sink base adds a lovely touch, with the extra benefit of hiding storage beneath.

Another idea is to introduce as much wood as possible—perhaps in the vanity's base, a framed mirror, or shelving. Wood flooring can be used successfully in a bathroom, so long as it's protected in high-traffic areas (such as in front of a sink) with extra coats of heavy-duty clear finish.

Consider installing a radiant heating system under a tile floor.

A High-Design Water Supply

For the sink and shower/tub, think about how the water should be supplied and controlled—that is, the design and placement of spouts and faucets. Consider a hand spray at the sink (for hair washing); it is a must for large soaking tubs or whirlpools (for ease of cleaning). Controls for a large tub need to be properly sized. Choose a larger tub filler or waterfall spout for increased water volume, so that the bath fills quickly (and doesn't get tepid). Locate controls at the front ledge of the tub.

A Not-Too-Deep Tub

Despite the allure of a sunken tub, they are very dangerous because they are tricky to get out of safely. Likewise, tubs set into a raised platform

Metal Finish Maintenance

LOW MAINTENANCE	MEDIUM MAINTENANCE	HIGH MAINTENANCE
▪ Satin chrome ▪ Stainless steel ▪ Powder-coated steel ▪ Matte nickel ▪ Porcelain- or ceramic-coat	▪ Nickel ▪ Anything polished: brass, chrome, nickel	▪ Unlacquered brass ▪ Bronze ▪ Silver ▪ Gold

and accessed by steps are accidents waiting to happen. Deep tubs need handrails or grab bars for safe egress; a lovely, deep tub is best set into a platform for the bather to sit on before entering.

Controlling the Shower

Showerheads and controls should be located for convenience, so that the user's head doesn't get wet just by turning on the control. (Note that body sprays require planning in advance and close coordination between plumber and tile installer.) Consider luxuries like rain bars vertically mounted on the enclosure walls, ceiling-mounted rain showerheads, a steam machine, or a deep bench for reclining. Closely follow all safety recommendations for steam machines, consulting with a plumber on the location of controls and automatic timers.

Choices for the Sink and Vanity

Basin choices will include the shape, depth, and material from which it's made, and whether to integrate a soap dispenser or dish. Choose between semirecessed style, surface-mounted, or under-mounted vessels, or one that's integral with the vanity. Materials to consider include porcelain, glass, stone, metal, and ceramic.

At the sink area, counter space is at a premium, but stylistic choices often win the battle: rectangular trough sinks make a unique design statement, but eat up valuable counter space; pedestal sinks are lovely but offer no storage and very little surface area. Vanities are good solutions for both challenges, and can help reinforce

the overall design aesthetic of the home. Open metal shelving can support a lovely stone top and vessel sink; a wooden or even a mirrored chest of drawers can be repurposed as a vanity, adding storage and character.

The basin, vanity, faucet/fittings, and mirror are enticing opportunities to create a beautiful vignette of shapes and materials. Yet it's important to keep in mind that abundant items both big and small tend to accumulate at a bathroom sink, and a good design anticipates how these will be stored, stowed, or displayed.

Playing It Safe Underfoot

The most important safety consideration in a bathroom is preventing slips and falls. While a high-polished stone or tile floor is tempting, the best finish is honed or subtly textured. In a shower, the smaller the tile module, the more slip-resistant it will be due to its grouted grid. Consider little hexagons or half-inch penny rounds.

A Word of Advice About Stone

If slabs of stone like marble or granite are used for countertops or shower enclosures, then any coordinating tiles must be carefully matched to the slabs and purchased at the same time. The patterning can be unpredictable, even within one box (or sourced from one area of a quarry).

Large footprints and open knee space below the sinks make for accessible bathrooms at the Universal Design Living Laboratory.

UNIVERSAL DESIGN

Accessibility for the aging, injured, and children is critical in a bathroom. The guidelines developed for accessible bathroom layouts outline the ideal placement of faucets, switches, and exposed hot-water pipes. Universal design also calls for adequate, textured grab rails inside the shower and bathtub to assist in stability. These have to be adequately anchored to the wall (with wood blocking behind the tile) to support weight. A minimum dimension of 6 by 8 feet is required to envision an accessible/universal, fully equipped space. Here are some common features to include in the design:

- In-wall plywood or blocking reinforcement around all tub, toilet, and shower walls—to allow installation of grab bars with 250-pound minimum load support capacity
- Securely mounted heavy-duty towel bars (250-pound minimum load support)
- Clear open space (30 inches wide, 27 inches high, and 19 inches deep) below sink for seated use
- Single-lever or ergonomic dual-lever sink faucet
- A mirror and medicine cabinet, both mounted with bottoms directly above sink-rear backsplash height

- Bathtub with nonslip bottom and adjacent 24-inch (minimum) full-length seated drying space
- Offset-mount lever-type controls near the entry side of the bathtub and the shower (control valve mounted at 38 to 40 inches)
- A curbless shower unit 36 inches wide (48 inches for wheelchair users) by 60 inches long (minimum), with a nonslip base
- Shower-spray unit with a 6-foot-long flexible hose and detachable handheld showerhead with water shut-off button or lever on head. Mount on a secure heavy-duty vertical slider bar unit (able to support a 250-pound minimum load).
- Elongated comfort-height type of toilet with seat-top height of 16½ to 17½ inches
- Linear light fixtures mounted vertically on either side of a mirror, or horizontally above; sconces flanking a mirror. LEDs are practically maintenance free.
- Recessed can light fixture above shower and tub, approved for wet locations
- Exhaust fan controlled by a separate vacancy-sensing switch with an automatic motion-sensing on feature
- Lighted shaving or makeup mirror mounted near sink

OUTDOOR SPACES

The boundary between indoors and out has become increasingly porous. Products conceived for alfresco environments are more design-forward these days, and manufacturers have expanded their roster of offerings. There are now outdoor lighting fixtures, fabrics, and even kitchen elements to rival the stylishness of their indoor counterparts. At the same time, these features are migrating inside the home as well, often where high-performance finishes are desired; consider outdoor fabrics like solution-dyed acrylic, which is often used to cover seating in family rooms or pet-friendly spaces.

Outdoor living mimics indoor life in terms of the type (and variety) of activities that take place there and the furniture arrangements and support services required. Each activity—dining, relaxing, snoozing, reading—needs proper seating, surfaces, storage, and illumination. The primary difference between indoor and outdoor spaces is that the latter must be designed to withstand sunshine, moisture, insects, and temperature fluctuations. Whether an open-to-the-elements shower, a breezeway sitting area, a screened-in porch, or a semienclosed pool cabana, the more exposed to the elements a space is, the more hard-wearing the finishes and furnishings should be.

An infinity-edge pool is the focal point for an outdoor living environment by David Scott. He created a series of more intimate arrangements—one for dining, one for sunbathing, one for group interactions, and one oriented around a fire pit for evening fun. A quiet complement of beachy hues for flooring (sandstone pavers), upholstery, and outdoor textiles keeps the focus on the conversation—and the view.

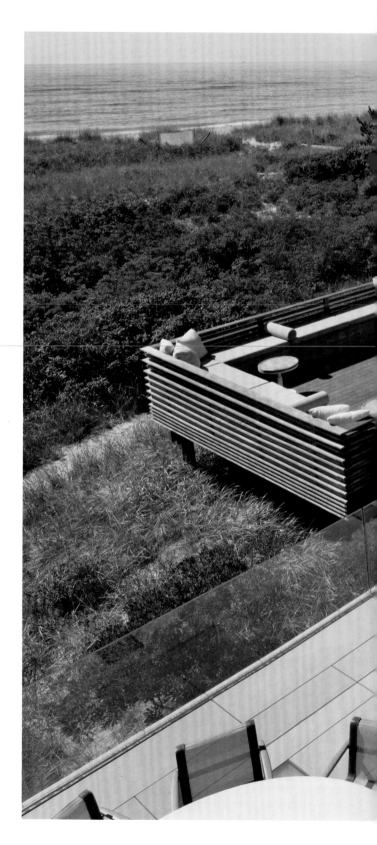

DESIGN
CONSIDERATIONS

The outdoor space should complement not only the surrounding landscape but also the aesthetic of the main house (or adjacent room). Stylistically, an outdoor space can be more casual than the interior, since it's typically devoted to relaxing and entertaining. Put the emphasis on comfort, hospitality, and ease of maintenance, in terms of storage and cleanup.

It goes without saying that materials for outdoor spaces need to be low-maintenance, washable, and moisture-proof or fabricated of a natural material that acquires a patina with age and exposure. Keep in mind how the structure is oriented on the site—for example, which side faces the morning or setting sun—as well as when the space will be used. This will inform the need for shading devices.

A weekend home by Suzanne Lovell features a covered living space that's open to the elements. (A folding glass wall retracts to connect the space with the adjacent kitchen in warmer months.) The designer specified indoor/outdoor textiles for the sofas, plus teak frames that stand up well to wind and moisture.

Outdoor Design Solutions

TO CONTROL	USE
SUNSHINE	<ul><li>An awning</li><li>An umbrella, freestanding or anchored into a table and at least 7 feet across to cover a seating or dining area</li><li>Tenting (with or without fabric screening)</li><li>Fabrics that are UV-stable and colorfast</li></ul>
HEAT	<ul><li>Shading devices (see above)</li><li>A ceiling fan (where possible)</li><li>Water features such as a fountain or swimming, plunge, or reflecting pool</li><li>Light-colored surfaces (versus dark colors and metallics, which trap heat)</li></ul>
COLD	<ul><li>A heat lamp, either freestanding or built-in</li><li>A fire pit or fireplace</li><li>Warm, tactile textiles, such as faux-fur throws and rugs</li><li>Radiant flooring (where applicable)</li></ul>
WIND	<ul><li>Furniture that's properly anchored or heavy enough to withstand hearty gusts or storms</li></ul>
MOISTURE	<ul><li>Durable, slip-resistant flooring: slate, flagstone, or rough-finished stone (such as flamed); antislip porcelain tiles; treated wood</li><li>Water-resistant furnishings such as teak or anodized aluminum chairs, polypropylene stools, or lounges in powder-coated steel and synthetic fiber</li></ul>
INSECTS AND OTHER PESTS	<ul><li>Avoid standing water, which can attract/breed insects</li><li>Screen walls or mesh curtains</li></ul>
PRIVACY	<ul><li>Tenting</li><li>Curtains</li><li>Planters with tall foliage</li><li>Folding screens</li><li>High-back lounges</li></ul>
DARKNESS	<ul><li>Battery-powered table lamps</li><li>Hurricane-type candleholders</li><li>Lighting torches</li></ul>
DIRT/DUST	<ul><li>Machine-washable textiles</li><li>Surfaces that can be hosed down (concrete, pressurized wood)</li></ul>

SPATIAL PLANNING

When setting up furniture for a deck or a patio, follow the same guidelines as you would for an interior living room. Poolside or at the dining table, create separate groupings for quiet retreat versus more boisterous family-and-friends gatherings. Keep things casual, flexible, and elegant.

FROM MOST EXPOSED TO MOST ENCLOSED

Plein air patio or deck

Pergola or arbor

Covered porch or veranda

Curtained porch

Screened-in porch

Pavilion or room enclosed in folding/sliding glass doors/walls

Room or freestanding cabana with one or more walls that slide open

Silvina Leone used color to give a large outdoor living environment cohesion. The exterior of the house—including the deck's ceiling—is painted crimson, a hue that threads through the upholstery details and patio umbrella. The color also plays nicely off the surrounding greenery.

Architect Donald Billinkoff designed a screened-in living/dining porch that spans one end of his home. Aluminum chairs, teak seating units, and outdoor fabrics are hearty choices that hold up to sun, cold, and rain; in fact, furnishings don't have to be taken inside during the cold winter months or covered in plastic—an important consideration when an interior is open to a porch or a deck.

An Insider's Guide
TO DESIGN DOCUMENTS & PROCEDURES

The following pages are geared toward designers who are establishing their own firms or otherwise new to the professional process. Included is a sample contract—fully annotated, with the fine print parsed—to familiarize emerging practitioners with the expected clauses and verbiage, and the standard methods for structuring compensation. Homeowners working with a professional will also find this section insightful, as it explains the formalities of the designer-client relationship. Both sides of the arrangement need to know each other's expectations and responsibilities.

Designers and homeowners alike can benefit from a step-by-step breakdown of the purchasing process. Highlighted are sample sales orders and purchase orders, contractual documents that designers must complete properly and thoroughly—and that clients must review and approve to initiate a purchase. Also decoded is the prototypical general contractor's contract, accompanied by a summary of the bidding process. As even a small job can require the services of a GC or other tradespeople, understanding these procedures in detail is essential—especially for homeowners who may be hiring and managing such workmen and artisans themselves.

THE DESIGNER CONTRACT DECODED

To officially initiate the working relationship with a client, the designer prepares a letter of agreement or a contract for the homeowner's review and signature. This contract is not just a formality to describe the project scope, but also an opportunity for the designer to explain his working process and billing methods. In it, the designer states mutual expectations about timelines, budgets, compensation, and procedures. "Our contract outlines what clients can expect from me—and what I expect from them," says designer Vicente Wolf.

The following is simply a guide—one example of what a letter of agreement could look like—and should not be construed as legal advice; designers and clients should review all contract templates with an attorney.

CONTRACT TEMPLATE

The document should be written on letterhead that lists the designer's legal entity, address, and phone number.

1. Basic Information

DATE: _____

NAME AND ADDRESS OF THE CLIENT: _____

PURPOSE OF THE AGREEMENT: This letter of agreement explains the scope of services to be performed by [legal name of firm] in connection with the interior design of [premises and specific rooms/areas to be designed] located at [specific address], and as shown in drawings[1] prepared by [name of architect or builder] titled or numbered [insert], as provided by the client.

2. Scope of Services

This "scope of services" section details the design work to take place. Consider itemizing services by phases, listing all that apply; this is typical of design contracts, and will create a reference point for the subsequent compensation section. If the scope of work varies by room, state this clearly, room by room. Services to be performed in connection with the aforementioned areas include:

---

1. Any building or architectural drawings provided by the client should be referred to here specifically, itemizing each drawing by title, sheet number, preparer/architect, and date.

- **Phase 1: Predesign.** Interviewing, programming, surveying the site, researching; preparing a detailed program of requirements.
- **Phase 2: Schematic Design.** Initial concepts, planning, layouts, color scheme development, furnishings selection, and materials schemes.[2]
- **Phase 3: Design Development.** Further developing the schematic design, including preparing specifications, drawings, and details required for initial estimates.
- **Phase 4: Contract Documentation.** Preparing interior design intent drawings and final sales orders, purchase orders, and specifications; coordinating with an architect (or other licensed professionals); releasing drawings for bidding by a general contractor (or other tradespeople); awarding contracts.
- **Phase 5: Contract Administration.** Reviewing construction and general contract documents; visiting the job site to ensure that any work by others (GC, etc.) is proceeding according to the drawings or specs; purchasing services as stipulated below.[3]

3. Compensation Clauses

This clause, which is essential to any contract, explains the fee structure in relation to the work performed in each phase.

BASIC COMPENSATION
- The fee for design services as described above in Phases 1 and 2 will be a flat fee of $_____, plus reimbursement for out-of-pocket expenses such as travel, parking, and printing costs.
- The fee for Phase 3 will be equal to 30% of the net cost of the items and services the designer purchases on behalf of the client, and 25% of the value of the general contract.[4]
- All contracts with vendors, suppliers, or tradespeople—including the GC—will be directly between the client and the vendor and, when issued by the designer, are done so solely on behalf of the client.[5]

ADDITIONAL COMPENSATION
- The client will pay the designer an additional fee for any additional work performed outside the agreed-upon scope. Such services should only be initiated at the written request of the client.

---

2. State how many design alternatives will be provided in phases 1 and 2. It is perfectly acceptable to provide the one design you consider to be the best for the project, allowing the client to request revisions and *minor* changes during the schematic-design phase. If a client wants more than one option to choose from, that will affect the fee; all requests for design work outside the original agreement will likely require an additional charge.

3. Be aware that the general contractor—and not the designer—is responsible for ensuring that the contract between the GC and the owner is being fulfilled; i.e., that any pertinent subcontractors are performing their work in accordance with the contract.

4. These percentages are at the sole discretion of the designer, and only suggested here.

5. In particular, the general contract must be formed between the end user and the licensed GC. Note that sometimes the designer will contract directly with a workroom, such as an upholsterer or a cabinetmaker, in order to resell the goods to the client.

- The fee will be billed at the designer's regular hourly rates,[6] as follows:
  - » Principal: $200/hour
  - » Associate: $100/hour

OTHER CLAUSES CAN INCLUDE

- Compensation for Working with a Sub- or General Contractor
- Fee for Purchasing Coordination Services

See next section for more detail.

4. General Conditions

- The client is responsible for paying all state and local sales taxes on merchandise, services, shipping, and interior design fees, as applicable.
- The client is responsible for paying all shipping, handling, delivery, and storage charges connected with any orders placed on her behalf.
- The client is responsible for any restocking fees or penalties incurred by the cancellation of an order by the client.
- Invoices are generally payable on a net 15-days[7] schedule along with any applicable late fees.
- With regard to implementing the approved design—or any item or service provided or installed by others—the designer is not responsible for any malfeasance, neglect, or failure of any contractor, vendor, workroom, or supplier to meet their schedules for completion, or to perform their duties and responsibilities under their agreements. All contracts with licensed contractors or tradespeople will be made directly between the client and the contractor, under separate agreement.[8]
- The designer is not responsible for the performance or workmanship of any services, contractors, workrooms, or sources, or for any items purchased directly by the client.
- The designer's drawings, schedules, and specifications are and remain the sole and exclusive property of the designer, whether or not the project for which they were prepared is executed. They may not be used by the client for other projects, for additions to this project, or for completion of this project by others (provided the designer is not in default under this agreement), except by agreement in writing and by appropriately compensating the designer.[9]

---

6. This work is best billed at the designer's hourly rate, since the scope of any additional work cannot be known in advance. Again, these percentages are at the sole discretion of the designer, and only suggested here.

7. Or sometimes net 30-days.

8. For instance, if the general contractor goes bankrupt midproject or the drapery workroom botches the job, the client cannot hold the designer responsible or withhold design or purchasing coordination fees, unless the designer himself has failed to uphold his responsibilities.

9. A designer's work—from concept and color scheme to design drawings—is considered her intellectual property, and belongs solely to the designer unless the contract explicitly states that it has been sold outright to the client. This means the client may not reuse the design in any way for any other project, or share it with others who may use it, without permission and proper compensation to the designer.

- Following completion of the project, the designer has the right to take photographs of the space for her own use and inclusion in her portfolio, website, or other social and print media.[10]
- Either party may terminate a letter of agreement in writing on seven (7) days' written notice, for any reason. If the agreement is terminated for any reason except default of the designer, the designer will be compensated for all services performed prior to receipt of written termination notice from the client, together with payment of reimbursable expenses then due. If the designer defaults during Phase 1 or 2, the designer will return all fees paid up to that date.
- This agreement is in effect until [date][11], and may be renegotiated thereafter.
- Unless otherwise specified, this agreement shall be governed by the law of [state/location of designer's business].
- Resolution of contract disagreements: Disagreements between client and designer must be settled through mediation[12] in the city of the designer's business.

The letter of agreement represents the entire understanding between the parties concerning the particular project to which it refers, and supersedes all prior negotiations concerning the same. This agreement may be amended only in writing, if agreed to by both parties.

If the above is satisfactory to you (the client), please sign one copy of this agreement and return it to the designer, retaining one copy for your records, along with a check in the amount of $_____, representing a nonrefundable payment required to initiate the design. $_____ shall be due upon presentation of the design.

Design fees for phases: The fees for Phases 2, 3, and 4 will be billed monthly, as these phases are completed or partially completed.[13] Fees for purchasing shall be billed as orders are submitted for client approval and signature prior to placement of the order.

5. Signatories

SIGNATURE AND TITLE OF DESIGNER: _____

SIGNATURE OF CLIENT OR AUTHORIZED SIGNATORY: _____

DATE OF THE SIGNATURE: _____

PRINTED NAME AND TITLE OF CLIENT/AUTHORIZED SIGNATORY: _____

---

10. The client may not unreasonably withhold permission, unless expressly stated in the agreement.

11. The effective date is determined based on the estimated date of completion, plus about 30 days for completion of punch list or outstanding items.

12. Or note other means besides mediation, as this is not always desirable.

13. Each phase requires the review and acceptance by the client, which should be indicated by a dated sign-off/signature on the drawings, specifications, or presentation materials, so that the next phase can proceed on a solid foundation. Once the client signs off on a phase, the designer is free to move ahead to implement all that follows. The designer is likely to bill hourly to address any requested changes to the approved design, post-signature.

HOW A DESIGNER IS COMPENSATED FOR WORKING WITH A SUB- OR GENERAL CONTRACTOR

A general contractor is a licensed professional, as are many subcontractors. Legally, a GC *must* work directly for the client. An interior designer who is not herself a licensed general contractor may not legally hire a subcontractor and then bill the client for the subcontractor's services. A designer who puts herself between the client and the contractor is misrepresenting that she is actually a licensed contractor, which is illegal.

Even when the work is not structural, as in the case of painting and wallcovering installation, a designer who hires the painter or installer and resells his services to the client is assuming all liability for the work quality, contract implementation, and any damage to or injury on the job site. In some localities, a designer may be legally required to become a licensed contractor in order either to provide design services or to resell the services of any other vendor. Contractors should have a direct relationship with the client (even if the designer is communicating with the contractor on the client's behalf).

However, the contractor is working from interior design intent drawings prepared by the designer, and accordingly the designer may charge a fee for professional services, such as verifying that the work is being done in accordance with said drawings. There are three ways to charge for this: by time and materials; by a percentage of the construction costs; or with a flat fee.

- TIME AND MATERIALS. The designer charges by the hour for all site visits, meetings, phone conversations, and any time spent coordinating and verifying the work in the office, plus expenses. When a design fee is based on time and materials, a client will typically ask for an estimate of anticipated hours/fees in advance, and may request an "upset" figure (or a "not to exceed" cap) on the total fee to be billed.
- PERCENTAGE OF CONSTRUCTION. The designer charges a percentage of the overall construction costs; payments to the designer can follow the GC's payment schedule. For instance, when the job is 25% complete and the GC bills for 25% of the fee, the designer can bill for 25% of his percentage fee. (Since construction costs can be very high, a designer sometimes—but not always—charges a lower percentage on construction than on purchasing coordination services.)
- FLAT FEE. From the client's perspective, a flat fee is a good way to control at least one project expense. However, this is the least desirable fee structure for designers. Budgets and scope invariably grow over the course of the project. Unless a designer is prepared to document in detail every additional out-of-scope task she is asked to perform, she will likely find herself doing more work for a set fee.

PURCHASING: THE ORDERING PROCESS & DOCUMENTATION

Depending on the nature of what item or furnishing is being ordered, the purchasing process—and the attendant paperwork—can be quite involved. A custom case good may need to be shipped from the cabinetmaker to a finisher for specialty treatments such as gold leaf or French polish. A separate purchase order will be required for each workroom. Delivery will need to be coordinated and finish samples approved (and sometimes redone several times). Any custom furnishing or element that involves fabric—such as an upholstered chair or window treatments—will also require that two separate orders be placed: one for the item, one for the yardage. Sometimes there is an intermediate step necessitating a third order: when a fabric requires a backing or waterproofing treatment, it needs to be sent from the textile showroom to a finishing house prior to being forwarded to the upholsterer. Factor in extra steps for shipping the fabric to the appropriate workroom, and again for sample approval.

The person at a design firm who oversees the minutiae of a project—including the purchasing process—is called, appropriately, a project manager. She is responsible for preparing and trafficking sales and purchase orders, among many other duties. Every firm follows its own process, but here is the manager's rough order of events:

1. Prepare specifications describing and illustrating every item and detailing all custom pieces.

2. Obtain quote/price from pertinent workrooms, showrooms, or other vendors.

3. For any fabric or wallcovering purchase, reserve the estimated yardage required with the fabric supplier, plus an additional 10 to 15 percent (called *overage,* to account for the complexity of lining up seams and patterns) from the same dye lot. (The upholsterer will identify the exact yardage to order.)

4. Prepare a comprehensive proposal or list of sales orders for the client, including all components of the items to be purchased so the client knows the total cost. For instance, an SO for a custom sofa will include the sofa itself, the fabric, and any trim, as well as delivery costs, sales tax, and designer's fee.

5. Get payment from the client. The client returns the signed SOs or POs to the designer, with the appropriate checks. The orders cannot be placed until the client has submitted a deposit.

6. Send each vendor a PO and deposit (or full payment) for the item(s) being purchased.

7. The vendor issues a written confirmation of the order to the designer. The acknowledgment states the order information, the deposit or payment received and balance due (if any), the terms of sale, and delivery information. The designer carefully checks the acknowledgment to verify that it matches the terms and details of the PO.

8. When the item in question is fabric or wallcovering, the vendor sends the designer a cutting or swatch for approval to verify the correct color and pattern. The designer conveys approval by signing and returning the form. If the cutting is deemed unacceptable, the designer rejects it (in writing) and requests another.

9. For fabric, the designer receives a shipping notice from the vendor advising that the fabric was sent to the appropriate upholstery or drapery workroom (or another destination). Wallcovering is sent to either the project site or the painter/installer. For furniture or an accessory, the vendor notifies the designer when the item is ready to be shipped or delivered, and requests payment of any balance due prior to delivery (or payment in accordance with the terms specified in the original PO). The shipping notice usually asks that the designer contact the vendor to schedule delivery.

10. The vendor sends a final invoice to the designer when an item is complete. It may have a $0 balance or include additional costs incurred during the production of the item; for example, freight charges not known when the order was placed.

11. The designer sends a final invoice to the client each time an item is complete and ready for delivery. Like a vendor's final invoice, it may have a $0 balance or include any additional costs.

12. Collect sales tax on the total purchase and related design fees when each item is complete; the tax amount should be included on the final invoice to the client. The office bookkeeper maintains a record of these payments and remits them to state agencies as required.

PURCHASING COORDINATION SERVICES

Designers spend a great deal of time coordinating the ordering of goods and services on behalf of a client. These activities include:

- Preparing detailed purchase orders
- Coordinating between two vendors or workrooms, as in the case of purchasing fabric from a manufacturer and having it delivered—properly marked—to an upholstery workroom
- Supervising the order process, from original quotation to order placement through vendor acknowledgment of order receipt, updates, and anticipated shipping or delivery date
- Visiting the workroom to verify the work in progress, if necessary
- Arranging for storage or delivery and installation
- Being present for installation
- Processing payments from client and to vendor
- Dealing with all problems regarding the order, including answering questions from the workroom regarding problems or specifications

Compensation for these services can be integrated into the basic fee structures or stand alone, which is called a purchasing fee. (When no construction is involved, the designer may coordinate the purchasing once the basic schematic design has been presented and approved.) The purchasing fee is due in full, regardless of whether the purchase is canceled or changed by the client.

For ethical and legal reasons, the method used to calculate any fee for purchasing and reselling *must* be stated in the letter of agreement. Here are some common fee structure options:

- Traditionally, a designer would use a percentage markup—or the difference between net and list prices—as the basis for calculating the fee for purchasing coordination services. For instance, a table is priced at $1,000 list, and the designer is able to buy it at $600 net. She may resell the table to the client at net plus 30 percent (or $780) or any other percentage; or resell it at full list price—or the opposite, with no markup at all.
- More common these days is for designers to charge a purchasing coordination fee, often calculated on an hourly rate—in which case, the purchased item is resold at the designer's cost (or net price) and the hours spent coordinating are billed separately.
- For purchases made independently by the client, the designer charges time and materials for all coordination services. For example, the client finds a chandelier on a website, and wants to buy it directly. The client asks the designer his opinion, wants to know if it is the correct size, style, and color for the room in which it is to be placed, and asks the designer to be present to receive the chandelier and let the electrician know the weight, proper location, etc. The designer charges for his time, using the stated hourly rate, for each service.

SAMPLE PURCHASE ORDER

Depending on the nature of the purchase, a PO can (and should) be quite detailed. The PO serves not only as a contract between designer and vendor but also as the primary communication vehicle between them—a place to describe the minutiae of any custom features or elements.

Date: _____

Purchase order number: _____

Design firm/company placing order: _____

Name: _____

Address: _____

Contact person: _____

Phone: _____

E-mail: _____

PURCHASED ON BEHALF OF

Client name: _____

Client address: _____

Ship to/delivery address[1]: _____

_____

VENDOR/SUPPLIER[2]

Company name: _____

Address: _____

Contact person: _____

Phone: _____

E-mail: _____

ITEM TO BE PURCHASED

Quantity (yardage, square footage, individual quantity): _____

Name of item: _____

Description: _____

- Dimensions: _____

- Style or catalog number: _____

- Color (and color number) or finish (and finish number): _____

_____

1. If furniture, specify the address of the client's home, the project site, or a storage/warehousing facility. If fabric, deliver to the appropriate workroom for incorporation into completed furniture, upholstery, drapery, or wallcovering. Include a note: "Delivery to be coordinated with designer prior to scheduling."

2. For example, the workroom, company, showroom, or contractor.

- **For Furniture**

  Photograph of item: _____

  Drawing of item: _____

  Upholstery swatch[3]: _____

- **For Fabric**

  Swatch of actual fabric: _____

  Notation of dye lot (if known): _____

  Request for cutting for approval[4]: _____

  Special treatments[5]: _____

PRICING[6]

Extended price (unit price × quantity): _____

Shipping or delivery cost or estimate: _____

Sales tax on the extended price *plus* the shipping/delivery cost: _____

Total: _____

Required deposit: _____

Balance due before delivery: _____

Stipulation of inside delivery, if necessary[7]: _____

SIDEMARK NOTATION[8]

Designer's name: _____

Purchase order number: _____

Client name and contact information: _____

Location of project site: _____

Code from numbered furniture plan: _____

---

3. When the fabric has been sourced elsewhere (i.e., not from the vendor who manufactures or is fabricating the actual piece), the acronym COM—for "customer's own material"—is used. For instance, a designer orders a specific model of sofa from a trade showroom. The showroom typically offers a range of fabrics for her to choose from, or she can specify the fabric from an outside source. (A related acronym is COL, which stands for "customer's own leather.") Always include a swatch of the chosen upholstery fabric, plus the name of the vendor or supplier (with a note of that PO number).

4. A cutting for approval (CFA) is a swatch of the in-stock yardage ordered that the vendor sends the designer to ensure it is correct.

5. Examples include latex, knit, or fabric backing, a stain-repellent treatment, and vinyl laminating.

6. The price for one, such as the price per yard or the price for a set of drapery.

7. Inside delivery means delivery to the inside of the home, as opposed to the curb. Note stairs or other delivery conditions here.

8. The sidemark notation helps the designer and vendor track which project the item belongs to and where on the site it belongs.

AUTHORIZED BY

Printed designer/firm name: _____

Authorized signature: _____

Signing date: _____

TERMS[9]

- Acknowledgment of this order must be received from the vendor within ten days of the PO date; otherwise, the order is subject to cancellation.

- The designer's name and PO number pertaining to this order must appear on all invoices, correspondence, delivery slips, and delivered items.

- All billing is to be directly to the client, c/o the designer, and submitted to the designer for approval.

- Seaming diagrams for all carpet orders must be submitted to the designer after field measurements are taken, for review and approval prior to fabrication and installation.

- Shop drawings for cabinetry and architectural woodwork must be submitted to the designer for review and approval within two weeks of receipt of this order, unless otherwise indicated.

- All work will be done in accordance with applicable building department and building management rules and requirements.[10]

- All items and installation conditions are to be field-verified by the vendor prior to delivery, including restrictions on elevator and stairwell sizes and access. All delivery dates are to be verified by the designer prior to delivery to the job site.

- The vendor (or its representative) is responsible for making arrangements for availability of elevators prior to delivery. They should also verify in advance that the piece will fit into said elevator.[11]

- No acceptance will be deemed to have occurred and neither title—nor risk of loss—will pass until after inspection of goods or service.[12]

- Acceptance of partial shipment does not waive any right with respect to the remainder of goods to be shipped.[13]

- Any goods or workmanship that differs from the sample or order—or that are not as represented—may, in addition to any other remedies provided by law, be returned at the vendor's expense.

- Merchandise will not be considered delivered until it has been placed in its designated delivery location, as noted.

- Failure to enforce any one condition shall not be a waiver of that condition or any other condition herein.

- No representations or warranties are made by the designer except those expressly provided herein.

---

9. Every PO must also contain conditions of purchase information (or "boilerplate"), which specifies some or all of these terms.

10. The designer should communicate any such stipulations to the vendor.

11. Some items, such as long sofas, are delivered in two sections and stitched together on-site.

12. This is a legalese way of saying that the designer needs to physically inspect the piece before accepting ownership.

13. Include this clause when the order is not being shipped all at once.

SAMPLE SALES ORDER

A sales order goes to the client from the designer. It is a simpler document than a full purchase order. If the designer's contract has stipulated the sales order method for client approval, then she will generate a document for the client that includes the following information:

Date: _____

Sales order number: _____

ISSUER

Designer name: _____

Address: _____

Contact information: _____

CLIENT

Client name: _____

Address: _____

Contact information: _____

Item or service(s) to be purchased (sometimes including a photo or a fabric cutting): _____

Cost, including any applicable tax: _____

Deposit requested and balance due: _____

Client name, signature, and date of acceptance: _____

CONSTRUCTION: THE BIDDING PROCESS & CONTRACT DOCUMENTATION

Many design projects will require a general contractor—not just large-scale renovations. The process of finding, hiring, and overseeing a GC typically falls under the interior designer's purview, as does the creation of certain drawings and documents. Here's how the process unfolds:

1. The designer and the architect prepare the final set of interior design intent and construction drawings that contain detailed specifications and quality standards (often referred to as the "boilerplate").

2. The architect files documentation—including the stamped and sealed construction documents—with the local building department or jurisdiction in order to obtain a building permit.

3. Prospective GCs (usually two to four) are identified and asked to provide three references from prior clients and from at least one architect or designer.

4. The designer gives each candidate an identical, itemized bid form (ensuring they can be easily compared) to fill out by a certain date plus a set of the construction documents marked "not for construction." (GCs will distribute copies to potential subcontractors in order to solicit competitive bids.) Expect the bid process to last up to eight weeks, which accounts for multiple rounds of revisions and negotiating.

5. The designer reviews completed bids in detail with each bidder. Ideally, the designer and the client interview each viable GC together. If necessary, the designer negotiates the bids until a quote for each line item is finalized.

6. The project is awarded to the top choice. The GC generates a formal contract that specifically references the set of construction drawings it was based on (citing its creator, date, title, and the titles of each individual drawing sheet). The designer and the client's attorney carefully review the GC's contract before the client signs.

7. After the client signs the contract and pays the deposit, the GC then hires individual subs.

8. The GC retrieves the permit at the building department. If construction is taking place in an apartment building, this and any required paperwork are submitted to management.

9. The project begins.

THE GC'S CONTRACT

The GC's contract should include a schedule for completion plus late penalties and rewards for early delivery. Here are some key elements:

- Date of contract
- Location of project
- Specific area in which work will be done
- Scope of work as described in drawings
  - » Prepared by:
  - » Dated:
  - » Sheets numbered:
- Legal entity or name of general contractor
- Expected date of commencement of work
- Expected date of completion of work
- Incentives for timely completion
- Penalties for late completion
- Representation that the GC is bonded and licensed to perform the work as described in the drawings and can provide proof of same. Rules governing licensed contractors vary, but it is imperative to use a GC appropriately licensed in the locale where the work is being conducted (this status can be verified through the state licensing board's website). General contractors are required to carry both workers' compensation and general liability insurance and be able to produce proof of such—in the form of a certificate of insurance (COI)—to the homeowner or building. Clients or buildings should be designated "additional insured" on the COI. This offers protection in the event of a lawsuit stemming from a construction-related injury or damage to adjacent property, such as a neighboring apartment or a common area.

- The total compensation for completed work
- The payment schedule. The deposit, generally due upon signing, typically equals 10% of the final bid. (This advance allows the GC to give his subs deposits for purchasing the materials needed to begin.) At every step of completion, the GC submits a request for payment of completed work. Traditionally, the client "holds back" 10% of the bill for every phase (often in escrow) to cover the final 10% that represents completion of postoccupancy punch list items (see below).
- In the event of a disagreement or nonperformance by either party, how the disagreement will be settled
- How the contract may be terminated by either party
- Contract termination date, determined by the needs of the project and the best intent of the GC. Penalties for lateness and rewards for early completion may be included. The term "substantial completion" is usually used to connote a project that is 90% finished, or when a client may move in or take possession of the premises. The remaining 10% is comprised of odds and ends—called the "punch list" items—that can be completed after the client takes possession.
- Names of authorized signatories for each party
- Original signatures of authorized signatories, with the date of signature

Again, the client must sign the contract directly with the general contractor (or any other contractor)—not with the designer.

ACKNOWLEDGMENTS

We would like to thank the hardworking, talented, and patient team from Clarkson Potter, for giving us the opportunity and support to create this book: associate publisher Doris Cooper, indefatigable editor Angelin Borsics, designers Ian Dingman and Rita Sowins, production supervisor Kim Tyner, production editorial director Mark McCauslin, and former editor Aliza Fogelson, who initially approached NYSID with the concept for *Home*.

A volume of such length and scope is truly a collaborative effort. We greatly appreciate the invaluable contributions of the following individuals, businesses, and organizations, who shared their deep industry knowledge, allowed us access to their portfolios, projects, and workrooms, and otherwise assisted:

Caleb Anderson

Dean Barger

Neal Beckstedt

Donald Billinkoff

Blanche P. Field LLC

Laura Bohn

Chip Brian

Geoffrey Bradfield

Allison Caccoma

Darryl Carter

CetraRuddy

Coffinier Ku Design

Adrienne Concra

Ellie Cullman

Kati Curtis

Marta Dani

Mercedes Desio

Joan Dineen

Jamie Drake

James Druckman

Pamela Durante

Carol Egan

Thom Filicia

Kristin Fine

Guillaume Gentet

Alexis Givens

Deborah Goldreyer

Judith Gura

Patrick James Hamilton

Bart Hamlin

Alexa Hampton

Addie Havemeyer

Harry Heissmann

Holiday House NYC

Linherr Hollingsworth

Karen Howard

Tamara Hubinsky

Hutker Architects

Ingrao Inc.

J+G Design

Steven Jonas

Jonas Upholstery

Kapito Muller Interiors

Steven R. Kaplan

Lindsey Katalan

John Katimaris

Addison Kelly

Cathy Kincaid

Kips Bay Decorators Showhouse

Terry Kleinberg

Kravet

Laura Krey

Amy Lau

Silvina Leone

Lillian August

Suzanne Lovell

Taruan Mabry

Zack McKown

Gideon Mendelson

Dennis Miller

Richard Mishaan

Benjamin Noriega-Ortiz

Daniella Ohad

Pamela Banker Associates

Amanda Parisi

Charles Pavarini

David Phoenix

Campion Platt

Tracey Winn Pruzan

Elizabeth Pyne

Katie Ridder

James Rixner

Ethel Rompilla

Carlos and Soledad Salgado

Barbara Sallick

Robert Schwartz

David Scott

Mark D. Sikes

Lisa Simkin

Peter J. Sinnott IV

Paul Siskin

Matthew Patrick Smyth

Stefan Steil

Sara Story

Mike Strohl

Alan Tanksley

Phillip Thomas

Calvin Tsao

Alberto Villalobos

Weitzman Halpern

Bunny Williams

Vicente Wolf

CREDITS

Brett Beyer: 74, 75, 93 (bottom), 423 (bottom left)

Antoine Bootz: 116 (right), 119, 341 (right)

Jean Bourbon: 72 (top), 73, 184 (bottom left), 236 (bottom right), 339 (right)

Bruce Buck: 113, 348

Marili Forastieri: 25, 276

Tony Giammarino: 193

John Gruen: 2, 26 (bottom left), 60 (right), 141 (top left), 253 (top right), 339 (left)

Nick Johnson: 146, 181, 287 (top), 288 (right), 341 (left)

Eric Laignel: 17, 353 (bottom right), 359

Peter Murdock: 1, 31, 45, 80 (bottom), 134, 172, 174, 247, 380, 401, 411

Jason Penney: 59 (top left)

Eric Piasecki/Otto: 85 (bottom), 94, 97, 138, 142, 145 (left), 152, 165, 313, 315, 343, 356, 363

Costas Picadas: 120 (bottom left), 153 (bottom), 423 (bottom middle)

Richard Powers: 183, 209, 245, 292, 328 (bottom), 404

Marco Ricca: 28–29, 59 (bottom left), 117, 126, 237 (top right), 249 (bottom left), 289, 309, 318, 354, 409

Peter Rymwid: 53

Universal Design Living Laboratory (udll.com)/Mark Leder: 378 (bottom right)

Universal Design Living Laboratory (udll.com)/Scott Cunningham: 378 (top, bottom left), 426

Copyright © Parish Family, courtesy of the NYSID Archives & Special Collections: 131

Courtesy of Dufner Heighes: 162

Courtesy of Kravet: 205, 206

Courtesy of New York School of Interior Design and Waterhouse Wallhangings: 186, 191

Courtesy of Terry Kleinberg: 93 (top), 267

All other photographs copyright © 2018 by Mark La Rosa Photography

All other illustrations by Taruan R. Mabry

INDEX

N

Natural fibers, 194
Natural light, 35
Natural wood flooring, 155
Needlepoint carpets/rugs, 252
Needs assessment. *See* Research
Neutral colors, 78
New York School of Interior Design, skills taught by, 8, 10
Nightstands, 384, 389, *389, 393*

O

Oil-based paint, 168
Ombré, for carpets/rugs, 251
Ordering process and documentation, 441–447
Organization. *See also* Documentation; Scheduling
    during design process, 90–92, *92, 93*
    inventory of belongings, *44,* 44–49, *45, 49*
    of measurements, 48 (*See also* Measurement)
    professional mind-set for, 16
    project management, 100–105
    spreadsheets and lists for interior design intent drawings, 90, 92
    spreadsheets for budgeting, 30
Outdoor spaces, 428–432
    design considerations, 430, *430*
    enclosures, 432
    indoor/outdoor connection, 63
    overview, 428, *428–429*
    solutions for, 431
    spatial planning of, 432, *432–433*

P

Paint, 168–179
    chemical makeup, 171–172
    color choice for, 172
    color for ceilings, 173, *174, 175*
    decorative painting and finishes, 176, *176–178*
    as element, overview, 168, *168–170*
    finish type, 171
    installation considerations, 179
    materials and, 173
    medium, 168
    surrounding surfaces and, 173
    wood finishes, 126
Pairs, of accessories, 294
Palette creation, 74, *74, 75*
Paneling, 116, *116*
Paper-backed textiles wallcoverings, 182
Paper wallcoverings, 180

Parquet wood flooring, 155
Passementerie, 219
Pass-machine tufting, 250
Patterns
    choosing, for big picture, 55
    draperies and, 228
Pearl paint, 171
Pelmet, 231
Photographs, recording keeping and, 105
Pile, of carpets/rugs, 250, 251
Pilling, 201
Pillows, loose, 221, *221*
Piping, 213
Place making, 13
Plank wood flooring, 155
Plastics, in wood composite, 123
Play spaces. *See* Kids' rooms and play spaces
Pleating, *229*
Polished (flame) slab stone, 165
Porcelain tile flooring, 157
Positive/negative space, 294
Premium quality woodwork, 127
Pricing
    designer discounts and, 98–99
    fabric and textiles, 203
Printed fabrics, 203
Programming (pre-design) phase, 22–27, *23, 25–29*
Project, defining, 22–27, *23, 25–29*
Project files, for recording keeping, 105
Project management
    changes managed with, 104
    general contractor (GC), overview, 100
    purchasing coordination services, 443
    record keeping and, 105
    role of designer in, 103–104
    role of general contractor (GC) in, 102
    scheduling and, 105
Project management and purchasing coordination, 98–99
Proportion
    as design element, 58
    of space, 34
Purchasing
    budgeting and, 21, 30–31, 299
    coordination services, 443
    customer soft floor coverings, 256
    from custom workrooms, 96
    designers' purchases for clients, 98
    fabrics and textiles, 202–203
    furniture, 223
    ordering flooring, 167

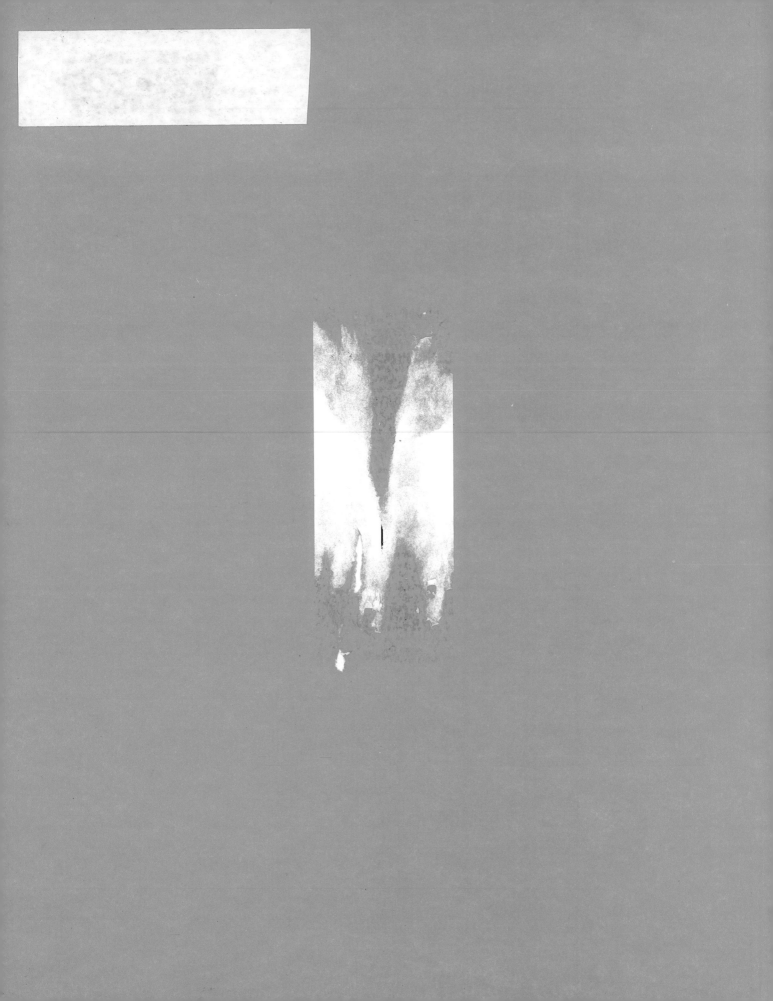